Thomas Heatherwick

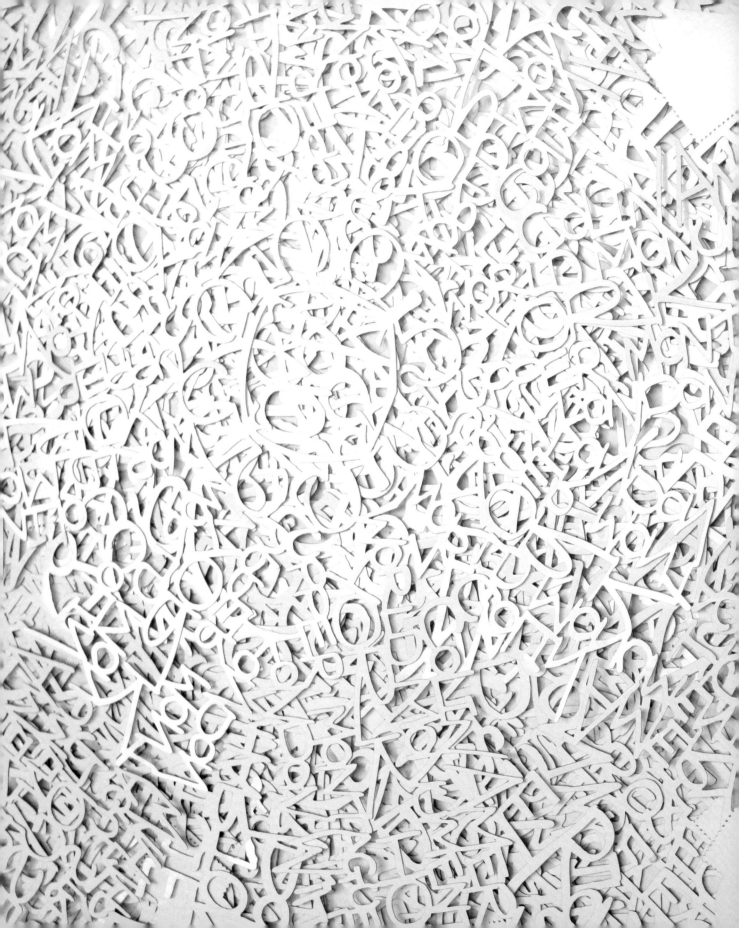

Thomas Heatherwick

Making

Written by
Thomas Heatherwick

With over 1,500 illustrations

Contents

From I to We

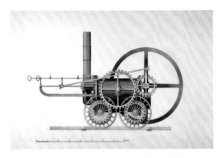

'Catch Me Who Can', Richard Trevithick, 1808

THIS BOOK ABOUT Heatherwick Studio's projects contains a selection of work carried out over more than three decades, presented, in this fourth edition, in reverse chronological order. The intention is not to persuade others to adopt any single approach to design or to promote any one philosophy but only to try to explain the thinking that went into each project and tell the story of how our ideas developed. Throughout the book, my voice may appear to fluctuate arbitrarily between 'I' and 'we' but the reason is that all except the earliest projects were undertaken by a group of people working with me to develop ideas. Thinking and experimenting together like this, we have found that we tend to guide ourselves towards ideas by finding a few key questions to ask ourselves. This is why every project in the book is introduced by one of these provocations. These descriptions may give the impression that ideas come easily, but almost every project, whether it is built or not, is an intense mixture of certainty and doubt, breakthroughs and dead ends, tension and hilarity, frustration and progress.

Elisabeth Tomalin, pencil on paper, 1989

I grew up in London and my early years were spent among people who pursued strong personal interests, exposing me to different influences and encouraging me to develop any natural aptitudes I might have. My grandfather, Miles Tomalin, was a writer and musician who wrote pacifist poems every year, which he sent as Christmas cards. He had been among those who had volunteered in the 1930s to go to Spain as part of the International Brigade, to fight the fascists in the Spanish Civil War. His study of the history of engineering convinced him that George Stephenson had been wrongly credited with the invention of the steam locomotive and led him to wage a personal campaign for Richard Trevithick to be rightfully recognized as its true innovator. My German–Jewish grandmother, Elisabeth

Hammock making

Hedge laying

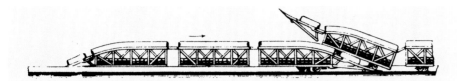

Stern's Improved Means for Allowing the Passing of one Vehicle by Another, 1904, 'Relates to systems of transport on single line or narrow routes whereby collisions may be avoided and travel carried on without interruption… It consists in passing one vehicle over the roof of the other, and of modifying the vehicle roofs and tyres to allow of such passage.'

An artistic way of hiding an unsightly view from a flat from 'How to Live in a Flat', William Heath Robinson, 1937

Citroën Karin concept car, 1980

Future Home 2000, Milton Keynes, 1981

Tomalin, had come to London after fleeing Dresden from the Nazis, and worked with the architect Ernő Goldfinger before setting up and directing the textile design studio of Marks and Spencer. Later she became a pioneer of the practice of art therapy.

Stefany Tomalin, my mother, was a painter and jeweller before becoming an authority on beads and bead-threading. For twenty years, she had a shop selling necklaces and beads on London's Portobello Road. Together we went to exhibitions, model engineering shows and crafts fairs, spending time with people who were forging iron, blowing glass, machining metal, erecting timber building frames, knotting hammocks, laying hedges, making sheep fences and constructing dry stone walls. Hugh Heatherwick, my father, trained as a pianist and at the age of fifteen joined the band of the Royal Marines, where he was also a boxer. Later he developed an expertise in fostering the creativity of children, adults, organizations and communities. Interested in innovation and in the future of cities, he took me to see Milton Keynes' futuristic housing prototypes and the new forms and technologies on display at international car shows. He subsequently played an important role in the studio and continues to help us to develop as an organization and evolve as a creative entity.

In childhood, I spent time drawing and making things as well as taking apart mechanical and electrical devices such as typewriters and cameras. I became curious about ideas, structures and problems being solved, and enjoyed my grandfather's books about great buildings and engineering, as well as the clever and comic inventions of Heath Robinson. After leaving school, I began a two-year diploma in general art and design, followed by an undergraduate degree in three-dimensional design at Manchester Polytechnic and then a two-year master's degree at the Royal College of Art in London.

In these seven years, my training allowed me to move freely between materials and processes that included working with plastics, glassblowing, welding, jewellery-making, ceramics, embroidery and timber joinery. Exploring different scales of problem-solving I was able to pursue my ongoing interest in the design of buildings and the built environment.

At this time I became curious about the historical figure of the master builder, who had combined the roles and skills of the builder, craftsman, engineer and designer, which meant that the generation of ideas was connected to the process of turning them into reality. However, with the establishment of the Institute of Civil Engineers in 1818 and the Royal Institute of British Architects in 1834, engineering and architecture seemed to have evolved into elite professions with separate identities from the rest of the building trade. Meanwhile, the craftsman became the employee of a new figure called the general contractor, whose interests were predominantly financial. Now, not only was the designer of a building discouraged from having a creative connection to materials and practical making, but the craftsman lost his prestige, beginning the slow decline in skills and expertise within the building industry.

My experience of making my own design ideas convinced me that understanding materials, and gaining practical experience of using them, was essential to developing ideas and finding ways of making them happen. In the research for my degree course thesis, I interviewed architects, self-builders and contractors about their education and ways of working. At that time, young architects were given no practical experience of making, such as casting a form in concrete, making a timber joint or constructing a brick wall. Given that buildings are some of the largest objects made and experienced by humans, it was surprising to find that the designers of these objects were so far removed from the craftsmanship

Using an ash tree that I had cut down to make furniture pieces, Manchester, 1990

Constructing hay stacks

Practical making skills

Constructing the Pavilion, Manchester, 1992

10

Making bread

Forging steel

Making the world's largest telescopic mirror

Motorway construction

of making them. I felt that this helped to explain why much of the new architecture I saw around me felt sterile and lacking in three-dimensional sophistication.

Having used my thesis to explore this subject, it felt logical to me at that time to use the final year of my degree at Manchester Polytechnic to experiment with a different model of building procurement. I found myself designing and making a full-size building, the Pavilion (pages 606–11), something that had not been done at the college before.

Studying at the Royal College of Art gave me space to think about the way in which I might practise as a designer when I left the education system. Instead of rigidly dividing artistic thinking into separate crafts and professions such as sculpture, architecture, fashion, embroidery, metalwork, and landscape, product and furniture design, I wanted to consider all design in three dimensions, not as multi-disciplinary design, but as a single discipline: three-dimensional design. Also, because each separate creative discipline seemed to be associated with a particular scale, there was an opportunity to take the aesthetic sensibilities of smaller scales of making, such as jewellery or bread-baking, and introduce these into the large-scale world of building design.

In 1994, I set up a studio in order to continue researching and experimenting with ideas and ways of making them happen. Since I had learned that I worked best in dialogue with others and wanted to do projects of a scale that a person could not do on their own, the studio was from the outset a collaborative venture. Since that time, it has been a mixture of people with backgrounds in engineering, architecture, product design, landscape architecture, project management, sculpture, photography, theatre design, craft and making. Today, Heatherwick Studio is based in London and works as a collection of overlapping teams, each formed around a project and led by experienced studio members.

The studio's design process has always depended on its workshop, which allows it to test and realize ideas through the making of experimental pieces, prototypes, models and full-size parts of buildings. In order to make a project happen, we have sometimes needed to construct all or part of it ourselves, beginning with the Pavilion (pages 606–11) and continuing with projects such as Autumn Intrusion (pages 550–59), Bleigiessen (pages 442–51) and the Aberystwyth Artists' Studios (pages 366–77).

When developing ideas for a project, we work as closely as possible with the project's commissioner and our team of collaborators. It is unusual for me to come into the studio in the morning with a drawing of an idea and hand it to my colleagues. Instead, we iteratively pare a project back in successive rounds of discussions, through analysis, questioning, testing, experimentation and interrogation, looking for the logic that will lead to an idea. If a potential commissioner asks for 'just a sketch', we have to try to explain that this is not the way we work. Since the budget for every project is limited, the focus of our creative thinking is often on how to make best use of limited resources. With the UK Pavilion (pages 308–20), our project was allocated half the budget given to many other Western nations and our design solution was led by our decision to concentrate these resources on a small proportion of the space, rather than spreading it thinly across the entire site.

In recent years, the studio has become involved in the strategic thinking that is shaping the future of cities and towns. It seems that the people who write the briefs for new buildings and infrastructure have more power to make places unique and special than designers. The greatest need for innovation seems to be in finding new ways to apply artistic thinking to the problems of a city, rather than automatically emulating Bilbao, where an extraordinary art gallery transformed the fortunes of

Studio, Camden Town, 1999

Constructing Bleigiessen, London, 2001

Constructing Artists' Studios, Aberystwyth, 2008

Studio, King's Cross, 2008

Studio workshop, King's Cross, 2009

Studio workshop, King's Cross, 2011

Studio, King's Cross, 2024

a city. For example, in designing a new bio-mass power station in Middlesbrough, there was an opportunity for the area to develop a new identity by investing in necessary renewable energy infrastructure, which would at the same time be a park, cultural facility and educational resource.

The studio's expanding interest in new types of public space is evident in our recent projects. In New York, we had the opportunity to create an entirely new space, at once a river pier, a world-class performance space and a public park (pages 142–53). And in our huge new district projects, London Olympia, Xi'an CCBD in China, and Azabudai Hills in Tokyo, we have been investigating what new kinds of public space can offer the occupants of a crowded city (pages 78–87, 34–45 and 88–101). Even when thinking on the broadest, most strategic level, the preoccupation is with how to use materials and forms at a human scale, the scale at which people touch, experience and live in the world.

Most recently, following the publication of my *Humanise: A Maker's Guide to Building Our World*, and my 2022 TED Talk, the studio has begun a global campaign to make the outsides of buildings in cities radically more joyful and engaging.

Making this book has been a bit like working on one of our projects, except that our projects are normally about three-dimensional space and form. This time, the task has been to find ways of crushing our own projects down into flat two-dimensional images and text, like putting flowers in a flower press, in order to squeeze them into a book. I hope that, as you turn the pages, these projects pop back up and come to life again as ideas and places in three dimensions.

Space Garden

Can humanizing space improve life on Earth?

WITH SO MANY PROBLEMS TO SOLVE here on Earth, affecting such huge numbers of people, the design of space habitats had never felt like a top priority for the studio. But in late 2023, following a series of exciting conversations, a collaboration with MIT graduate and space design entrepreneur and researcher Ariel Ekblaw began the studio's first project for space.

In recent years there have been many articles about different proposals for settlements on the Moon or Mars, as alternatives to living on the surface of the Earth. To many, space has been increasingly regarded as a fall-back solution for humans if life on Earth becomes unfeasible. Yet, the more proposals being prepared to get away from Earth, the more precious and amazing life on Earth felt.

At the same time as the natural world on Earth is in crisis, it has also become increasingly clear that the idea of an idyllic 'planet B' for future generations is completely unrealistic. Earth remains the best home for humans, so our priority must be to save and improve our way of living on it in better harmony with nature.

As perverse as it may sound, however, we became fascinated by the potential of space to let us live better lives on Earth itself. Was there any way we could use the huge potential of the unique 'backyard' of space, otherwise known as low Earth orbit, to improve life on our own Blue Planet?

What if some of Earth's most damaging processes and heavy industries were moved off-planet, and the unique environment of space was safely used for processes and products that could benefit broader humankind on Earth? Research already shows that certain high-tech vaccines and microchips are better manufactured in a low-gravity environment. Plus, some of our most polluting industries could become solar powered if transferred outside Earth's atmosphere, in easier reach of the sun's rays. The potential for innovation in using space to benefit the Earth seemed endless. This plan also seemed far more practical and possible than other more extreme solutions of mass human inter-planetary migration to far less hospitable climates for sustaining life.

For this new space economy to work, a number of people would be required to live and work for periods of time in low Earth orbit – not just robots or highly trained astronauts, but ordinary civilian workers to facilitate the amazing technology. However, making the lifestyle of space suitable and conducive to

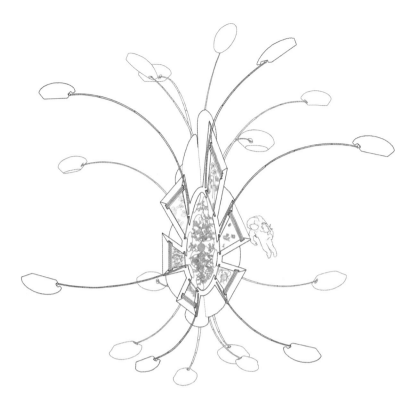

regular people would need a different mindset about how to make living and working environments in space. Given how tiny the living areas of space have to be, due to the physics of creating them at all, how can they be humanized? What are the mental health impacts of the potential design decisions when people may be stuck living inside them for many weeks at a time? It quickly became apparent that there was a role for nature to play a bigger part. Just as people during the Covid lockdowns had bought vast amounts of potted plants to soften their indoor environments, could planting also help to humanize the confined settings of space?

The studio has always been passionate about integrating nature into architectural design, so the idea emerged for a significant experiment to make a community garden in space – a laboratory for plant growth, where research could be done on sustaining life in space and on Earth from horticultural, nutritional and mental health perspectives. Unless we make it possible for humans to live more comfortably in space, how can we hope to remove many of the industries from Earth?

The studio's design team worked with Ekblaw's Aurelia Institute to imagine a Space Garden with thirty-six controlled growing environments, each housing a different plant species, sent into orbit for a twelve-month research experiment. The team started by researching the architecture of space travel and exploration. Despite the cultural hold that space has in the popular imagination,

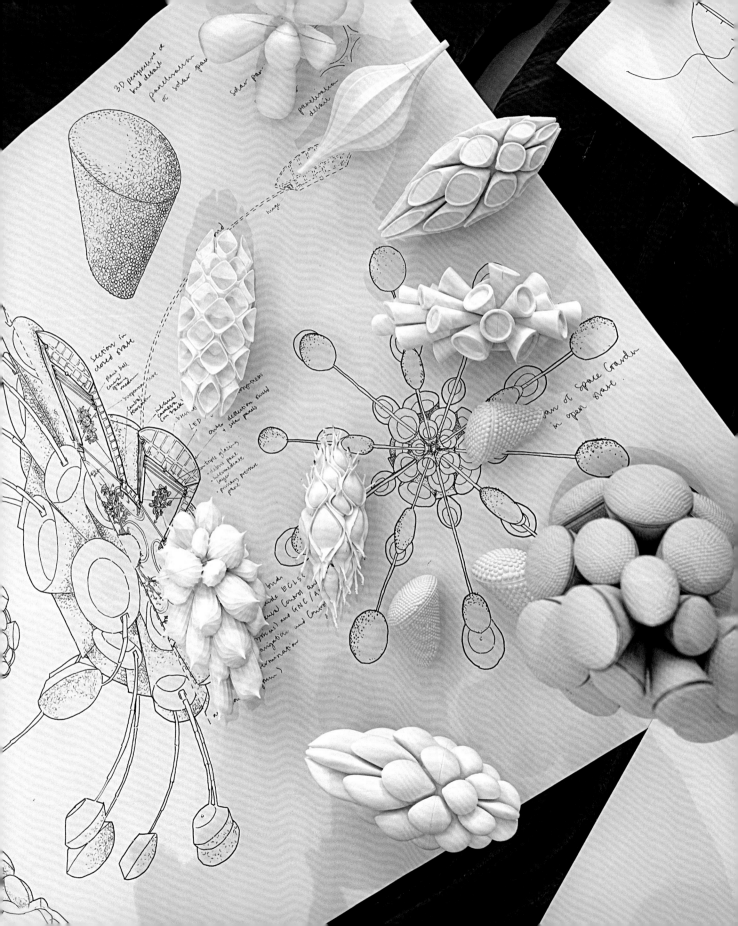

from the retro futurism of the 1950s to the sleek, modern ships and planetary bases showcased in *Star Wars* and *Star Trek*, in reality, space design has always been functional, industrial, relatively ugly and inhuman. Up until now, spacecraft seemed to be designed to show they can survive, rather than thrive, in space. We felt there was an opportunity to create something that could cope with the hostile environment of space, but also evoke a greater sense of humanity and emotion. It was time to establish a more aspirational visual language for space.

From a scientific perspective, there was also an opportunity to experiment with growing more plant species than had ever before been cultivated in space – potentially crucial for long-term nutrition and mental health. Up until recently only a handful of plant species have been attempted in space. How could we dramatically change this with our project?

Unsurprisingly, the challenges of the project are significant. The garden structure has to be able to fit into the payload fairing (the nose cone) of a commercial space rocket in order to be lifted into orbit, meaning the plants and their habitat itself have to be designed to survive the impact of dynamic pressure and heat during launch through the atmosphere. The structure at launch can therefore be no taller than 10 metres and no wider than 5 metres. It also needs a sophisticated shading system to constantly maintain the Earth-like light levels required by the plants during the garden's repeated ninety-minute orbit around the sun.

The team explored different possible shapes for the garden, influenced by principles of biophilia and the beauty found in nature. A structure of clustered pods, which each houses a species of plant, was chosen, with each chamber having a plant grown from a community garden on Earth. These pods are organized around a central chamber featuring a hero species of particular fascination or cultural significance, such as a fig tree (one of the first plants to be cultivated by humans on Earth). The smaller chambers have glazed openings that allow the sun's rays to enter, while a telescopic arm attached to a protective cover can expand or retract depending on the optimal shading position for it at any one time. These covers also protect the glass from the impact of flying space debris showers. The outcome is that the whole shape of the biophilic craft can change radically and organically in different scenarios. Finally, the outer surface of the orbiting Space Garden is covered in tiny solar panels to capture power from the sun.

The project is currently in development to create a proof of concept, with the intention that in the not-too-distant future it will be a new kind of beautiful landmark in low Earth orbit. We also imagine it as an inspiring vantage point from which to look back at Earth and appreciate it as our only home in the universe, and somewhere we must protect at all costs.

Universidad EAN

Why do columns have to be straight?

AS PART OF ITS CAMPUS in the heart of the city, Universidad EAN in Bogotá, Colombia, wanted to build a new design school, asking the studio to create the building.

After the Covid-19 pandemic, the university's leadership team had been thinking about the importance of togetherness in educational settings. Their aim was to motivate students to come back into the classrooms after years of isolating lockdowns, where online learning had become normal.

Colombia is the world's second most biodiverse country, and Bogotá is considered one of the leading cities for sustainable development. As signatories to the C40 Urban Nature Declaration, city leaders had pledged to maximize the use of nature throughout the city.

Surrounded by huge, lush mountains, Bogotá itself is inspiring, with its diverse architectural styles, from Tudor-style houses to modern glass buildings, to lots of brick structures. Almost every street is framed by views of the amazing 'cloud forest' mountains that encircle the city.

The brief was for a seven-storey building on Calle 72, one of the city's main arteries. The school would be surrounded by taller buildings and so had to stand out as somewhere special, interesting and colourful. It also had to have a relationship with a series of existing heritage houses around it, which we had been asked to revive and retain. Facilities needed to include classrooms, workshops and seminar rooms, but also public offerings like cafés and a yoga room.

Researching local craft traditions of Bogotá and the nearby communities, the team was particularly struck by a form of weaving unique to Colombia's Wounaan indigenous people called Werregue basketry. Loving the colour, texture, patterns and variety in the baskets, we wondered how to bring some of this joyfulness to the new building.

Together with local communities, the team developed the design of different patterns for colourful, ceramic-clad columns made of basket-like forms piled on top of one another.

In designing perhaps the most colourful building in the city, there was a sincere desire to create a campus that students would be proud and excited to enter. And even for non-students, there is an accessible communal oasis of a public square amidst the hard urban surroundings.

The project, scheduled to begin construction in 2025, was launched at a university event to an audience of hundreds of past and present students. One of the client team, speaking on stage, captured the wishes for the long-term impact of the project: 'Hopefully, this will lead to more buildings in Bogotá that humanize the relationship between infrastructure and people.'

Tree of Trees

How can an object inspire people to plant more trees?

IN EARLY 2022, representatives of Queen Elizabeth II asked the studio to help draw attention to the Queen's Green Canopy initiative. The campaign had been set up to encourage people from across the UK to 'Plant a Tree for the Jubilee' to benefit future generations and to offer a living legacy in honour of the Queen's seventy-year leadership of the nation.

The brief was to create an object that would motivate people to plant more trees at the same time as communicating a message of hope, regeneration and optimism. And it also needed to provide a focal point and moment of togetherness for the scheduled Jubilee celebrations at Buckingham Palace. As a symbol, this structure would be seen by tens of thousands of people in London, and many millions watching on television around the country and across the world.

With an immovable Jubilee deadline and two weeks of design time before construction needed to start, the team immediately began to experiment with different ways of visually celebrating the act of planting trees. As we were designing, we were inspired to learn that Queen Elizabeth II had planted over 1,500 trees in her lifetime.

70 ft / 21m

Trees are the superheroes of our towns and cities. Most of us know instinctively that planting more of them is a good thing for the world. They absorb pollution, offer shade, provide homes for ecosystems and improve our wellbeing. The question in our minds was how to motivate people to actually do it? We realised we would need to find a way to make people see trees with fresh eyes.

Instead of making a structure about the subject, could the finished piece be a tree-planting nursery in itself? This idea evolved to create a commemorative 'Tree of Trees' to support hundreds of saplings, which would then go on to be planted after the Jubilee celebrations were over, as a lasting contribution to the Queen's initiative.

Collaborating with a team of engineers, arborists, fabricators and nurseries, we rapidly developed the final concept for a

temporary 21-metre-high structure, made of reclaimed steel, with 80 'branches' that would support 350 British-grown saplings in spun-aluminium pots.

The project was installed outside Buckingham Palace in the days leading up to the Platinum Jubilee. Working with a tree nursery in Cambridgeshire, we selected 350 saplings from nine native species – alder, field maple, hazel, hornbeam, larch, rowan, silver birch, small-leaved lime and whitebeam – to ensure they could be planted successfully in different parts of the UK after their time in the spotlight, during which they would be kept healthy by a bespoke watering system that ran across the entire structure. As the project neared completion, 'Junior Foresters' from Coppice Primary School and William Torbitt Primary

School in Essex helped us place the saplings in the pots and cover the Tree of Trees in lights.

On the evening of Thursday 2 June, during a special ceremony, Queen Elizabeth II pressed the button to illuminate the Tree of Trees as the Jubilee's Principal Beacon. Forming the first in a chain of 1,500 beacons lit across the UK and Commonwealth countries to mark the occasion, the Tree was an ever-present backdrop for parades, concerts and ceremonies over the next few days.

After the Jubilee weekend, the 350 saplings in their celebratory pots were given to 350 community groups across the country.

Trees matter much more to our lives than we realize. Over the course of two tree-planting seasons, the Queen's Green Canopy initiative directly led to the planting of over three million trees across the nation – one of many lasting tributes to Queen Elizabeth II's extraordinary service.

Xi'an CCBD

Can a modern, large-scale
development have character?

IN EARLY 2020, the studio was invited to design a project for the Chinese state development company, China Resources Land, on a prominent plot to the south of Xi'an. The city is the oldest surviving capital of ancient China, at one end of the important Silk Route between Asia and Europe. Even though the site was close to an important temple and not far from the pits where the famous Terracotta Army was discovered, it had no historic structures on it.

We were asked to imagine a whole district that would integrate towers and significant public space, with below- and above-ground shopping next to a busy road. The Xi'an Centre Culture Business District (CCBD) would need to cope with the local climate, which ranges from minus 10 to plus 40 degrees centigrade throughout the year. In the context of such temperature extremes, the design team became even more interested in finding ways to create sheltered public space in which people could come together.

The demands of the project could easily have lead to the typical response, seen all around the world, of a single gigantic podium building with towers above. Instead, we wanted to find a system that would allow us to break down this podium arrangement to accentuate the human scale, making the place feel as porous and accessible as possible, and encouraging visitors to explore the district.

36

The team gradually evolved the idea of giant, glazed ceramic table-shaped frames interlocking with each other, infilled with different shops, restaurants and level changes. Rather than designing rectangular frames, we were inspired by the sophisticated, undulating forms used in traditional architecture in China, and experimented with curving the edges of the table frames to give them a soft, playful quality. At the centre of the site, in the same way an elephant stoops down to let a passenger climb onto its back, these tables gradually reach down to the ground so visitors can walk up to the landscape on top. In this way, there is a blurring of the boundaries between ground, roof, staircase and terrace.

To avoid the surfaces of the table frames feeling clinical and industrial, the team found a number of specialist pottery manufacturers willing to experiment with making large quantities of ceramic panelling with a handmade, artisanal quality. We were excited at the potential to use unusual, varied, natural ceramic glaze finishes that would create visual complexity close-up as well as from a distance. The team made hundreds of test tiles of extruded ceramic pieces with different glazes applied using enormous heat to achieve an almost volcanic effect. For us, the more natural imperfections visible within them, the more precious they felt. We did not want a strict quality control where we inadvertently ended up losing material idiosyncrasies that could potentially affect the emotions of the visitor.

Within the mass of our interlocked table buildings, the team worked hard to make the main shopping environment feel characterful and special. The interior space is warm and welcoming through the introduction of skylights shaped like leaves and paving patterns of soft-edged stones to create interleaving textures on the floor. Handrails are made from hand-carved wood and the visible edges of the floors are cast with an unusual organic form developed to reduce horizontal monotony.

For the exterior landscape design, the team was particularly influenced by Xi'an's own tradition of people promenading in the city's public spaces. Wherever you are in the world, people welcome opportunities to be on display themselves, as well as to people watch. On warm evenings in Xi'an, the atmosphere is amazing, with incredible festive night-time light shows and citizens strolling along the city's famous historic walls.

At the heart of the new district is a project called the Xi'an Tree, inspired by a famous local 1,400-year-old gingko at the Gu Guanying Buddhist temple that still blossoms spectacularly every year, situated at the centre of the temple complex. There was a need for a public focal point in the district, but instead of making an inert sculpture that people only looked at, the team wondered if there could be a special centrepiece that grew up from the lower level and invited everybody to climb it to get new views and perspectives of the surrounding city.

As Xi'an had been at the end of the famous Silk Route, we created a monument celebrating the route itself on a grand scale, with a unique walkable structure. It contains 337 steps, 60 huge structural 'leaves' and takes visitors on a journey through gardens representing the seven different climate zones of the regions on the Silk Route.

The team worked with the famous horticulturist Mr Guo from Xi'an's botanic gardens to develop a landscape design featuring a complex layering of biodiversity and planting heritage. Across the Tree are many gathering points. At the halfway point, 250 people can come together for events, talks or just to look out across the city, and at the top there is space for 100 people, and more intimate spaces and gardens. In total, there are over 150 trees, hundreds of rocks as part of the locally inspired landscape, and almost 2,000 square metres of shrubs, bushes, flora and fauna – all connected by flights of reclaimed timber steps.

New evidence is emerging about the serious impact of big areas of built environment on our mental health, and it is starting to be possible to measure the degree to which they affect people, whether positively or negatively. The studio is interested to learn from large projects like Xi'an CCBD and Azabudai Hills in Tokyo (pages 88–101) and to see what lessons can be passed on to others involved in creating big new pieces of city.

安全是生命之本 违章是事故之源

Hainan Performing Arts Centre

Can performance halls be part of the community?

IN 2020, THE STUDIO was approached to enter a design competition for a performing arts centre in Hainan, a tropical island province at the southernmost point of China. The local government intended the new complex, including an opera house, a large concert auditorium and a multi-functional hall, to become a landmark in the new cultural quarter of the capital, Haikou.

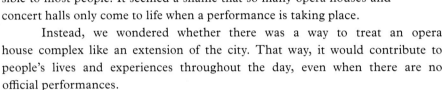

Researching these types of cultural venues around the world, the studio found that they are often imposing and cut off from their surroundings, sitting empty for a lot of the time and generally inaccessible to most people. It seemed a shame that so many opera houses and concert halls only come to life when a performance is taking place.

Instead, we wondered whether there was a way to treat an opera house complex like an extension of the city. That way, it would contribute to people's lives and experiences throughout the day, even when there are no official performances.

In any city, public, weather-protected space for people to gather together is precious. It is even more rare in a tropical climate like Hainan where it is typically only offered by shopping malls.

The competition-winning design developed by the studio provides three performance spaces that come together as focal points. They frame a large amount of public space under a sweeping canopy, which, in turn, creates a cooler microclimate as well as protecting everyone from the tropical rain. This roofscape parasol shelters a mix of different areas that form an open-air village, of which the halls are a part.

The idea is that everyone has a reason to visit here – whether or not they have a ticket for a show. There is an opportunity to take the formality of performance and blend it with the informality of the island's culture, to make a place that feels accessible and welcoming to all.

Covering 10 acres of land and integrating thousands of solar panels, the dynamic roof is influenced by the volcanic landscape and the costumes, colours and movement of Hainanese Opera. To optimize the building's functionality in the island's tropical climate and to provide the best possible place for thousands of people to come together, a technical team of makers and engineers has rigorously tested the design through physical and immersive digital modelling and data analysis.

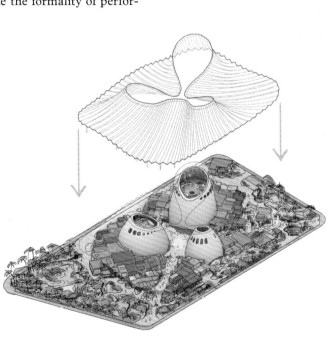

When finished, the building will stage international productions, from large-scale opera, ballet and musicals to avant-garde drama, fashion and immersive multimedia performances. While having performance capacity for 3,800 people, it will also, crucially, be creating public space for many thousands more.

48

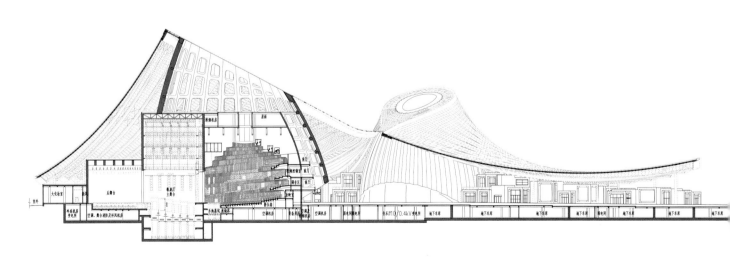

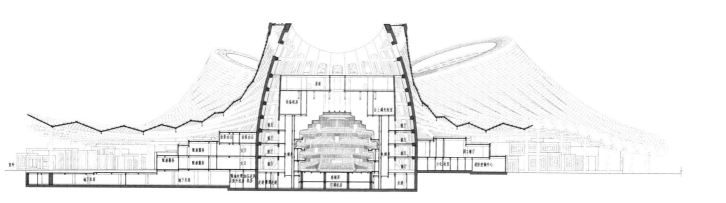

West Bund Orbit

*Can you let the public climb
your building?*

THE STUDIO WAS ASKED TO DESIGN a public exhibition hall on Shanghai's West Bund waterfront, located next to the Long Museum and directly opposite the site where the studio's UK Pavilion stood at the World Expo in 2010 (pages 308–25). Hongkong Land, the commissioner, wanted to create a riverside landmark, as well as a cultural heart for the new financial hub it was developing in the city's Xuhui District.

Imagining the building as a lookout post over the river, the design team did not want to simply decorate the exterior of a big exhibition box. Instead, we became interested in the idea that the outside of the building could be brought alive by the visitors by encouraging them to actively explore and climb the structure itself.

The visual language of the project evolved from looking at the elegant moon bridges found in Chinese parks, where flights of stairs are combined with graceful, flowing movement. A vision emerged for a structure whose exterior is made from interwoven ribbons that twist as they wrap around the form, creating a sense of rotational motion and a building that is accessible to everyone from a full 360 degrees – all the way around itself.

With no obvious front or back to The Orbit, visitors are invited to journey up and around the structure via accessible staircases, bridges and terraces. These lead to a rooftop garden where cultural events take place and multiple viewing platforms overlook the river.

The outside of the staircases and terraces is made of glass-reinforced concrete embedded with small pieces of mother-of-pearl aggregate to catch the eye with its special luminosity. One of the first events at The Orbit, which launched in 2024, was the Art Waterfront International Forum, immediately establishing it as a new cultural destination for Shanghai.

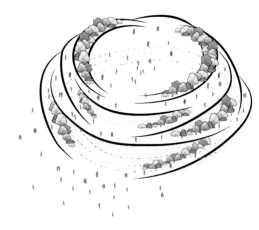

The main exhibition space at the centre of the building is supported by further facilities on the upper levels. A second gallery wraps around the main hall to catch the attention of people passing outside, who can look in through glazed openings.

The Orbit's location on the bend of the river means it stands out like a jewel that is open to all, whether visitors choose to go inside to an exhibition or not.

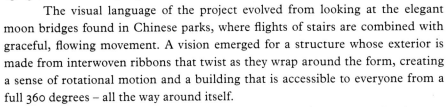

Airo

Can a car clean the air?

HAVING WORKED ON THE London bus (pages 258–65) some years earlier, the studio was invited by one of China's largest vehicle manufacturers to design a new electric car. Knowing that every car company in the world was developing electric vehicles as part of the biggest revolution in the automotive industry in decades, we were curious to find a fresh approach.

Rather than just restyling the outside of a car, the team set itself the task of creating more meaningful change. During our research, we were struck by the fact that electric cars are typically less good for the planet than we had realized. While it is true that they are non-polluting at the point of driving, from a fossil-fuel perspective, they still give off damaging particles from their tyres and brake pads that are inhaled by passers-by.

Gradually an idea for a new electric car evolved, based on two core aims. The first was to make a vehicle that would actually clean the air around it as it moved. Like flypaper, it would capture the polluting particles it produced, as well as the ones emitted by the cars, buses, lorries and motorbikes around it.

We had seen HEPA (high-efficiency particulate air) filtering technology being used on double-decker buses in the UK in a very limited and experimental way, and we were interested to see how powerful it might be if applied to a vehicle produced in its millions. At that scale, the impact could be significant.

It was also fascinating to learn that there are approximately 1.4 billion cars in the world, but they are typically used less than 10 per cent of the time – mostly they are sitting idle. That seemed absurd considering that there is a crisis of space happening for many of us around the world. And, most modern cars typically have seats that are more comfortable, and audio systems and temperature control that are better than what many of us have in our own homes. This led us to our second idea. We became excited at the potential of

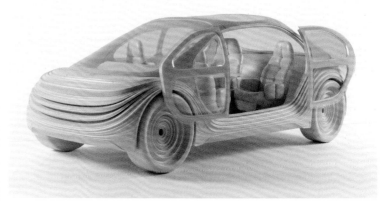

60

making a car designed to be used as an extra room for your life, and not just as a transportation device.

The breakthrough was discovering that by rotating the driver's seat and the passenger seat by 180 degrees, we could think of this much more like the cabin in an aircraft situation. In business-class seats on aeroplanes it is possible to comfortably work, eat, rest and be entertained. So similarly, if you have four car seats that come together, with a fold-out table in the middle, you could suddenly have the potential of useable space with multiple functions. When not being driven, the car could be a meeting room, a gaming pod, a bedroom, or a lounge.

Adding pairs of sliding doors (rather than traditional swing doors) would save more space and increase accessibility. This was now a concept for a car that was also, simultaneously, a moving pavilion: it could transform depending on its location, whether in a city or in nature.

Giving the car the name Airo, the studio started to make full-sized prototypes and mock ups, experimenting with the types of interior space that could be created by avoiding conventional plastic car interiors. Borrowing from the language of interior design and introducing colour, warmth, natural materials and flattering lighting, we designed a space more like a lounge than a car.

For the exterior of Airo, we moved away from the typical smooth, flat surfaces of modern car design, adding ripples, folds and creases to provide texture and echo the flow of air across the car body. It was thrilling to collaborate

with experienced car-modelling companies who are used to taking complex, three-dimensional surfaces and exploring how subtle changes can shift viewers' perceptions.

In 2021 a full-size prototype of Airo was exhibited at the Shanghai and Guangzhou motor shows as well as Goodwood's Festival of Speed. My hope is that one day it will become a reality, and I can finally upgrade the Citroën 2CV I have driven for three decades (page 12).

64

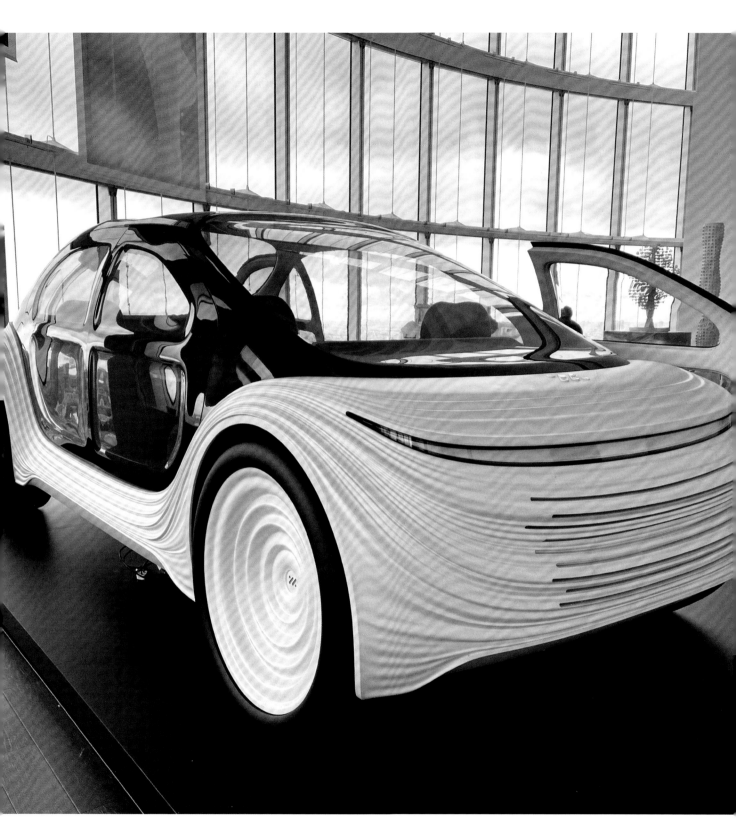

Stem

Can a desk support your mental health?

THE COVID-19 PANDEMIC led to a major shift in how many people lived and worked all over the world. Many of us found ourselves under lockdown and forced to work from home. Instead of having real conversations face to face, we pretended to be highly productive while speaking to pixellated screen images of each other on software few of us had ever used before. Rather than walking around a living design studio, standing up for much of the day, our team members were trapped at home. Some of us had not sat down for such long periods since being teenagers taking exams at school.

Out of the blue during this time, we were invited to join an experiment to create a desk and chair suitable for this new reality. Reflecting on our own new feelings of isolation and sense of environmental monotony at being stuck indoors, we began to wonder whether nature might have a part to play.

In the studio's work with buildings, we had become interested in Attention Restoration Theory, which was developed by psychologists Rachel and Stephen Kaplan in the 1980s. It argues that exposure to natural environments for just forty seconds makes very real improvements to how our brains function and how our minds replenish themselves in-between periods of concentration.

That made us think even more about the mental-health benefits of nature within interior spaces, and we wondered whether we could use our own desks to incorporate more living plants into our workspaces. We decided to design a table that incorporated luscious plants into it.

To make the table, our client asked us to look at using sustainable American hardwood. For inspiration, we turned to the craft of wooden spoon carving. And, instead of actually designing a desk, we created a modular system of special legs topped with planters of all different heights and diameters. These can be combined and simply clamped onto any desk surface – from a piece of glass or stone to an IKEA tabletop – to prop them up.

We then worked virtually with the high-quality timber craftsmanship company called Benchmark via online sketches, emails and video calls. They were able to carve the tactile, ripple-patterned components out of maple wood, using a computer-controlled carving machine. Each leg is sculptural in its own right and can be adapted to add cupboards, trays and lights.

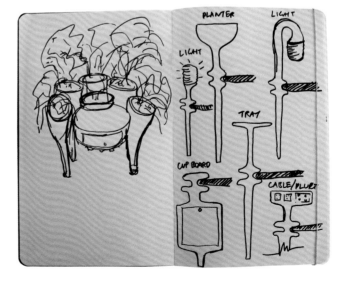

Our first version of the table, which we called Stem, used a glass surface to place all the emphasis on the legs and plants (including two cacti, a huge Monstera and an African Jasmine). Once the Covid lockdowns ended, the table was displayed at London's Design Museum as part of an exhibition called *Connected* in 2020, which celebrated people physically coming back together again.

The prototype now lives in our studio, where we still use it to take video calls to this day.

Friction/Expanding Furniture

How can inanimate objects change shape?

MY TEAM AND I HAVE ALWAYS BEEN fascinated by the idea of transformation, particularly that moment of revelation when one thing becomes something else. And a number of different projects that move, unfold or unfurl – from the Rolling Bridge (pages 436–41) to the Olympic Cauldron (pages 174–81) – seem to have truly connected with people.

In 2004, the studio designed a carpet that could dramatically change its proportions and pattern using a pivot mechanism. Seeing the prototype gave us the idea for an expanding table as the ultimate expression of this concept (pages 72–73). While a square table-top became a long, thin rectangle, a circular version mutated into an eclipse.

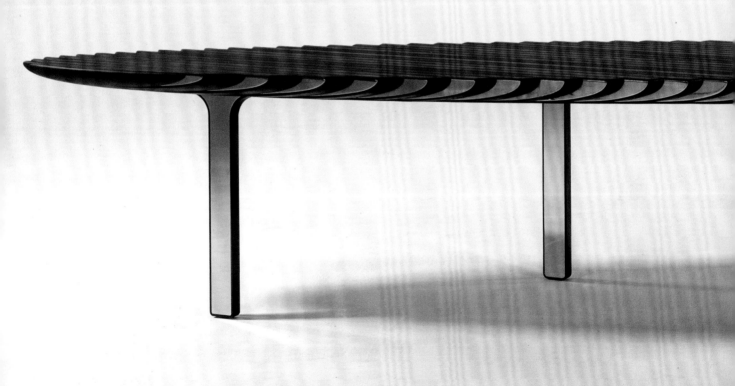

Then, the team asked itself if it were possible to use multiple layers of the pivoting trellis mechanism to generate a fully three-dimensional material that could be carved into any shape. We then developed a large bowl (pages 74–75) that transformed into an extraordinary elongated elliptical form.

All that thinking has culminated in Friction (below): a 1.8-metre round table for six people, which, via a simple mechanical lattice device, shapeshifts into an enormous, stretched ellipsis, with space for twelve to sit around it comfortably.

The 45 slats that form the table-top are individually machined in two parts to make certain that every single joint on the table is in the right place. Then, 193 pivot points are precisely placed, pinned together and calibrated to

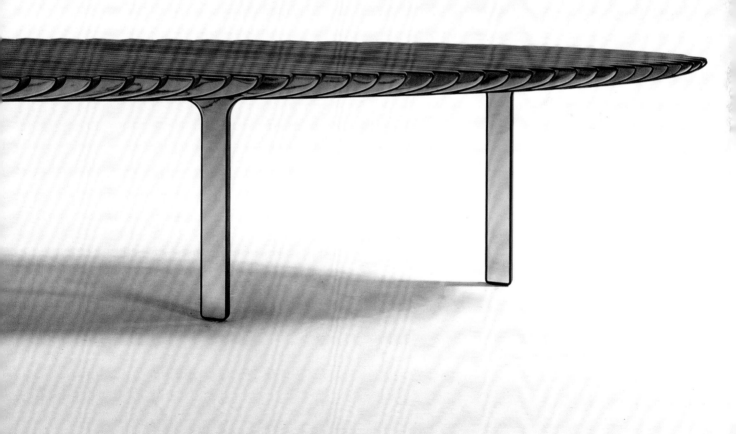

72

ensure that the table is perfectly level, balanced and opens smoothly. When extending to its full width of 4 metres, the legs transition into the underside of the table.

While this is a very engineered object, the studio also wanted it to feel like a piece of traditional, hand-crafted furniture. We partnered with Millimetre and Bill Amberg Studio to wrap a ludicrously precise polished aluminium structure in leather – a by-product from the food industry reused to limit waste – with the aim of crafting something soulful and rich in materiality.

Ultimately, the aim is that Friction is an heirloom that looks better as it ages and never loses its power to delight and surprise.

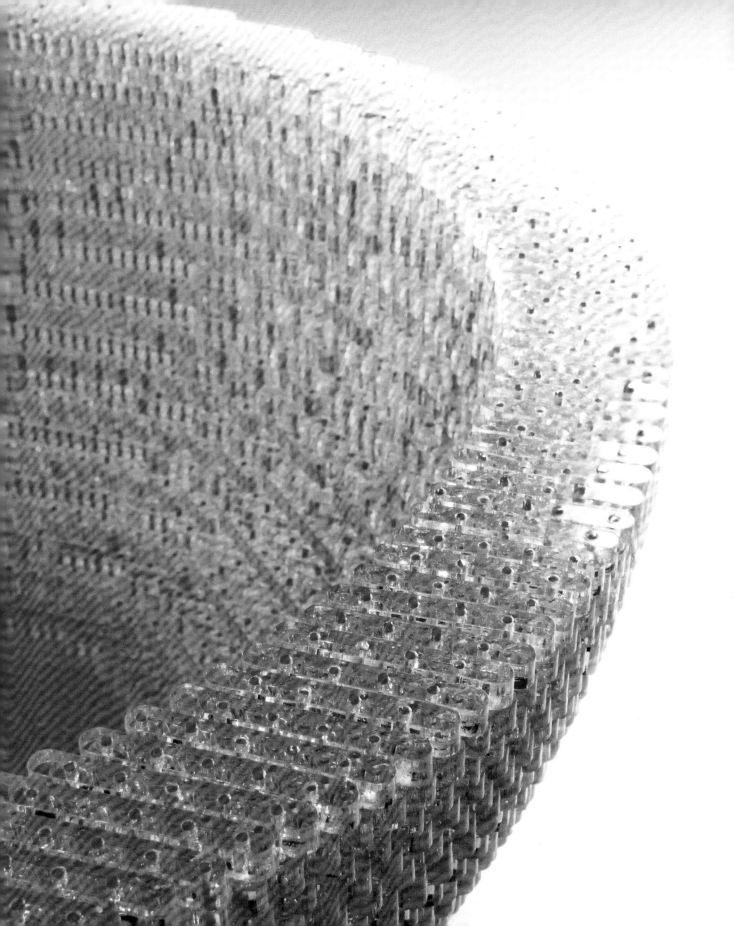

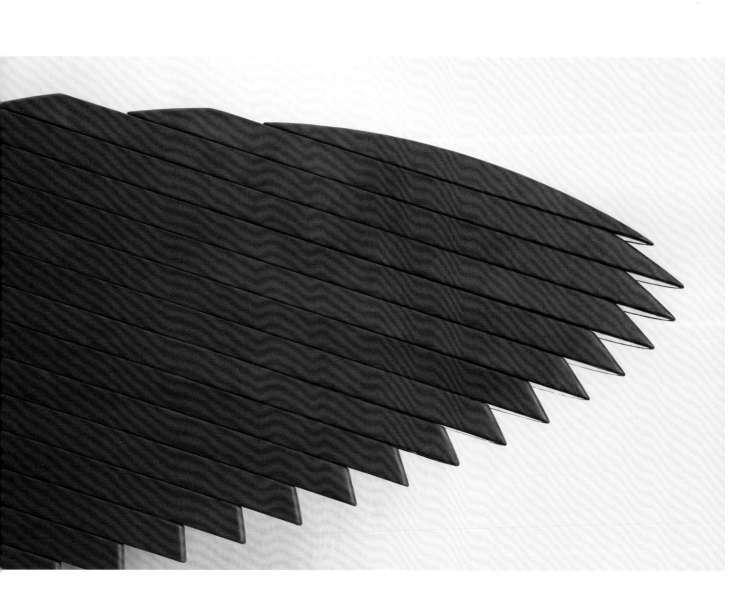

London Olympia

Can you make public space on roofs?

2017

OLYMPIA HAS ALWAYS HAD a special place in London's cultural scene. Conceived as a collection of major exhibition spaces, it opened in December 1886, with Henry Edward Coe's Grand Hall, with its barrel-vaulted roof and pleated-glass façade as the centrepiece.

Over its 140-year history Olympia has been the setting for a huge range of gatherings, celebrations and exhibitions attended by millions of people. It is an extraordinary meeting place of entertainment, innovation and business, from circuses, horse races, and rock concerts by Jimi Hendrix and Pink Floyd, to car, boat and motorbike shows, chess tournaments, beer festivals, Crufts dog show and London Fashion Week.

By 2017, however, when the studio was approached by Yoo Capital and Deutsche Finance International to reimagine Olympia, its 14-acre site had evolved into a confusing mixture of buildings, which felt closed off and fortress-like, and impossible for the public to enter without a ticket or a lanyard. Despite being the last major exhibition halls in central London, Olympia had become a strange island of half-dead space in the middle of the city. Unless you were going to an exhibition or conference there, it was no longer a destination in its own right for Londoners.

The studio took responsibility for the master-plan concept, in collaboration with SPPARC architects, and began to look for opportunities to build on Olympia's success as a collection of exhibition spaces, but reimagining it to be more generous to its visitors and its neighbourhood. The original Victorian exhibition buildings had been conceived as a people's palace, welcoming to anybody, so the team's ambition was to transform the site back into a vibrant cultural quarter.

At first look, however, this seemed to be an impossible task, with the existing halls taking up most of the street level. How could any hall be removed to make new public space? The team's unusual solution was to lift up the public

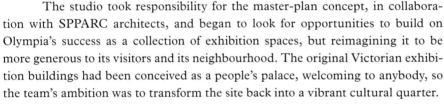

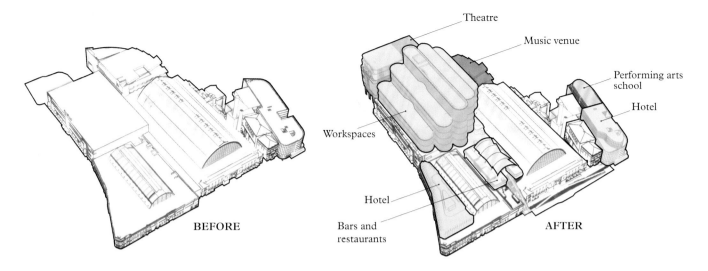

Theatre

Music venue

Performing arts
school

Hotel

Workspaces

Hotel

Bars and
restaurants

BEFORE

AFTER

realm by two-and-a half storeys to sit between the curving glass roofs of the National and Grand Halls, creating a street in the sky.

This 2.5-acre space on the roof has never before been accessible to the public and is now intended as a lively meeting place lined with generous planting and shops, cafés, bars and restaurants. The design team also developed the idea of adding a third barrel-vaulted glass space to create an open-sided rooftop garden with incredible views across London. The elevated public realm would also be the main access route to a new concert and event space seating 4,400, and a brand-new 1,575-seat theatre (London's largest since the National Theatre opened in 1976). Complementing these and accessed from the street, the plan includes a conference centre, two hotels and a school for the performing arts.

This elevated new public realm would also connect to a new 550,000-square-foot complex of workspaces called Olympia Central, consisting of five curving towers. Floorplates spill out from each tower to create big outdoor terraces. The massing of Central steps back, reducing its visual impact, while creating some of the largest office terraces in London, giving workers open-air spaces in which to exercise, socialize and enjoy the views.

The impressive pleated-glass walls of the Victorian Grand Hall influenced the design team to carry through this idea to many elements on the site, such as the new glass over the roof garden, the walls of Olympia Central and the aluminium cladding of the new theatre. Even the new hotel designed by the studio that sits on top of the National Hall has stepped rooms inside, which give it a concertina profile outside. The scheme also has pleated door handles and specially designed details like the lift buttons with unusual intergrated signage.

Finally, the team was excited to honour the heritage of the site by retaining and carefully renovating back to their former glory both the Grand Hall and the National Hall. Planning permission for the scheme was granted in January 2019, and the new buildings are on target to open in late 2025.

Olympia will be welcome to all, as a generous and humanized people's palace. It will be a place to feel joy, excitement and wonder in an incredible city, playing a crucial part in maintaining London's place as a global cultural destination.

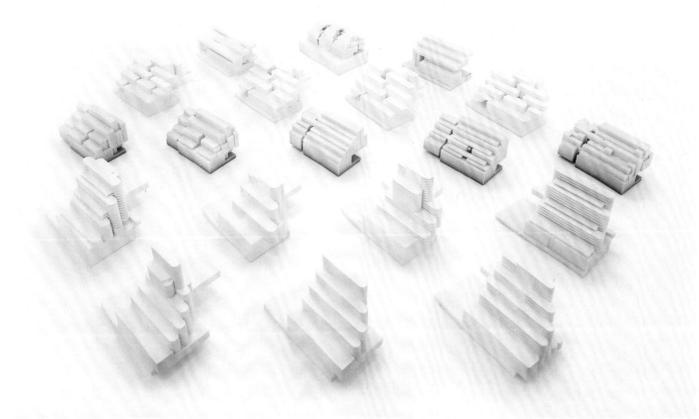

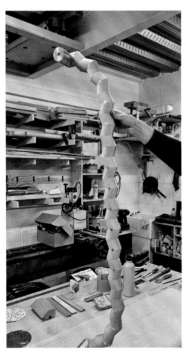

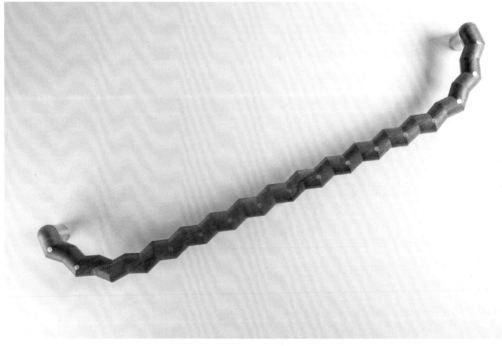

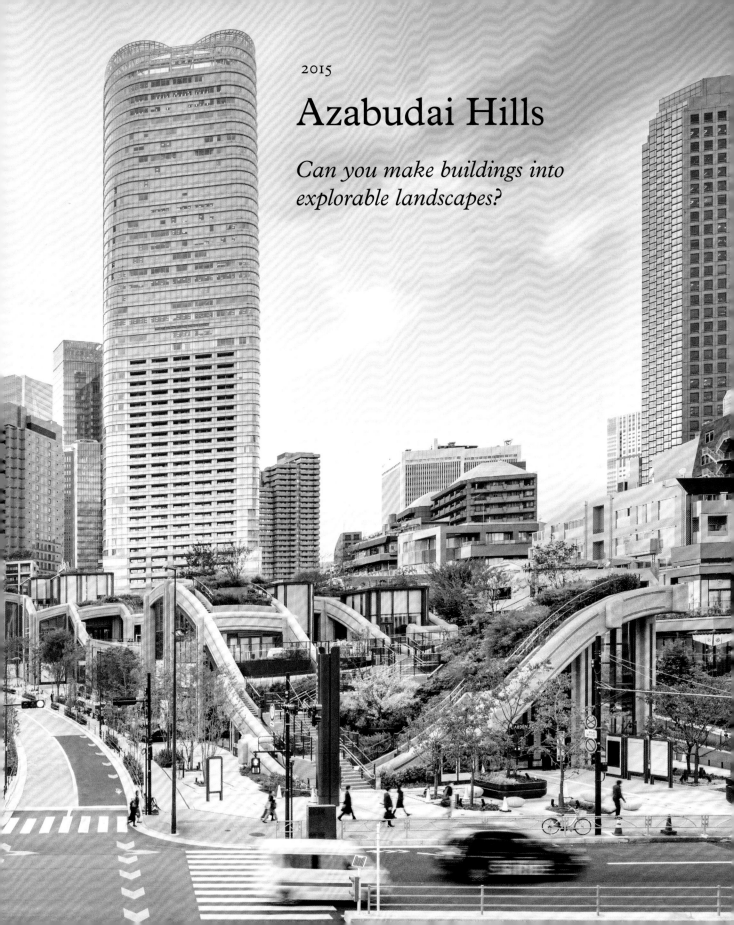

2015

Azabudai Hills

Can you make buildings into
explorable landscapes?

JAPAN'S FOREMOST PROPERTY DEVELOPER, the Mori Building Company, invited the studio in 2015 to lead the regeneration of a 20-acre district in central Tokyo: a Y-shaped piece of land straddling the commercial quarter of Roppongi and the business area of Toranomon. The team had designed big buildings before but had never built an entire district.

By the time the studio joined the project, a consortium formed of Mori, the residents and local businesses had been discussing the proposal for nearly thirty years. The district's master plan already allowed for three towers, one of which would be the tallest in Japan, but Mori now needed an overall vision for all the buildings and the landscape between the towers.

The existing neighbourhood was made up of more than two hundred buildings, which had been hastily constructed after World War II. There were homes, temples, nurseries, offices, dry cleaners and florists, squeezed together at a variety of scales. The buildings had lots of character but were in bad condition, and the residents were actively involved in debating what might replace them.

The big question was how to build a new piece of a city that respected its history and community, but did not create the same sterile, soulless feeling for residents and visitors that so many brand-new developments of this size do.

The team became interested by Mori's concept of building a vast main tower that generates a big income, financially justifying constructing the district's surrounding buildings at a more human scale and in a more varied way. This, in turn, would give the area a special atmosphere and character. It was intriguing to explore how much public green space a new development such as this could give back to the city. Compared to London, where 20 per cent of the city is green, in Tokyo it is only 8 per cent. Could the buildings themselves contribute to this percentage of greenery, and not just the spaces between them?

Having researched rectangular garden pergola structures, which have lush planting growing through them and over them, we wondered whether we could take this idea and imagine it at a neighbourhood scale. A system emerged where a huge structural frame could bend upwards and downwards to create planted buildings with planted spaces in between.

Punching through the gaps in this structural 'net' would be an organic assembly of pavilions of different sizes, as well as affordable apartments, workspaces, restaurants, shops and galleries. At other points the net could swoop down to create a sunken courtyard or be

pushed aside to make room for a new temple. It could also be used to frame the location for a school for eight hundred children.

Going forward to build the project, the net system helped us to embed a large amount of nature within the district – in total, 24,000 square metres of greenery and 320 species of plant. As well as creating a playful and accessible landscape in the heart of the city, we were able to introduce precious pieces of wilderness. Such natural planting encourages biodiversity and provides a home for beneficial pollinators in the city.

Green space was also very important in the design of the school. However, unlike most schools, which are typically very spread out due to their various playgrounds and sports pitches, this one was in the centre of the city and would need to be relatively high-rise. We were keen to see how many external sports and play areas we could still give it. Also, next to the other smaller shopping pavilions we would be building nearby, we wanted to make sure it would have a clear identity of its own. Therefore, we designed it as a collection of overlapping terraces filled with planting and spaces where children could play, learn and connect.

With a feel more like an urban treehouse than a single big box, the finished school was built with the same yellow brick tiles that used to cover the post office that had existed previously on the site. The studio was able to find the original factory that made the brick tiles and used their 'reject' tiles, to give the final surfaces of the school more built-in imperfection and visual fascination.

To make the architectural pergola frame more engaging to look at, and earthy rather than clinical, we cased its steel beams and columns in panels of glass-reinforced concrete with a mix of warm-coloured pebbles on the surface.

The intention was for the frame to look dramatic and sweeping from a distance but to also be interesting and tactile up close.

At the core of the scheme is the main open central garden conceived by the studio. And at its heart is an event plaza for the whole district, which needed a large canopy to protect whatever happened below it from the rain and sun. Instead of thinking about it as another part of the undulating landscape structure, we saw an opportunity to mediate between Japan's tallest tower and the smaller pavilions around it. Inspired by a photograph of Mount Fuji with a saucer-shaped cloud hovering above it, and also the curling and complex forms made by the craft of paper quilling, the team developed a dynamic structure of swirling and unfurling steel plate, supporting a layer of glass, on top of three towering columns.

A distinctive thing about the finished project is the way in which ambiguity manifests itself. Because of the changes in level, visitors are faced with discoveries and surprises: one minute they are in a green plaza, the next a sunken amphitheatre. The team has attempted to create moments of joy and fascination everywhere. It is not possible to capture the whole district in a photograph – you have to walk through it to discover it. Instead of big empty plazas or wide, blank boulevards, a street is at the heart of the project. There are large-scale heroic parts, but also humbler areas, where the emotional connection can sometimes be stronger for visitors or passers-by. The final district sits against the backdrop of the existing tapestry of the city, as a series of interwoven layers: small scale with bigger scale, nature with buildings, the new and the old.

Named Azabudai Hills, the completed district was opened on 23 November 2023. Almost a generation after the project began, 90 per cent of the district's former residents have decided to move back in, including the 99-year-old head of the redevelopment committee, who had lived in the neighbourhood his whole life.

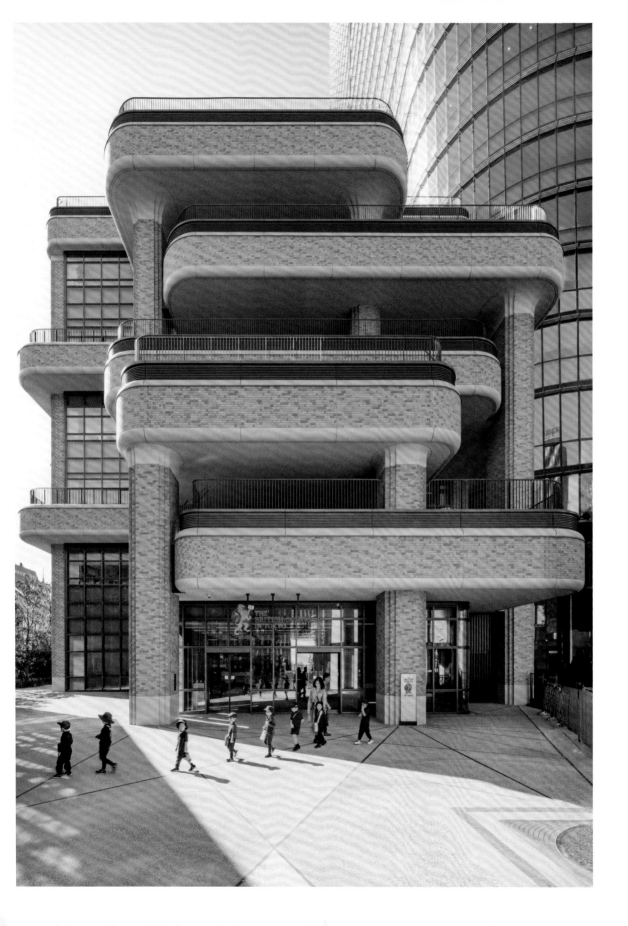

Glasshouse

2015

Can a roof get out of the way when it's not needed?

THE WOOLBEDING ESTATE in West Sussex was described by former British prime minister Benjamin Disraeli in the late 1800s as 'the greenest valley with the prettiest river in the world'. In 2015, the Woolbeding Charity asked the studio to design a glasshouse within the historic 1,000-acre estate.

Over three decades, philanthropist Simon Sainsbury and his partner Stewart Grimshaw had restored the grounds, including 26 acres of gardens. Sainsbury passed away in 2006, and five years later the grounds were opened to the public, and a grant was put aside for the Woolbeding Charity to create a new garden and glasshouse, managed by the National Trust.

The design team began by researching England's rich tradition of gardens with glasshouse structures. After consultation with Grimshaw and swapping thoughts with horticulturalist Fergus Garrett and his acclaimed Great Dixter House and Gardens team, the idea emerged to create a garden inspired by the famous Silk Route that historically linked Europe to Asia. Such a concept did not exist in another British public garden.

A plan was developed for a meandering pathway taking visitors past three hundred species of plants on a journey from Mediterranean Turkey to China, culminating in a collection of subtropical plants, including umbrella trees, magnolias and bananas, all within a glasshouse. But the team had a dilemma. On the one hand these subtropical plants needed protection from the potentially damaging effects of British winters, but on the other hand the health and strength of the plants relied upon unhindered exposure to wind and sun.

A design for the Woolbeding glasshouse emerged, influenced by the Wardian cases and terrariums of the Victorians. The structure has a radially symmetrical jewel-like plan with a pitched roof to allow enough height for the tall plants to grow inside.

But it also holds a surprise.

On warm days, the gigantic triangular pieces that make up the roof move, opening and stretching outward using a mechanism of hydraulic pistons. The transformation sees the shape of the structure dynamically change from a gem to an open flower to allow sunlight and breezes to reach the plants inside. The completed structure is 15 metres high and covers an area of 143 square metres, with a system that lets the subtropical plants inside have the best of both worlds: full sun and natural exposure in the summer months and the necessary protection from the elements during the winter.

While the extraordinary glasshouse transforms on a daily basis, the plants inside and the Silk Route garden beyond evolve and flourish more gradually. They are two constantly changing habitats designed to be educationally fascinating, as well as full of wonder.

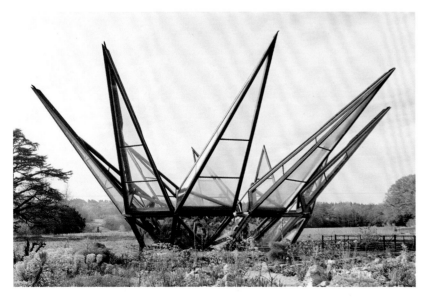

Lantern House

Why do windows have to be flat?

IN 2015, THE STUDIO was commissioned to design apartments in the Meatpacking District of New York, near the former docks where deliveries used to arrive by boat.

Once an industrial part of the city, the area was in the process of being regenerated, triggered by the creation of the High Line Park on the former railway line, which ran directly through the middle of our proposed site, splitting it in two. Alongside brick warehouses and the remnants of industry, new buildings by many different architects were springing up, and millions of people were now walking around the area.

Researching different apartment projects built in New York in recent times, the team was interested to learn that those

built from brick or stone typically sold quicker and for higher prices than those made from metal and glass. This did not seem to be influenced by whether something was more historic looking or newer looking. Rather, it seemed to be about the use of materials and the emotions they evoked in people. Typically, the outside surfaces of metal and glass buildings feel thinner and flimsier, while brick or stone structures suggest permanence, durability, longevity and a connection to the earth. Following these learnings, we looked at using brick. We knew we did not want to imitate an old building, but could we still make something that felt true to its location and heritage?

Unlike some architectural projects where you have lots of sculptural freedom, the form of our building in the Meatpacking District was almost completely controlled by a combination of the city's zoning laws, with limits to maximum height and buildable floor area, and the team's own research, which confirmed that ceiling heights over 3 metres in apartments mean that they are more likely to sell. It was clear that this project would need to consist of two towers, one of eleven storeys and one of twenty-two storeys, either side of the High Line. Our job was to make these simple forms come alive.

In the studio's early days, we were fascinated by the overall shape of buildings, but over time, we have come to understand that humans are often more emotionally affected by a building's texture, materiality and detail than by its overall form. It is possible to experience a building with an extraordinary shape, yet made from sterile, featureless materials, and be left feeling very little. The decision was made to allow the simplicity of this project's overall building form to stay as it wanted to be, and instead to focus on its materials and the three-dimensionality of its surface.

We were also very influenced by the rigidity of New York's 'grid' layout, which is famous for being formed of a pattern of regular rectangular blocks. Our building's blocks would be part of this, there was no other option. But we wondered if we could get away from the tyranny of squareness by making the windows less square. This evolved into the idea of reinventing the traditional bay window. Looking at examples of windows from late-Victorian and Edwardian-era buildings, we became intrigued by the thought of making our pair of buildings be all about their windows.

We had previously created curving windows for a museum project in Cape Town, Zeitz MOCAA (pages 196–207). However, the technical requirements there had been much simpler. The same solution would not work in New York due to the huge increase in scale of the project, the New York weather, plus the city's more onerous building regulations.

Fortunately, the client owned their own window-manufacturing company, and we were able to work with their specialist engineers and craftspeople to develop an entirely new system of high-performing

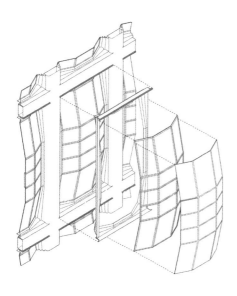

windows made with rectangular glass and sophisticated opening mechanisms. There was also the opportunity to make the corner windows wrap around to create curving lantern shapes, and to have sculptural frame details with corners that tuck inwards, with folds like origami paper.

The result is a building made from windows that sparkle unexpectedly in the sun and give unusual reflections of the sky, because the glass panes that make up the window point in different directions. And the same windows used on the upper floors for living rooms, bedrooms and bathrooms, make dynamic three-dimensional shop windows at ground level.

Lantern House's bricks are also special, made in collaboration with Taylor Clay Brick, a company that has been producing bricks for New York since the 1800s. Drawn to the artisanal process they use, we worked together to develop a range of custom brick types for the project. Three different textures, wire-cut, blade-cut and die-finished, were used, and one type of brick was hand-carved. Slurry and ceramic mineral coatings were then used to give the bricks an earthy, distinctive finish.

Visitors enter Lantern House underneath the High Line itself. The reception consists of a special roof hung like a hammock between the two buildings, pierced by the riveted steel legs of the High Line.

From inside, the extraordinary bay windows break the rectangular geometry of a typical room, allowing the residents to immerse themselves in the views. From outside, thousands of passers-by experience the building from 12th Steet, or from walking along the elevated park between the towers. Up close, there is lots of fascination from the jewel-like faceted windows, while further away, the buildings' curved yet regular forms playfully catch your attention.

Lantern House opened in 2021. Once the project finished, I had a lovely moment in a conversation with a friend who works in architectural reclamation. She was explaining how 99 per cent of buildings constructed over the last century have virtually nothing of emotional value to reclaim. Meanwhile, with older buildings, people often save columns, mouldings and panelling because these items feel complex and special enough to give character and personality to new uses. When I showed her the windows of Lantern House, she looked at them and said immediately, 'Oh, they look great. When can I reclaim one?'

Google Workspaces

Can you make whole buildings from solar panels?

THE DIGITAL REVOLUTION of the last three decades has profoundly changed the world, and, for many of the companies driving this innovation, Silicon Valley in California has been the geographical heart.

Pioneering the use of the search engine to make information accessible to everyone, one of the main companies was Google, but by the mid-2000s it had

grown so quickly that it was using up all the existing buildings in its neighbourhood of Mountain View. With lots of the technology firms going through a similar transition, the race began to be as inventive with its workspaces as with its technology and attract the most talented people in the world to work for the company.

The studio was approached by Google about the possibility of designing its new headquarters, which would be home to eight thousand people, on a large piece of land it owned near its existing offices. As the company was constantly shifting and changing to evolve at the same speed as the fast-moving technology industry, it needed spaces that would be extremely flexible.

Google was already known all over the world for its distinctive approach to interior workspaces within existing older buildings. However, with this new headquarters, envisioned as a campus formed of several buildings, there was an opportunity to create something far more impactful. The company also wanted to challenge the typical Silicon Valley model from the 1980s: brick and concrete office-building boxes sitting in seas of tarmac parking lots, surrounded by cars. The studio was fascinated by the opportunity to see if it was possible to invent the best possible physical environment that might inspire each person in the organization to do their most imaginative work.

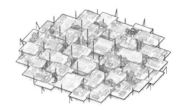

Following a lengthy competitive process, the studio was selected to work on the project alongside Danish architecture firm Bjarke Ingels Group (BIG) as equal partners in an equal collaboration. The two teams immediately began working together to produce a master plan.

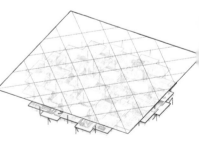

An early visit to Moffett Federal Airfield on the edge of the site was particularly influential. Owned by NASA and leased to Google, it contains three airship hangars – spectacular, enormous, singular spaces built in the last century to house what at the time had been seen as the transport of the future. This led to a breakthrough, when the team wondered whether the challenge of needing space for thousands of employees could be solved by building something similar. Instead of creating floor upon floor of conventional office space, could we instead reinvent the notion of vast, flexible airship hangars as spaces in which people could work in many different ways?

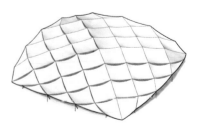

120

Under big, large-span canopy structures we imagined spaces with a landscape like a small ever-changing town, with streets, shortcuts and courtyards that open up for gatherings. There could be cafés, gyms and rest places, while, sitting on the roofs above this streetscape, could be a huge, interconnected level of workspaces. This floor would consist of stepped platforms like large-scale furniture that could be reconfigured to accommodate different team sizes and tasks.

As the hangar idea evolved, it developed into giant, semi-rigid tents that touch the ground lightly and have soft, draping forms with generous 40-metre-high spaces inside.

In a conventional hierarchical office only a few people near the windows have access to views and daylight. We moved away from this by designing canopy structures that are split apart in many places by smile-shaped clerestory windows, allowing light to flood in equally to every desk space.

Mountain View has an extraordinarily broad landscape, reaching out to the bay. However, the nature had been poisoned by many years of silicon chip production, so the team wanted to detoxify the land, bring back wildlife and give more space to horticulture. With such large spanning canopies acting as vast umbrellas, there was also the opportunity to store the rain running off them in big ponds for use throughout the buildings. Helped by the best experts in the world, the team designed a geothermal system that takes the cool temperature from the earth below ground and uses it to naturally bring down the buildings' temperature and reduce the need for extra energy.

The team also contemplated how to harness the energy from the sun's rays that are so abundant in California. It seemed a shame that buildings are typically constructed and then, almost as an afterthought, a few, often ugly, solar panels are put on the roofs to provide a bit of energy. What would happen if the entire surface of the building itself was made of solar panels? With the weather so sunny for much of the year, the team considered what the maximum possible power was you could get from completely covering the roof with a high-efficiency roofing system that captured solar energy. We had never seen this done before at this scale. Working with specialist firms we developed bespoke panels

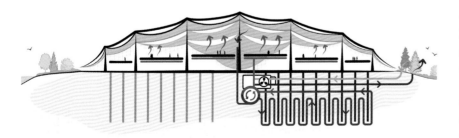

that overlap and drape over the curved shape of the buildings like the scales of a dragon and generate 40 per cent of the total energy needed.

The first three buildings on the campus, called Bay View, opened in the summer of 2022, while the largest structure, called

Gradient Canopy, opened in 2023. Accessible pedestrian and cycle-friendly pathways thread around these dramatic buildings and through the surrounding wetland environment, creating a campus that is a generous neighbour to both its natural habitat as well as local community.

The ambitious new workspaces opened as the global Covid-19 pandemic was ending and conversations were happening all over the world about what the workplace of the future might look like in a post-pandemic world. These buildings, developed seven years earlier, already felt like the workplaces of the future: flexible and stimulating places, utterly unlike your home, where you could be together with your colleagues in the most creative environment. In the world of architecture, it is now better understood than ever that to be truly sustainable any new structure must be 'long life, loose fit'. So, it was exciting to see the first employees move in and hear them enjoying the idea that their new buildings would be able to be endlessly rethought and adapted in the decades to come, in the same way that we have learned to reconfigure the large flexible warehouse spaces created in the Victorian era as fantastic versatile workspaces.

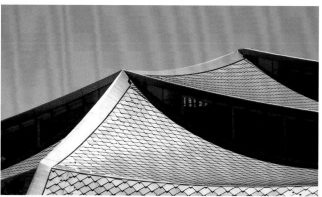

Finally, the completed buildings were awarded the prestigious LEED Platinum certification, the highest environmental sustainability certification possible. At the time of the award, they were the largest LEED Platinum buildings in the world.

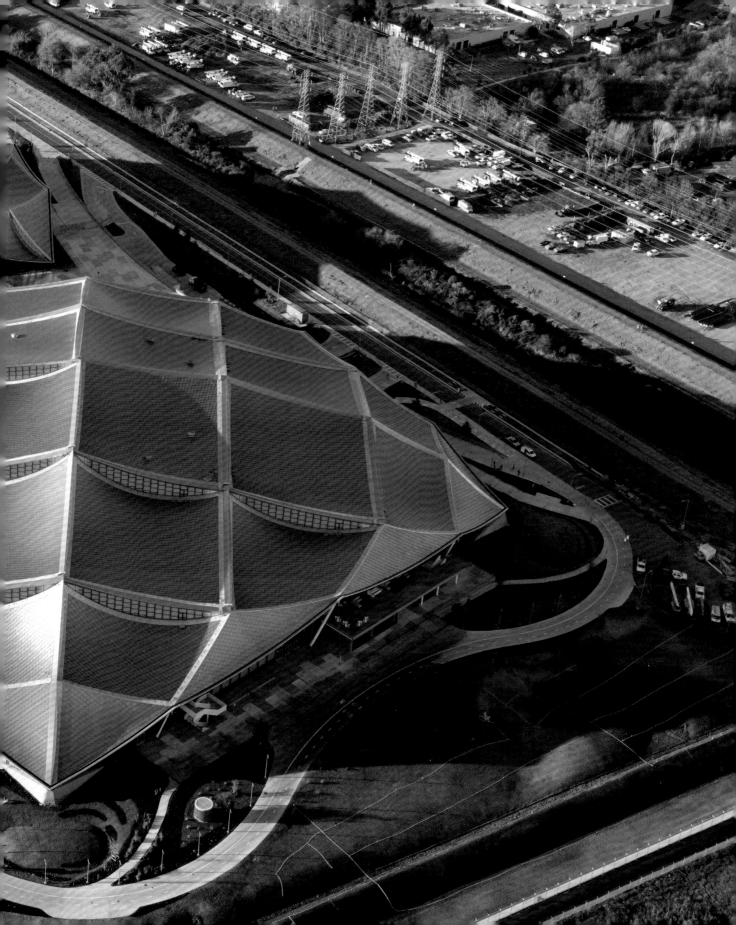

Coal Drops Yard

How can two buildings become one?

FIFTEEN YEARS AFTER OUR FIRST conversations with London property developer Argent, the studio was asked to look at a pair of mid-nineteenth-century industrial buildings in King's Cross that had fallen into disrepair.

Coal Drops was originally where the coal that powered much of Victorian London was brought into the city by rail. Trains came from the north of England, pulling into railway tracks raised above brick and cast-iron structures. The coal was then dropped into storage hoppers below, ready to be loaded onto horse-drawn carts and distributed across London.

When I started my studio in 1994, I found a space to live and work inside a former button-making workshop not far from Coal Drops Yard. Back then, King's Cross was known as a bad area with a reputation for drugs, crime and prostitution. Coal Drops itself was full of warehouses, one of which was now a notorious night club called Bagley's, which a lot of people, including government ministers, have memories of going to. I was never a clubber, and, instead, my main memory was driving down there in my Citroën 2CV to pick up a butcher's block from a junk dealer to use as a table for meetings and meals in my small studio. This wild, industrial, lawless-feeling place felt very run down, and I wondered what would happen to it. Two decades later, the team was excited to be designing a project there.

Initially, the developers had suggested creating two special bridges to connect the surviving Victorian warehouse buildings that were being cleaned up to become retail spaces. This pair of bridges would allow visitors to travel from one side of shops to the other. However, having already worked extensively in Asia at Pacific Place in Hong Kong (pages 348–61), the studio had learned a lot about retail design. During many design workshops our ideas had been accepted or rejected with unarguable logic over several years, honing our understanding of the behaviour of people in shopping environments. Back then, the studio had

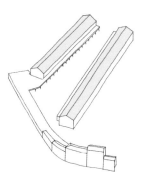

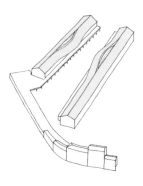

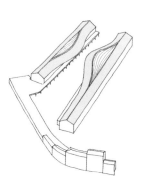

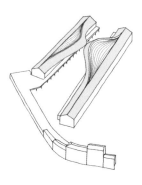

proposed the kind of bridges that were now wanted for Coal Drops, and this had been firmly kicked out for a very good reason: in a shopping area you want thousands of people to flow through it, almost unthinkingly. If a connecting link in a shopping mall is too interesting you risk people stopping to look, and so flowing less well.

We had also learned that shop fronts opposite one another in shopping malls are typically around 13 metres apart, because that is the distance most people see something or someone, find it engaging and move towards it. Any further than that and a shopper is less attracted and more likely to go home. But the distance between the buildings at Coal Drops was 26 metres at its narrowest and 39 metres at its widest – double bad and triple bad! Even more challenging, the two volumes were like a pair of splayed skis, getting further apart with no enclosure or sense of heart. We are not feng shui masters, but we imagined that they would not be happy if we showed them this situation.

Instead of two fancy bridges, the studio team challenged the brief and proposed conserving resources for a single bigger intervention that could give Coal Drops its heart. Our idea was to fuse the two buildings together above people's heads to create a third floor with 2,000 square metres of additional shopping space, while simultaneously making a large rain-protected outdoor public heart space below.

When these buildings were first made, they were never intended for public use or to frame public space. The Victorians were building industrial structures. The IKEA sheds of their time. It is ironic that while the contemporary British construction industry attempts and usually fails to make interesting public places, the Victorians and their industrial structures managed it when they were not even trying.

Normally, when historic buildings are renovated in the UK, a predictable formula is applied: sensitive restoration of existing building fabric, combined with new additional extensions (to the roof or other parts of the building) in the form of timid glass boxes. But that seemed at odds with the pioneering and ambitious architecture that the Victorians tended to create.

The roofs were in need of replacement, having suffered fire damage many years before. We wondered whether this was an opportunity to avoid simply adding a boring glass box and instead to introduce something more dynamic, with new surfaces that would grow, bend and stretch, like elastic, before connecting in the middle at multiple points.

However, the process of getting planning permission was not smooth. The UK heritage body Historic England liked our design, but the city planner from the local authority was not convinced. He commented that by forcing the two roofs to fuse, we were not sufficiently respecting the sense of the warehouses as a pair. We went away dejected, sure that we were right, and frustrated that he was just not understanding us. But then, as a thought experiment, we decided to take his feedback on board and play some more with the roof idea. This time, instead of fully joining one side to the other, we tested whether there was a way we could make these roofs simply kiss each other.

And surprise, surprise, we found the project got stronger and more interesting. I was proud of my team for not always thinking we were right and embracing the challenge we had been given. I am also grateful to the planner for having pushed us to make something better. His job was to represent the public and we are passionate about the public too. We both wanted the same thing. I love this story because he was right and we learned from him. And normally the world of building design characterizes city planners as the people who water down, rather than strengthen, designers' proposals.

The final constructed roofs are made with slate from the same quarry (Cwt y Bugail in North Wales) that supplied the original material nearly two hundred years before. And because of the particular way the roofs curve and meet each other, we needed both left-handed and right-handed roofing craftspeople to lay the tiles. In the end we even found a special left-handed and right-handed father-and-son team to do the work.

The finished building has a sense of its history, but also feels new and dramatically different. While working within a tight budget, we chose to put

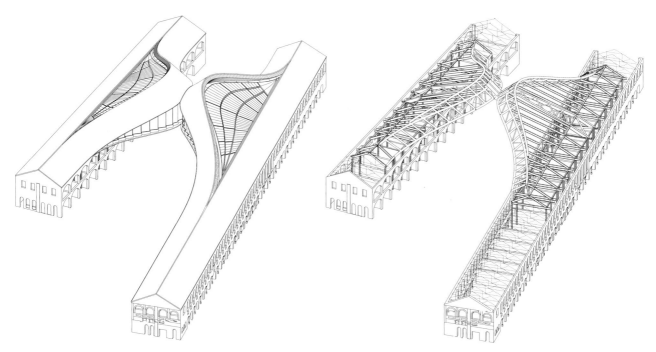

particular care into the lift buttons, as we were aware that they are often the only things visitors touch in shopping centres. Focusing on making those moments memorable, we made six different designs, one for each of the six different lift cores. Our goal was to give a tiny moment of unconventional joy to anyone interacting with them. We even ended up casting one of these moments to look like a bouquet. But fashioned from lift buttons rather than flowers.

When the project opened, it was nice to find that such humble and relatively inexpensive details could be just as interesting for people posting pictures on social media as photographs of the big kissing roofs themselves.

Little Island

How do you make public space on a river?

FOLLOWING A DESIGN COMPETITION, THE
Hudson River Park Trust, and businessman
and philanthropist Barry Diller, appointed
Heatherwick Studio to build a new pier on
Manhattan's southwest riverside. The location was the original Pier 54, where the
survivors of the *Titanic* disaster docked.
Together with his wife, fashion designer
Diane von Fürstenberg, Diller, who has a
long history of working in film, television
and performance, had been a key supporter

of the newly created High Line park in New York. Following this he started a
partnership with the Hudson River Park Trust to make a new structure as part of
a wider series of public spaces being created in this former industrial area.

The brief was to design a new pier as a public park and incorporate world-
class performance spaces.

The team's first thought was not simply to rebuild a new pier on the site
of the previous one. Instead, we believed it was more appropriate to consider the
whole area between the two remaining functional piers of Gansevoort and Pier 57
as a single body of water, and to place the new structure in the middle. We were
also fascinated by the hundreds of wooden piles sticking out of the water now
that the pier decks they had once supported were gone. These blackened pieces
of maritime history formed an amazingly atmospheric reminder of the city's
economic boom in the early twentieth century.

With so many technical challenges in building new structures in a major
river, the studio began by looking at how other piers in the city had been built,
restored and redeveloped. Concrete piles are hammered into the thick silt of the

riverbed until they reach the bedrock, and from this base a new concrete pier deck is constructed, which usually hides the tops of the piles as they emerge from the water.

As much of the nearby water was characterized by the leftover piles, the team wondered whether, rather than denying their existence, the new pier's identity could come from focusing on them instead. The idea evolved to take the new concrete piles and to continue them out of the water, extending skyward to raise up sections of a green landscape. Fusing as they meet, these individual piles would come together to form the topography of the park.

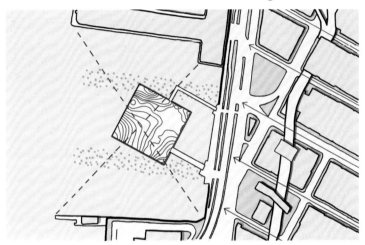

The existing highway running along the western edge of Manhattan created a dominant sense of vast flatness in the area. We became convinced that we needed to offer a contrast to this by concentrating on the vertical three-dimensionality of the pier. Raising a new piece of undulating park up into the air would not only counteract the presence of the big road but also make the park more noticeable from a distance. A more three-dimensional park landscape would also work well with the need for outdoor theatre and performance spaces, as raked seating could be shaped into the landscape to give the audience better views.

The resulting design developed as a system of repeating piles that each form a generous planter at their top. Every planter connects in a tessellating pattern at different heights to create a single manipulated piece of landscape.

More than a hundred different species of indigenous trees and plants suited to the harsh extremes of the New York climate were then planted in the thousands of tonnes of new soil within this landscape. The result is a unique topography that can be experienced as you walk underneath to enter, as well as from above as the 280 piles rise out of the water with no horizontal cross-bracing between them.

Opting for a simple square plan, we felt we would not only be able to hold an audience more effectively but it would also allow the undulating park landscape to be more interesting when viewed in elevation.

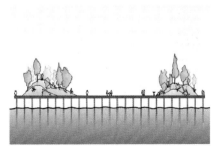

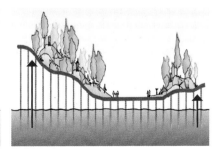

Also, instead of aligning the new pier with the other piers, the square plan is rotated perpendicular to New York's grid plan. This in turn creates a dynamic rather than parallel relationship with the walkway along the river edge and aligns the new pier structure in an unusual way with surrounding cross-streets, in particular 14th Street.

Construction of the project involved many amazing collaborators.

In 2021, the project officially opened under the name Little Island. Over one million people came to see it in the first year. As well as being a spectacularly landscaped public park, the completed project is a hardworking object that contains an outdoor theatre for 700 people, a smaller performance space for 200, a main space for 3,500, and many pathways and viewing platforms. The key to the experience for visitors is the planting, led by Signe Nielsen at MNLA Landscape Architects, which moves from pastel shades in spring to more intense colours in summer before dramatic autumnal hues. The landscape also attracts a large variety of wildlife, including species of birds rarely seen before in New York.

It is thrilling to see people exploring the park, watching one of the hundreds of free cultural performances and workshops, navigating the winding paths, meditating on boulder scrambles or reading books on the park benches. The new park allows visitors to feel they are having a break from the hecticness of the city.

The studio recently completed a research study to measure how socially impactful Little Island has been. Speaking to visitors, artists and park staff, we learned that the park attracts 1.5 million people each year, a significant percentage of which is New York residents. Additionally, 94 per cent of the many people who took part in an independent survey said that the park felt like a place for people like them.

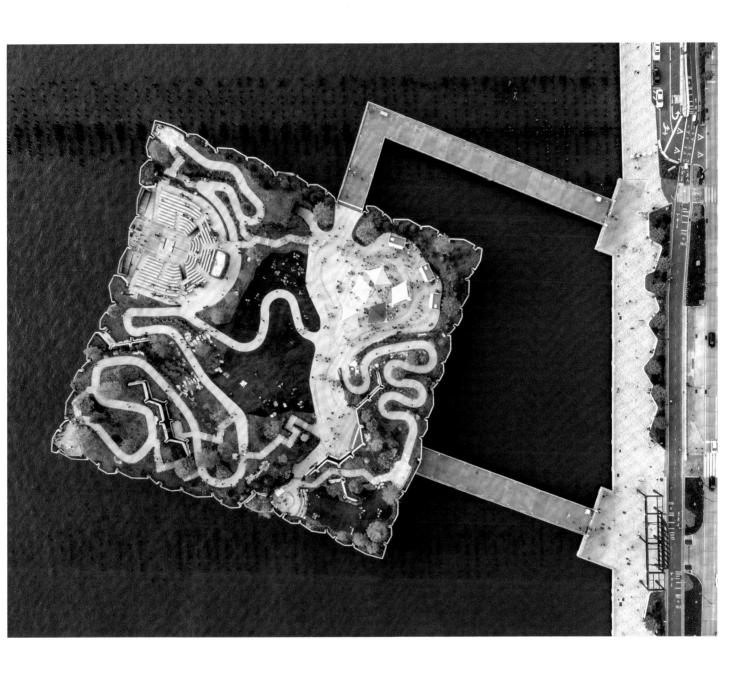

148

Maggie's Yorkshire

Can a building help you heal?

MAGGIE'S CANCER CENTRES, named after their founder Maggie Keswick Jencks, were set up as a counterpoint to the dehumanized medical buildings we have come to expect, which often make patients feel like they are part of a vast, unsympathetic health system. In 2012, the charity asked the studio to design

a new non-clinical centre for St James's University Hospital in Leeds, one of the biggest cancer treatment hubs in the United Kingdom.

The challenge was to find a way to make a building that could be empathic, as well as inspirational, yet still be affordable to build. For people experiencing some of the most difficult moments of their lives, this new environment would need to have larger areas for patients and staff to gather, as well as more private spaces where someone could cry. The centre needed to be a vital refuge not just for patients, but also for their families.

As one of the hospital's last precious patches of green, open space, the steeply sloping site was wedged between two busy roads and consisted of little more than a thin layer of grass laid over the leftover construction waste from building the adjacent car park. However bleak and poor quality the green space, the team was reluctant to design something that would remove it when scientific research has shown that looking out at greenery and nature improves recovery time for patients. Instead, was there any way that the process of creating a new building could make the site dramatically greener?

The studio realized that the solution was to avoid making a single big box that would swallow up the plot, and instead to make the building from three large wooden 'planters' filled with richly biodiverse landscaping. By constructing these from huge pieces of sustainably sourced spruce plywood, each planter could be slotted together simply and quickly, rather like a child's wooden dinosaur kit. The interlocking pieces of timber create a series of arching ribs that support the heavy weight of the spectacular natural wild gardens above, at the same time as making a series of intimate enclosed spaces within the bases of the planters.

At the heart of this Maggie's Centre is a kitchen where visitors are welcomed and can sit down for tea at a specially designed cork table, acting as an icebreaker to help everyone feel at home straight away. People entering the centre may be dealing with the shock of diagnosis, experiencing deep grief, or worrying about the knock-on effects for their family, so the homeliness and familiarity of sitting at a kitchen table seemed powerful and important. Arranged around the main kitchen and public open space are more private counselling rooms, as well as social areas for group meetings, a small library and a large space for practising yoga.

The rooftop gardens of the finished building were inspired by Maggie Keswick Jencks' love of gardening and are crammed with 23,000 bulbs and 17,000 plants local to Yorkshire, with all visitors to the centre encouraged to help take care of them. Holding up this extraordinary garden is the structure of spruce timber blades, giving the interiors a feeling of warmth. The walls in-between these blades are plastered with natural lime render, which allows the surfaces to breathe, and helps to maintain the right humidity level inside the naturally ventilated building.

As treatments become more targeted and effective, and cancer diagnoses do not necessarily mean the end of our lives, hope, inspiration and resilience are needed more than ever to get through. Researching and constructing Maggie's Yorkshire made the studio team even more convinced of the powerful effects on people's feelings and on their ability to heal when society designs its buildings with more empathy.

2013

Garden Bridge

Can a bridge be a place?

LONDON IS ONE OF VERY FEW CITIES that can claim to be a thought-leading capital of the world and at its centre is the 0.25-kilometre-wide River Thames. In 2013 London's transport authority held a tender for proposals to improve pedestrian links across the river. The studio decided to develop and submit an idea it had heard a decade and a half earlier from actor and campaigner Joanna Lumley. Her notion was to create a major garden in the middle of the city on a new bridge structure that would better connect north and south London. On it people could linger above the river and enjoy the wonderful views all around.

When we originally heard of the idea the studio had been gripped by its power, but the moment had not seemed right to take it forward. However, many years later, the success of London's 2012 Olympic Games seemed to take everyone in Britain by surprise and there was an interesting new confidence in its people. The optimism that remained afterwards, as well as the success of New York's High Line, built on a derelict piece of elevated railway, seemed to create a rare possibility of realizing such an ambitious project. With this in mind, in late 2013 Lord Mervyn Davies launched the Garden Bridge Trust, a UK-registered charity dedicated to the creation of the project.

We were interested that in Paris the River Seine is approximately a hundred metres wide, whereas London's River Thames rips the city apart by almost three hundred metres, profoundly separating it in two. Many Londoners rarely go to the other side and London's *Time Out* magazine has even been known to print special north and south issues with different cover designs. It was clear that this powerful river has historically been seen as a major obstacle to breach. However, Joanna's idea was for a bridge to be not just a link, but also an extremely special place in its own right.

The site chosen for the project was in the centre of the city between Blackfriars and Waterloo bridges, connecting Covent Garden and the West End to the north and the South Bank arts district to the south. A new bridge here, aligned with Arundel Street and the crescent of the Aldwych, would fit naturally into the tight city grain. A study recently undertaken by the *London Evening Standard* had even recalculated the exact centre of the city to be the public bench a few metres away from this location on the north bank. When you compared the frequency of other nearby river crossings, there was also a larger gap between the neighbouring Blackfriars Bridge and Waterloo Bridge, which this project would fill.

For many years there had been the assumption that the north bank area in the city centre was fine and that the south was in perpetual need of more development. But the south had been revived over

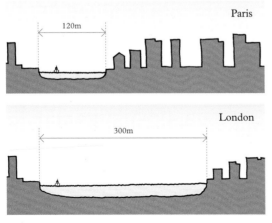

Paris

120m

London

300m

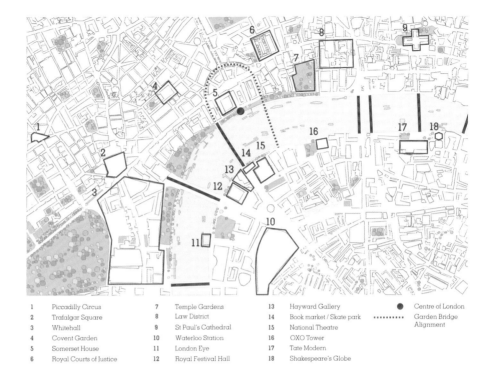

1	Piccadilly Circus	7	Temple Gardens	13	Hayward Gallery	● Centre of London
2	Trafalgar Square	8	Law District	14	Book market / Skate park	·········· Garden Bridge
3	Whitehall	9	St Paul's Cathedral	15	National Theatre	Alignment
4	Covent Garden	10	Waterloo Station	16	OXO Tower	
5	Somerset House	11	London Eye	17	Tate Modern	
6	Royal Courts of Justice	12	Royal Festival Hall	18	Shakespeare's Globe	

the past two decades to become a vibrant arts district attracting large numbers of visitors to its galleries, theatres, music halls, restaurants and outdoor entertainment. And in reality it was the north bank that was sliced away from the vitality of the river by the dual carriageway of the Victoria Embankment. The new bridge would go from a disused piece of ground on the south side, in front of the London Television Centre, to touch down directly on top of Temple tube station, which, despite being the most central Underground station in London, was strangely one of the least used on the network. Unlike most other stations nearby it is located right on the river, plus it has a little-used public space on top of it. The bridge offered the perfect opportunity to breathe new life into this place that had been under-utilized for so many years. On both sides of the river there was now an exciting opportunity to grow and nourish neglected areas at the same time as providing new walking routes, away from cars and traffic, to and from places such as Covent Garden, Soho and Waterloo.

With its rich and diverse horticultural heritage of heathlands, parks, squares, allotments and community gardens, London is one of the greenest cities of its size in the world. British gardens are particular to its climate, with their clammy, slightly musty, moist earthiness, complete with mouldy leaves and worms. To do proper justice to Joanna's idea, the hero of a garden bridge would have to be the garden and not the bridge, and to capture this we would need to make a substantial piece of horticulture.

To do this Dan Pearson was chosen for his distinctive and naturalistic planting style. The idea he developed was to use more than six hundred Northern European species in a design that will gradually change in mix and density as it moves from across the river. With Dan's passion for seasonality we were excited to imagine how, whenever you come and visit throughout the year, as its many plants come in and out of leaf and flower, the bridge will always feel slightly different.

However, to provide the real piece of nature for Dan to work with would require many hundred cubic metres of soil. All this wet soil would be extremely heavy and create a significant structural challenge to hold up.

We worked with the respected engineers of Ove Arup to see if we could turn this intriguing idea into something that could really be built. But as the garden needed to be the focus, the tallest things on the bridge would have to be the plants themselves and these could not be allowed to be obscured by any structural columns and cables. To do this, and for a blade of grass or a small tree to really be the tallest thing on the bridge, the structural engineering would have to happen from below. Around this time the harbour master for central London,

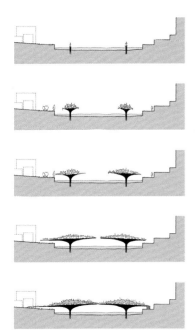

Captain Terry Lawrence, gave us the two precise locations in the water where we could build new piers. The challenge was now to take the great structural load and transfer it down to these piers.

The resulting design begins with two 20-metre-deep foundations dug into the clay at the base of the river; these each rise upwards and out of the water to form a pair of very large planters in which the two halves of the garden can be planted. There was then a simple logic to the shape of the bridge following the engineering. The result is that the soil is able to be deepest at the middle of each planter, where it is directly above the structural columns, and becomes progressively shallower as it reaches out across the river. It was interesting that over time the planting will ever so slightly echo the engineering as plants will naturally grow taller closest to the centre points of the piles.

The detailed form of the structure then evolved through thinking about the radial structural fins that the bridge would need to transfer the weight of the garden back to the structural columns. Instead of smoothing the silhouette into large and expensive three-dimensional curved surfaces, we wondered if we might allow the form of the external surfaces of the bridge to be articulated by drawing attention to this radiating geometry and celebrating it. Also, rather than

designing a go-faster form that would subliminally encourage people to feel they should walk speedily across the river, we were excited that the scale of each articulated rib could make a series of places on the top surface of the structure where you could linger and look out at London.

As the historic north part of London has been associated with stone and brick, while the more modern South Bank has become inextricably known for its use of concrete, the choice of materials was extremely important. We felt that we needed to create a project that did not appear to have any overt allegiance to the architectural palette of either side. It was also essential to find a material that would have an inherent warmth; something concrete or stainless steel might not be able to give. Our engineers then introduced us to a special metal called copper-nickel, suited to the aggressive corrosive situation of the salty tidal waters of the river, which would not need painting or regular re-coating. Its particular appeal was its warmth, in contrast to stainless steel, which has similar performance characteristics but cold and clinical associations. Used in the manufacture of offshore oil rigs and other marine applications such as ship propellers, copper-nickel is durable and even more

desirable because it stays relatively light in colour over time, rather than oxidizing to a very dark tone. As the underside of the bridge would need to be beautiful and not gloomy, this non-darkness would be important.

As well as being a direct and fast route for a commuter, the Garden Bridge also offers the possibility of being the slowest way to cross the river. Even though it is a major piece of infrastructure it will contain an unusual human scale and sensibility that people can feel comfortable to nestle in, where a group of friends or a family can stop, a place for a tryst or even a marriage proposal.

Success for the project might be that someone walks on, reads their book on a bench and leaves the same side they came, having never even reached the other side. Or a person who walked briskly across at seven o'clock on their

North Landing

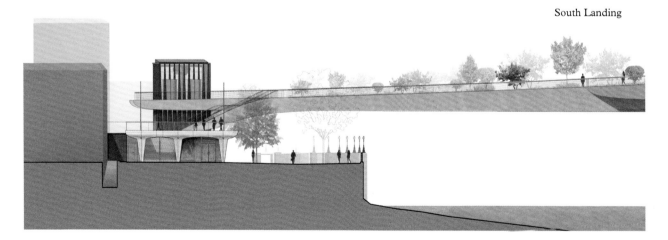

South Landing

morning commute and then returns in the evening, zooming past on their way to the British Film Institute. Whether lingering or zooming, the choice being made is not only one of convenience but also of exposure to a pocket of specialness in the heart of an incredible city.

Garden Bridge has yet to be realized.

Since this project, others like Little Island in New York (pages 142–53) have shown that unexpected public places can bring joy and optimism to millions of people. While the Garden Bridge has not found its moment yet, one day, just maybe, it will.

Olympic Cauldron

How can every country in the Olympic Games take part in making and lighting the Olympic cauldron?

THE STUDIO WAS INVITED by the organizing committee of the London 2012 Olympic Games and Danny Boyle, creative director of the opening ceremony, to design the vessel for the fire that burns throughout the games, which is known as the Olympic cauldron. Ignited ceremonially in Greece and brought to the host nation, this fire makes a symbolic connection to the flame that was kept burning throughout the original games that took place in Ancient Greece almost three thousand years ago.

While parts of the world grow increasingly secular, the Olympic Games seemed to us to represent a faith that everyone can subscribe to, transcending the boundaries of nation and religion to unite the world in a celebration of human achievement. With the stadium as its temple and the Olympic protocol as its liturgy, this faith even gives us the modern-day equivalent of miracles – except that these are human miracles, which we can all see with our own eyes and believe in. It felt to us that the Olympic cauldron is the high altar of this faith.

Given that the games only last a few weeks and the cauldron can never be re-lit, we wondered what would become of this big object afterwards. Olympic cauldrons are sometimes converted into monuments or water features but once they are stripped of their ceremonial function and context, it is difficult for them to look anything but forlorn. This made us want to give London's cauldron a meaning that went beyond its identity as a physical object.

Rather than the cauldron itself, it seemed to be the ritual and theatricality of lighting the flame that people remembered. Moments of drama, like the archer igniting the cauldron with a burning arrow at the Barcelona Olympics, had become embedded in collective memory while cauldrons as objects had been largely forgotten. Instead of finding an unforgettable way of lighting a forgettable object, we wanted to look for a connection between the cauldron as an object and the ritual of lighting it. Could the cauldron itself be a manifestation of the way it was lit?

We also noted that it was normal to locate the cauldron on the roof of the stadium, far removed from the spectators, and since stadiums had grown in scale over the years, Olympic cauldrons had tended to become larger and larger in order to make the greatest impact. But it interested us that in 1948, when London last hosted

the Olympic Games, the cauldron had been placed inside the stadium. This precedent suggested that rooting it to the ground among the spectators could again give the cauldron a more intimate relationship to the crowd. Also, it felt arbitrary to us to pick one particular bit of the roof on which to place the cauldron, since no one part of its circumference had greater significance than any other. Instead, it occurred to us that the most powerful point of a circular space is its absolute centre, and so it was here that we chose to place the cauldron.

As well as connecting with the circularity of the stadium, this central position seemed more fully to express the cauldron's ritual importance as the altar of the Olympic Games. Bringing the cauldron closer to the crowd enabled us to give it a more human scale. Also, during the opening ceremony, the cauldron could become a way of organizing the crowd of 10,500 parading

athletes. Rather than milling around in a disorganized throng, teams could be arrayed around the cauldron like segments of a pie-chart, with the colours of their uniforms forming vast radiating patterns, connecting the athletes themselves with the combined geometry of the cauldron and stadium.

Instead of trying to reinvent the shape of a bowl of flame mounted on a column, we started looking for an idea that would relate more directly to the phenomenon of countries around the world gathering together in pursuit of sporting achievement and not squabbling with one another. Because this only lasts

a few weeks, we wanted to make a cauldron that would only exist during this time. Our idea was that each country would bring a unique object to the ceremony and these pieces would come together and cooperate to form a cauldron. When the games ended, the cauldron would come apart again so that each country could take home their piece of it as a national memento of the event. Every one of the constituent pieces would be distinct from every other, their size and shape in no way reflecting the relative wealth, size or global status of any one country.

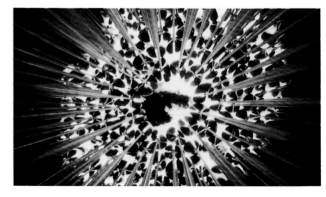

178

This idea was realized at the Olympic opening ceremony on 27 July 2012, when the 204 teams paraded into the stadium, each one led by an athlete carrying its national flag and a child carrying a polished copper object. As the competitors gradually assembled, each copper piece was unobtrusively attached to one of the slender rods that radiated from the exact centre of the stadium. Then the Olympic flame was carried into the arena and handed on to seven young athletes. As they ran into the centre of the stadium, spectators now saw the 204 copper elements arrayed on the ground and watched while the athletes

ignited individual flames within them. When the last ones were alight, the flames began to lift gently upwards on their metal stems. During the next forty seconds, the individual flames rose in waves and converged in the darkened stadium before surging together into a single great flame of unity, a symbol of the peaceful gathering of nations.

During the Olympic closing ceremony, the cauldron opened out once more, the blaze was extinguished and the cauldron was dismantled, each copper piece patinated with iridescent colour after its exposure to extreme heat. For the Paralympic Games, the cauldron was fitted with a new set of elements and ignited for a second time.

In bringing the idea to reality, we found that a height of 8.5 metres gave the object a scale that was appropriate to its position in the centre of the stadium. We gave each of its 204 pieces the approximate size and proportions of an A3 piece of paper, small enough for a young child to carry. With gold, silver and bronze already having their place in the Olympic tradition, we chose polished copper for the elements because of its distinctive warm colour and the extraordinary patination of its surface after heating. Each element was inscribed with 'XXX Olympiad London 2012' and the name of its country.

Since every element had its own gas supply, igniter and burner head, and was individually operated by pivots and levers, the cauldron was a sophisticated device with more than a thousand moving parts. The rods were set out in ten rings and attached to ten circular drive plates, enabling the cauldron to lift in ten waves of movement. In the tradition of British engineering, this mechanism was precision-machined and assembled in the north of England and the copper pieces were hammered by hand from sheets of flat metal using a craft technique that is usually used for restoring the body panels of historic cars.

Until the moment when the cauldron was lit, none of the eighty thousand spectators in the stadium or the billion viewers worldwide watching on television knew where it was located, who would light it or what it would look like.

2011

Nanyang Technological University Learning Hub

*Can a building help change
the way we learn?*

THE STUDIO WAS COMMISSIONED to design a new educational building for the Nanyang Technological University in Singapore as part of its £360 million campus redevelopment programme. The structure, known as the Learning Hub, was to contain fifty-six tutorial rooms and be used by the university's 33,000 students.

The project was particularly exciting to us because it called for a new kind of environment, one more relevant to contemporary methods of learning, which have been radically changed by the advent of the internet and resulting digital age. One of the reasons students used to go to university was because it was a place where you could access specialist computers and books. But now that most of us carry computers in our pockets and bags in the form of smartphones and tablets, from which you can access the world's knowledge, you do not necessarily need physical university buildings at all. In theory you could even stay at home in bed and get a PhD with your devices.

If you can now learn anywhere and digital technologies don't necessarily require you to interact with anyone else in person, the role of a university building becomes most emphatically to bring people together. A new university building should be where you might meet your future business partner or someone to develop an incredible idea with. It must surely be a place that provokes and encourages as much face-to-face dialogue as possible between staff and students across different disciplines.

However, the original buildings on the campus had been planned around many miles of characterless corridors lined with multiple closed classrooms. This sterile environment, with endless passages and no sign of what was happening inside each room, seemed the least likely place where you might stop to have a conversation, meet someone, or share ideas. Students were likely to feel they were nothing more than a tiny cog in a massive machine for learning.

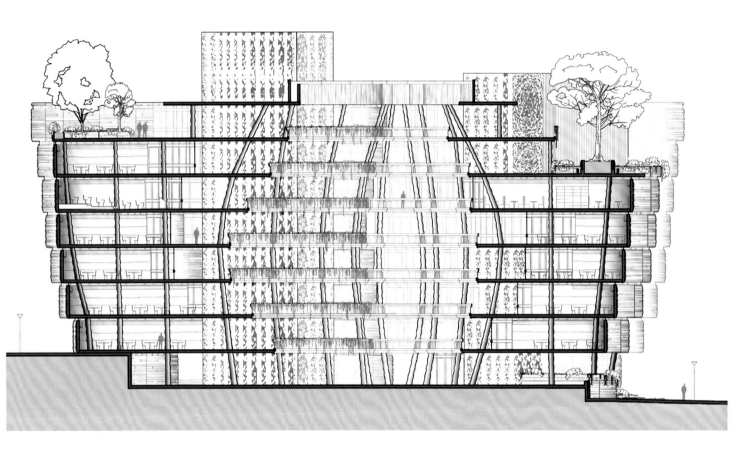

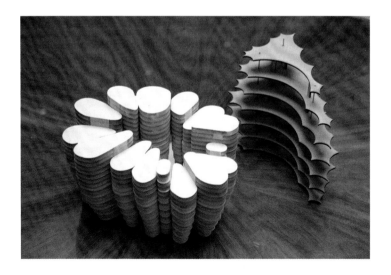

185

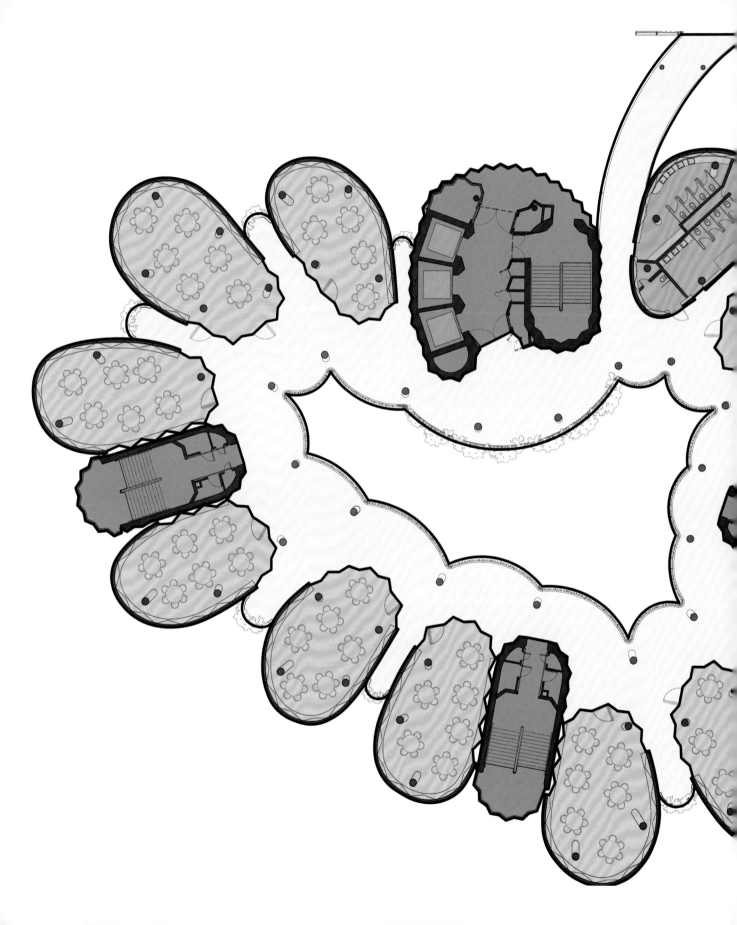

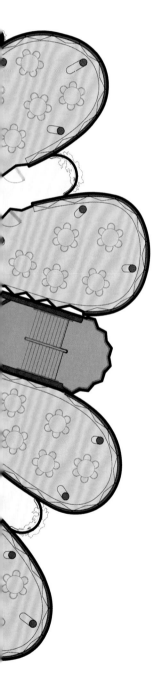

The university teaching staff had also stipulated that the building needed to be accessible twenty-four hours a day and should help to change the traditional format of lecturers delivering knowledge to students from the front of a classroom. Instead they wanted an environment of learning in the round and asked us for each room to have no corners – an order we obeyed. With no obvious front, back or corners, the thinking was that each new tutorial room and its furniture could be designed so that students worked together around shared tables with the tutor as facilitator.

We set ourselves the task not only to break free from the conventional hierarchy of professor and student relationships, but also to escape the tyranny of dead corridors; instead we would design a building based on making students and teachers bump into each other as much as possible. Rather than design a typical new big university building box, the studio chose to give the structure a more human scale by focusing instead on the tutorial rooms and stacking them on top of each other to make a series of smaller buildings. The resulting NTU Learning Hub is formed of twelve such piles of tutorial rooms, interspersed with open spaces and gardens, all clustered around an open but glass-covered central area. Making every tutorial room face onto this distinctive shared space allows students to be visually connected to each other and to the activities happening in the building. But the central circulation space does not just drive students from one room to another, it also provides lots of places to stop, talk and think, including garden-framed balconies with views across the rest of the campus.

As Singapore has year-round temperatures between 25 and 31 degrees centigrade, the naturally ventilated central space gives the ability to maximize air movement around these towers of tutorial rooms and to allow students to feel as cool as possible without the need to air-condition a large atrium. Each individual tutorial room is then cooled using silent convection, a pioneering new use of the technology to cool a room without the need for any noisy, energy-guzzling air-conditioning fans.

Our thinking about the construction of the building was dominated by the combination of a strict construction budget, stringent Singaporean building codes and an aspiration to achieve the highest possible environmental sustainability performance for the structure. The more we reflected on these factors the more it became clear that the project would have to be constructed entirely from reinforced concrete: concrete columns, concrete floor slabs, concrete structural cores and concrete external cladding. Concrete is unquestionably an incredible construction material, but from a British perspective the use of so much of it brings to mind the Brutalist post-war buildings of London's South Bank; for many people the associations of such large, grey expanses of this material are not positive. With this challenge – to alter how concrete could be perceived – we became interested in seeing if its surface could be given qualities of detail and warmth that people would not expect. Within our studio we described this to ourselves as trying to find ways to give the concrete 'love'. To do this without significant cost implications we had a maximum allowable depth of 25 millimetres to manipulate the concrete's surface before affecting the steel reinforcing structure underneath. To soften the appearance of the material and to make that small piece of surface deviation count as much as possible, we developed a process using warm, rather than grey, coloured concrete and casting it with cost-effective reusable silicone moulds to create real three-dimensional texture in the surface. Artist and illustrator Sara Fanelli specially made us seven hundred individual drawings, which we embedded three-dimensionally within the zigzagging surface of the structural concrete stair and elevator cores of the superstructure. These hand-painted ink drawings, referencing everything from science to art and literature, were deliberately ambiguous 'thought triggers', designed to leave space for the imagination of every student or professor to interpret them in any way they wish.

When creating the sixty-six columns that rise through the Learning Hub's eight floors we also attempted to get away from the familiar cylindrical concrete columns seen in most new buildings. We began experimenting with how light falls across the surface of these cylinders, seeing what potential interest we could add with shadows produced by our 25 millimetres of surface deviation. We found that a gently undulating surface, with each undulation the approximate size of a human belly, gave every column subtle shadows and an unusual silhouette as well as even encouraging you to touch it, an urge that rarely exists with a conventional concrete cylinder.

Another particular effort was made with the concrete cladding panels for the outside of the building. A special adaptable mould was designed that allowed the thousand pieces to be individually cast into subtly differing curves with differing articulation of ridges. Each one was different despite being made from the same tool.

A surprising outcome of the building's various raw treatments of concrete is that the project feels almost handmade – as if it has been fashioned from wet clay on a potter's wheel. Unlike familiar cladding materials there are no flat, dead surfaces that feel too sharp and shiny or perfectly straight.

The finished building opened to students in 2015 and has been awarded the highest Singapore environmental award of Green Mark Platinum. At its ground-breaking ceremony in 2012 Singapore's Education Minister joked that he hoped this human-scale building might even help improve Singapore's birth rate.

Zeitz MOCAA

How do you turn a building full of tubes into a building full of art?

CAPE TOWN'S GRAIN silo was built in 1921 as an industrial harbour facility where grain from throughout South Africa was graded and stored, ready for shipping. The building has remained a prominent feature of the city's landscape, which sweeps down the skirt of Table Mountain to meet the sea, and for half a century the silo was the city's tallest structure.

However, the advent of modern containerized shipping meant that by 2001 the silo had become redundant, and it fell into disuse. Recently the harbour it dominates has been regenerated into one of Africa's most visited destinations, a vibrant place of leisure and tourism known as the Victoria and Alfred Waterfront. But the silo has suffered deterioration and was in need of a new purpose.

The harbour's developers approached Heatherwick Studio, looking for help with defining a future vision for the silo.

At that time there was no programme and no design. The studio led a three-day workshop in Cape Town to examine potential future uses. It found that although the Waterfront already contained retail, hotels and residential areas there seemed to be an opportunity for a new cultural space.

South Africa has largely missed out on the development of large-scale cultural organizations being founded around the rest of the world in recent years. But rather than another historical museum, this special site offered an opportunity to found a new institution that was utterly contemporary. At the same time, the Zeitz Foundation was looking for a permanent public home for industrialist Jochen Zeitz's world-class collection of contemporary African art. The vision emerged to transform

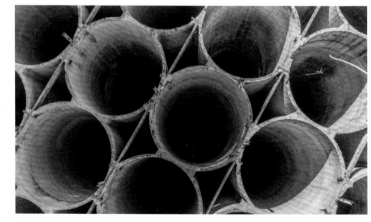

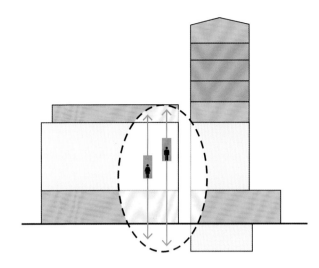

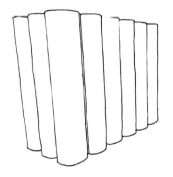

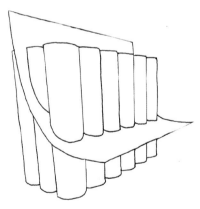

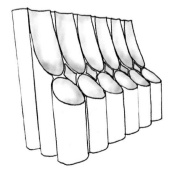

the derelict silo into the Zeitz Museum of Contemporary Art Africa (Zeitz MOCAA) and to create Africa's first museum of its kind.

Heatherwick Studio was asked to produce a design concept and our first thoughts wrestled with the extraordinary physical facts of the building. Despite appearing like a single structure, the silo actually consisted of two separate buildings that combined to form a huge machine.

Vast quantities of grain had been raised up many storeys inside the taller elevator tower, from where it was graded, funnelled and finally stored in the forty-two vertical concrete tubes of the lower second building. These tubes were 30 metres tall and 5 metres in diameter. The tower still contained large pieces of heavy machinery, great rusty chains and piping.

There was no large open space within the densely packed tubes, making it impossible to experience the volumes from inside. Rather than strip out the evidence of the building's industrial heritage, the studio wanted to find a way to enjoy and celebrate it. We could either fight a building made of concrete tubes or enjoy its tube-iness.

We realized that we needed to create a single large space or void to unify the two buildings and allow visitors to experience their remarkable interiors. Unlike many conversions of historic buildings that have grand spaces ready to be repurposed, this building had none. The project became about imagining an interior – how to make large gallery spaces in a way that celebrated the existing building.

The concept developed by Heatherwick Studio was to carve galleries and a central circulation space from the silo's cellular concrete structure. The form of the central void is a single enlarged grain of corn, puncturing the tubes to reveal a new geometry. The chemistry of these intersecting geometries creates an extraordinary display of edges, achieved with advanced concrete-cutting techniques.

The finished carved tubes above the atrium space allow daylight in through thick layers of laminated glass, fritted with a pattern designed by West African artist El Loko. The frit creates a walkable surface for the upper-level sculpture garden, allowing daylight inside while preventing too much heat building up inside. Meanwhile, cylindrical lifts rise inside bisected tubes like huge plungers, and stairs spiral upwards like giant drill bits.

The silo's monumental façades and the lower section of the tower are maintained without inserting new windows, and thick layers of render and paint were removed to reveal the raw beauty of the original concrete.

From outside, the greatest visible change is the creation of new glazed panels, which are inserted into the existing geometry of the tower's upper section and bulge outward as if gently inflated. By night, this transforms the building's upper storeys into a glowing lantern or beacon in the harbour.

Zeitz MOCAA creates a series of dynamic spaces in which Capetonians and visitors can experience the best contemporary African sculpture, film and performance, as well as public events.

The museum was officially opened in September 2017 by the late Archbishop Emeritus Desmond Tutu. Over 70,000 visitors went to see the building and its exhibitions in its opening month. Of these, 35,000 were free entrants, underlining one of Zeitz MOCAA's primary principles: access for all.

Today, the museum's galleries feature rotating, temporary exhibitions with a dedicated space for the permanent collection. There is also a Centre for Art Education and a project space for emerging artists.

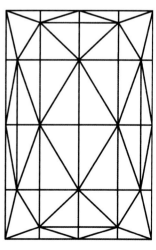

Boat

Can a whole boat be made of its hull?

IN 2007, THE CITY and regional authorities of Nantes, in France, set up 'Estuaire', an innovative project led by the city's progressive mayor. The aim of the project was to construct a large work of art in every waterside community situated on the banks of the River Loire, between Nantes and the port town of Saint-Nazaire. The strategic decision was also taken to strengthen the connection between Nantes and Saint-Nazaire by commissioning a new river boat that would travel between the two towns, to symbolize their closer union. The studio was invited to propose a design for this vessel.

As well as running daily trips along the river to see the artworks, the boat would provide a place for politicians to hold civic functions and meetings. In addition, it would be made available for hire, so its accommodation needed to be very flexible. Instead of facing forwards as they do in a bus, the two hundred passengers would want to look in different directions to get good views of the landscape and the specially commissioned artworks. As it would take people to the mouth of the River Loire estuary the boat had to be seafaring, but also manoeuvrable to bring people up close to the artworks in the shallow waters at the edges of the river. The most suitable type of vessel seemed to be a catamaran, a boat with two connected hulls, which is agile and stable and has a shallow draught.

River boats of this size are, it seemed to us, normally given the aesthetic character of a sports car, with a showy, go-faster design. Although this vessel should be able to go at high speed, we wanted it to be equally adapted to pottering along at a relaxed pace. We also noticed that, although the hulls of boats and ships are frequently very beautiful forms, the top of a boat rarely has much of a relationship to the hull. We gave ourselves the challenge of making the upper part of the boat, which sits above the surface of the water, relate to the part that lies under

the water. This meant that we should avoid treating the twin-hulled catamaran chassis as a pair of skis with something separate on top.

Instead, we developed the notion of growing the complete boat from a single hull element that is manipulated to form the boat's two hulls below the water as well as its accommodation and decks above. The continuous strip is a closed loop, which, having formed both hulls, crosses over itself to create two storeys of decks and indoor cabin space.

The vessel is to be constructed from aluminium in the shipyards of Saint-Nazaire.

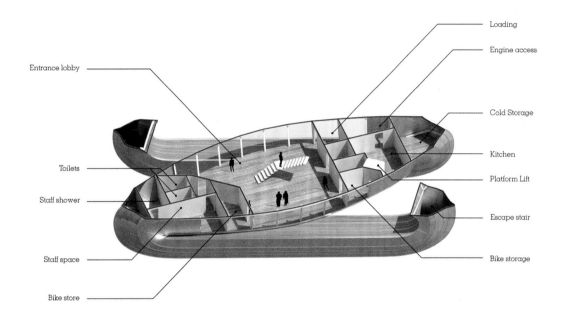

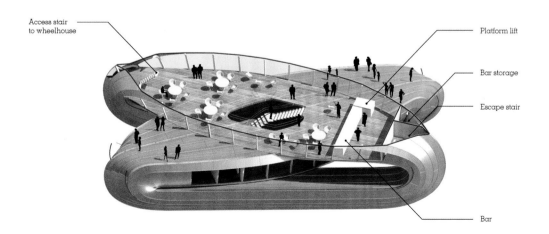

2010

Bombay Sapphire Distillery

Can industrial manufacturing be joyful?

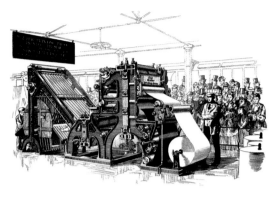

TEN YEARS AFTER WINNING a design prize from gin-maker Bombay Sapphire for a glass bridge idea, the studio was commissioned to lead the master plan and design of the company's new distillery in the south of England.

Having previously operated from shared production facilities, this was to be Bombay Sapphire's first dedicated distillery and headquarters and was an opportunity for the company to consolidate its manufacturing ability and improve efficiency.

The site in the village of Laverstoke straddles the River Test, one of England's finest chalk streams. Originally operating as a corn mill, the land was acquired in 1718 by Henry Portal and developed for the manufacture of paper to produce the world's bank notes. Over the following two centuries it grew into a sprawling industrial complex, including a series of Grade II listed buildings such as the mill owner's house, the workers' cottages and the main mill building. The result was an uncoordinated accumulation of over forty buildings, which made the site chaotic and confusing to find your way around. Equally challenging, the River Test which runs through it had been narrowed and hidden within a steep-sided concrete channel making it almost impossible to perceive.

To bring clarity to such a disparate site it became obvious to us that it would not be enough to simply restore the existing historic buildings, but that we needed to reveal the River Test once more and to use it as a device around which to organize everything. We also felt that the site's new master plan would only work with the creation of a central courtyard as a gathering area and focal point.

To turn these thoughts into reality we worked with government agencies English Heritage and English Nature to meticulously restore twenty-three of the existing historic buildings, to conserve the local wildlife and also to negotiate the

removal of nine of the most recent industrial structures and a poor quality bridge. The other significant move was to substantially widen the river and reshape its banks to form sloping planted foreshores in order to make the water visible and valuable once more. Each careful decision to take away a building structure in turn gave space for the surrounding rich English countryside to be glimpsed again from the heart of the site. At the same time we became very conscious of not wanting to lose a sense of the evolution of the site. So wherever a modern dilapidated building leant against an older historic structure we removed the modern addition but left its mark on the remaining building fabric as a trace of where it had been. This selective process of decluttering the site was as necessary on the inside as on the outside.

The initial master plan brief had also included the creation of a visitor centre. However, on seeing the vapour distillation process and the sculptural

Before

After

forms of the large copper gin stills, one of which is more than two hundred years old, we became convinced that witnessing the authentic distillation process would be far more interesting and memorable for a visitor than any simulated visitor experience. This production technique, different from those used by other gin distillers, is still carried out in accordance with a recipe devised in 1761 and involves infusing the gin with the vapours of ten tropical and Mediterranean herbs and spices.

This led us to think about growing these botanical herbs and spices on the site, which in turn pointed us towards a rich British heritage of botanical glasshouse structures. The Victorian curiosity and passion for the new science of horticulture had driven the creation of everything from the extraordinary palm house at Kew Gardens to the craze for Wardian cases, ornate indoor glasshouses for growing and displaying collections of exotic ferns and orchids. We wondered whether this could be the world's first botanical distillery and whether we could let visitors see the real distillation process rather than having a separate visitor centre.

The studio developed the idea of building two intertwining botanical glasshouses as a highlight of the central courtyard, one tropical and the other Mediterranean, to house and cultivate the ten plant species that give Bombay Sapphire gin its particularity. Excitingly, as the industrial vapour distillation process produces excess heat that otherwise has to be taken away, and as the

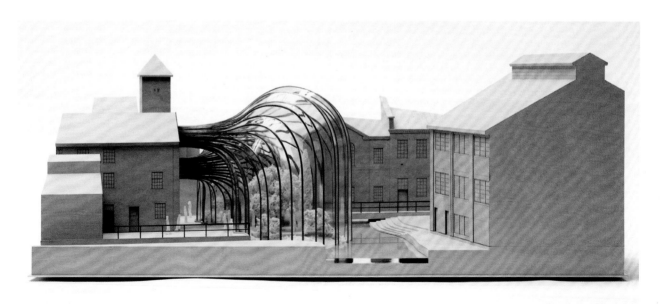

creation of tropical and Mediterranean climatic environments in the British context requires additional heat, there was a potential virtuous circle if we could tie these two things together.

The resulting glasshouse structures spring from one of the historic mill buildings, now re-appropriated as a gin distillation hall, recycling the spare heat from the machinery to make the perfect growing conditions for tropical and Mediterranean plants. The two glasshouses then embed themselves into the flowing waters of the newly widened riverbed. Working with a team from the Royal Botanic Gardens at Kew as horticultural collaborators, the ten exotic botanical plant types grow in the two structures alongside over a hundred additional plant and herb species that provide the accompanying ecosystem required to maintain them.

The resulting complex geometries of the new asymmetrical glasshouses took many months to calculate, engineer and refine. The finished built structures are made from 893 individually shaped two-dimensionally curved glass pieces held within more than 1.25 kilometres of bronze-finished stainless steel frames. In their entirety the glasshouses are made from more than ten thousand bespoke components.

On arrival, visitors walk to the newly opened-up river, before crossing a bridge and making their way along the waterside to the main production facility, located in the centre of the site facing into the courtyard and new glasshouses. Through careful restoration of the historical buildings, widening and revealing the River Test and the construction of a new gin factory system including new glasshouses, this project juxtaposes Laverstoke's historical past with an interesting new future.

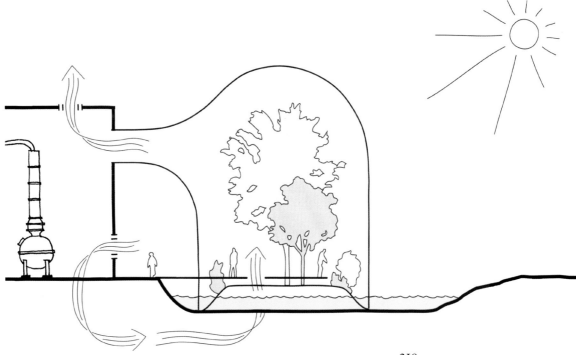

The distillery opened to the public in autumn 2014 and was awarded an 'outstanding' BREEAM environmental sustainability rating for its design, making it both the first distillery and first industrial facility, as well as the first refurbishment project, to have been awarded this rating.

1000 Trees

Can a new development be both enormous and human?

FOLLOWING THE SUCCESS of the UK Pavilion for the 2010 Shanghai World Expo, the studio was introduced to a number of potential Asian commissioners.

It was a surprise to find that, unlike their Western property developer counterparts, they had fewer assumptions about the visual language that building designers would apply to projects. The ambition and work of a designer was more important than an aesthetic style. Just because the right solution for the UK Pavilion had been a hairy structure (pages 308–20), they did not presume that a design for something else, such as an office building or hotel, would also result in the same aesthetic approach.

One of the most interesting new conversations was with a developer who had a 15-acre site next to Shanghai's main art district, M50, located 3.2 kilometres (2 miles) to the west of Shanghai's central Bund district on the Suzhou Creek tributary of the Huangpu River. The site sat next to a public park, was split over two plots separated by a narrow strip of government land and incorporated several historic buildings from the large Fou Foong Flour Mill that used to occupy it.

The brief was to create a new 300,000-square-metre destination, with a wide mix of uses, within a residential area whose repetitive concrete towers surrounded it on three sides. There was no urban heart in that part of the city, but there was some life and activity next door among the former industrial buildings of the art district, which galleries and artists had fought to save from demolition.

Most new property developments in China had become increasingly enormous during the country's rapid urbanization. This one followed the trend,

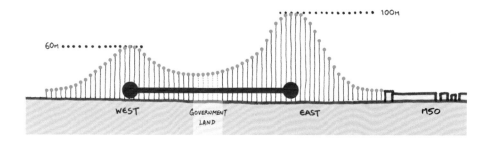

yet the studio was struck by the fact that the size of humans had changed so little over thousands of years. How could an unchanged human scale be reconciled with ever-larger chunks of city? If it is widely accepted that the places people enjoy and feel comfortable in are characterized by small-scale interest and variety, how could any architectural idea ever be appealing enough to sustain a building that is almost half a kilometre long?

The site had existing planning consent for a conventional format of two vast podium shopping-mall blocks with glass towers perched on top. The team was aware that the design of mixed-use projects is often limited to tweaking the façade of such big boxes. We were convinced that a new large-scale building development would not sit well with the neighbouring art district and park. Not believing that making attractive architectural wrapping paper for boxes was the right thing to do, we asked ourselves how to build a 400-metre-long development that responded better to its surroundings?

The existing park and art district already had successful human-scale interest and detail. We could not bring ourselves to design a separate massive building that turned its back on them, so we decided to see whether our project could be an extension of them instead. The team also searched for ways to counteract and soften the endless dry feeling of the surrounding towers while at the same time meeting the brief to construct the full permitted buildable area.

Following an instinct to break the huge, boxy building into smaller pieces, we became interested in the vast number of structural columns that a construction project of this size would need. Typically building designers hide these columns behind external skins or internal shop façades. However, we imagined the columns holding up structural floors in the same way that a substantial tree trunk holds up heavy branches, making each column suddenly more significant. In our own studio we had once naively imagined that having a large column-free space would create a nirvana of spatial flexibility. However, some years later we moved into a new workspace with a regular grid of pre-existing columns and realized that the columns gave character to the layout as well as being very useful for organizing the way people work.

This time, could we celebrate the columns that wind their way up from foundations many metres underground, through multiple storeys of parking, shops, restaurants, cinemas, hotels and service spaces, then out into the open, as the heroes of our building? By giving prominence to them over the façade, the bulk of the building would feel more articulated and less clumsy. The internal volume would then fill in the gaps between the columns.

We had also noted the contrast between the surrounding brutal buildings and the green planting of the adjacent public park, which felt full of life. Could we counteract the barrenness of an unchanging, gigantic new building by integrating planting as a natural balancing element?

If so, how might we include generous planting of trees and bushes in the building without adding significant structural problems? Flat, planted green roofs have become increasingly popular as a way to soften and humanize the impact of a building, but frequently require

larger beams between columns to carry the weight to the nearest columns. The team realized that the most efficient way to transfer the structural load straight down to the foundations would be to place the planting directly on top of each column. In this way the top of every column would become a large planter, each holding one or more trees, and the entire project would be built around a collection of columns of different heights, like a vast, agglomerated treehouse city. This celebrated the building's columns and extended the notion of the existing park across the site. Many models, including one made of spaghetti, helped the team arrive at the right topography.

Based on the Local Building Department's obligation to break the project down into two recognizable plots, each with different government-permitted building heights, the studio drew a standard orthogonal grid of columns that raised up the park incrementally, with the columns replacing the façade as the defining aesthetic element. The low edges of the building reduce the discernible threshold between the new development, the art district and the park. To the south, however, where the neighbouring city buildings meet the development, the new topography is sliced away to create a sheer façade, as if it has been cut open to reveal its internal cellular nature and contents to the world.

Even though no commercial activity is permitted to span the government land between east and west plots, the team felt that to work both commercially and symbolically the site needed a physical connection between them. We conceived the inner public circulation as a figure-of-eight plan, weaving a shopping-mall spine through the building's columns like a cat's cradle. The narrow

228

crossing point of the figure of eight bridges the government land, while the loops at the ends create major public spaces for the east and west sides of the development.

Another important part of the project was to retain all of the historic flour-mill buildings on-site, integrating and harnessing them as focal points within the wider scheme. The most special of these is the administrative office that sits at the centre of the column-stilted building. The width of the two sites grows up entirely around it, celebrating and enclosing it as the centrepiece of a new great public space. Other administrative buildings are used as entry points from the river, or are left as freestanding structures that sit as complementary elements embedded within the landscape.

Construction on the first phase, the west of the development, was completed in 2021. In the months before the opening, we collaborated closely with local and international artists to create giant artworks, both indoors on enormous murals and the lift shafts, and outdoors integrated across the entirety of the south façade. The result is a giant collection of street art that celebrates the cultural heritage of the M50 neighbourhood.

Visiting the project now, we are thrilled to spend time on some of the hundreds of outdoor terraces across the site. From them you can always hear the buzz of insects and the singing of birds, and enjoy the abundance of planting that is actively contributing to the city's biodiversity. These spaces also reveal the hum of human activity from sunrise to sunset. Some terraces hold food trucks, others cafés, while many feature displays of furniture or pieces of art and design. They have become places where people gather – to socialize, to join a fitness class, to practise yoga – which feels more important than ever.

At ground level, the riverside park has truly become a new green everyday space for the city. In addition to the daily walkers, thousands of local people come each spring to enjoy the cherry blossom festival, and the park sits adjacent to the starting point of the annual city half marathon.

In 2026, the mountainous east phase of the project is set to complete, bringing workspace, hotels, shops, a cinema and an even larger riverside park. There will be many more large-scale artistic collaborations. The studio is excited to see the entire 1000 Trees finished – it will stand as proof of how we can break down large-scale developments to a human scale that is engaging and interesting, whether you are looking at it from across the river, across the street or up close.

236

Al Fayah Park

Can you make a park out of the desert?

THE STUDIO WAS ASKED to re-conceive a major piece of public land in Abu Dhabi. Following the rapid pace of the city's recent development there was a desire to provide a local park as a public space devoted to the wellbeing of the people of the city.

Designing a park in the desert presented the studio with a series of challenges, the most serious of which was how to provide protection from the hot desert sun for visitors, as well as for the park's plants and vegetation. Offering a place for relaxation and leisure for those using it, the park also needed to be energy efficient and sustainable in its use of water to irrigate vegetation. The existing public space evoked the style of a European park by covering the desert with a blanket of grass, which required a significant amount of purified irrigation water to counteract evaporation caused by the intense sunlight. The process of creating desalinated water, which is produced industrially from salty sea water, is costly and energy-consuming.

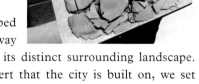

The idea for the park's design developed in response to these challenges and as a way of celebrating the beauty of the desert and its distinct surrounding landscape. Instead of denying the presence of the desert that the city is built on, we set ourselves the task of making a park out of the desert itself.

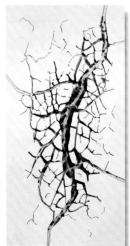

We became interested in the patterns of the desert landscape and looked at the shapes created when earth cracks from the heat of the sun. We also became fascinated by how, in earlier times, people living in such intense heat had grown their vegetables in the shade of palm trees to reduce the strength of the sun's rays. Experimenting with the idea of a structure drawn from a fractured desert crust, we developed a scheme based on revealing partially shaded planted spaces below a desert surface.

The project evolved as a series of cracked pieces of desert surface raised on columns to form a gentle dome across the site. These elevated pieces create a perforated canopy of partial shade under which a lush garden can grow, protected from the harsh excesses of the desert sun. This sunken oasis becomes a thriving landscape of plants and mature trees, forming a series of interconnected public recreational spaces.

The 20-metre-high shaded garden is conceived of as a place for families to gather and picnic, as well as a place for learning and festivals. Visitors will find cafés, play spaces, a library, pools and streams, as well as date palms and community vegetable gardens. By creating partial shade for the planting, the canopy aims to reduce the amount of water lost to evaporation and so will improve the park's energy efficiency and sustainability. While providing the shade for the oasis in the daytime, the elevated plates also become a network of social and meeting places in the cooler evening hours.

Christmas Card

Can you make someone open your Christmas card twenty-four times?

THE DESIGN OF THIS CARD is based on the Advent calendars that are given to children at the beginning of December to allow them to count down the days to Christmas Eve. We hoped to recreate the feeling of opening the tiny doors of your Advent calendar to find the coloured picture behind each one.

The card we sent out at the end of November consisted of twenty-four miniature manila envelopes, glued to each other to form an object that was the shape and size of a normal postal envelope and could be posted for the cost of sending a first-class letter. Each day, you opened an envelope and a small card popped out, held by a tiny stalk. The cards appeared to show nothing more than a few letters, a random word or some disconnected lines but, as the month of December went by, they accumulated to reveal an image and caption. The illustrator Sara Fanelli, who we invited to collaborate with us on the content of the envelopes, chose a phrase that was both beautiful and apt, with a final word that was hard to predict until Christmas Eve, when the full picture revealed itself.

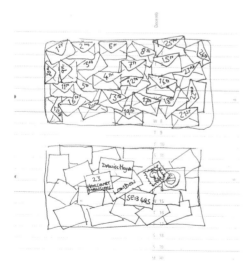

LIZ AND ANDREA
MORGANTE
FLAT 1
172 KENSINGTON CHURCH ST.
LONDON
W8 4BN

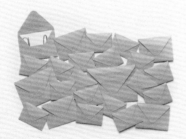

Jiading Bridge

How can a traditional Chinese moon bridge meet today's standards of accessibility?

AS THE CHINESE CITY of Shanghai expands rapidly, the satellite settlements on its outskirts are undergoing an intensive process of planned growth, with new high-speed rail links connecting them to the main city. The mayor of one of these towns, Jiading, invited the studio to design a new pedestrian bridge with a span of 20 metres to cross one of the town centre's many waterways.

Referring to the historical Chinese bridge form, we encountered a phenomenal heritage of interesting structures. Traditionally, while European bridges tended to take the form of a basic convex arc, often raised on stilts, the typical Chinese bridge was based on using two S-shaped curves, one at each side of the bridge. This concave–convex–concave curve form gives the steeply hump-backed Chinese bridge a distinctive and beautiful elevation, similar to the shape of an eye, but it requires steep flights of uneven stairs, which present obvious access difficulties. Crossing such a bridge is like climbing over a steep little mountain; difficult enough for an able-bodied person, challenging for the elderly and impassable for a wheelchair-user. As well as allowing boats through, Jiading's new bridge needed to meet today's standards of accessibility. The question was how to do this without giving it ramps that were steeper than the 1:20 gradient, which is agreed to be a safe and comfortable limit for wheelchair access. At this gradient, the bridge would either have immensely long ramps or be too low to let boats through.

Rather than import a European idea of a bridge, we wondered if there was a way to employ this s-curve form, which we loved, but make it more functionally relevant to modern needs. Could a bridge with that gorgeous shape be made to flatten itself? Or, conversely, could a flat bridge transform itself into this shape?

The idea is for a bridge made from threading together C-shaped sections, each one forming a single step with its own piece of balustrade. Each section is able to move relative to the others. In their flattened state, the sections align to form a level surface that allows a wheelchair-user to cross the bridge, before rearing up to produce a flight of steps and allowing boats to go underneath. Unlike a conventional opening bridge, which splits in the middle as it lifts,

making it temporarily impassable to pedestrians, this bridge can be crossed in any position – up, down or somewhere in between.

Despite its apparently complex movement, the bridge is operated by two rotating arches that run through every step section of the bridge and which, spanning the river, are made to rotate parallel to each other by hydraulic rams. As the bridge is lowered, the arches begin to tilt over towards the water, causing the step sections to shift and gradually transform the stepped deck into a flat surface.

The bridge sections will be constructed with machined steel on their external surfaces and bronze on the faces that move past each other, the contrast between the materials visually accentuating the transformative movement of the bridge.

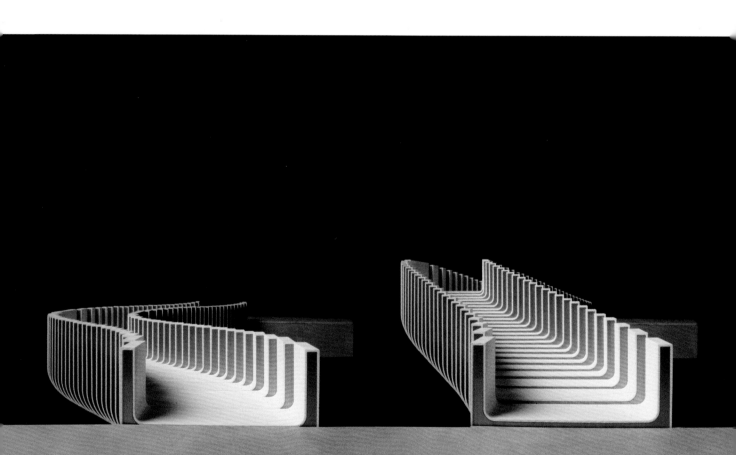

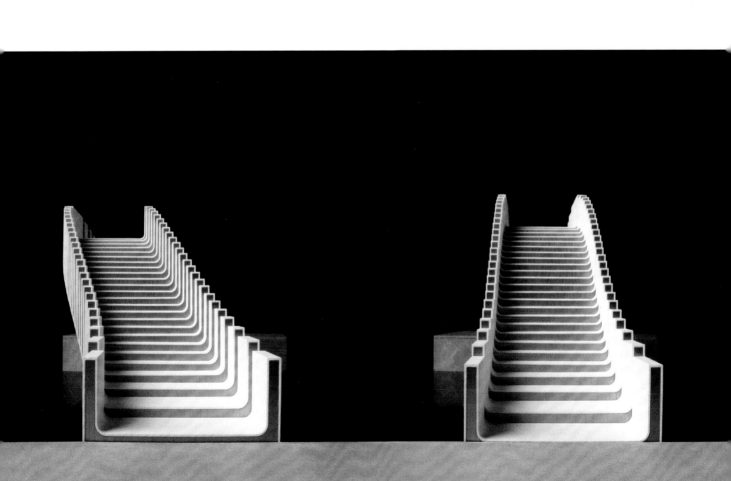

Towers of Silence

Can a structure you can hardly see have a strong presence in your mind?

LEADERS OF THE PARSI COMMUNITY of Mumbai, India, commissioned the studio to help them solve problems that have arisen in relation to their ancient burial practices. As practitioners of the ancient Zoroastrian faith, it is their custom not to bury or cremate their dead, but to place the bodies in a ritual space known as a Tower of Silence, or Dakhma, where they are exposed to the elements and consumed by vultures. Although the Parsis originated in Persia, they are most numerous in Mumbai, where the community holds many hectares of forest land in the centre of the city in which these sky burials are carried out. However, the faith faces serious challenges to its future.

First, since it requires both husband and wife to be Parsi to carry the faith on through the family line, the population of Zoroastrians is in decline. Second, a veterinary painkiller called diclofenac, widely used to dull the pain of working cattle, has proved so toxic to the vultures that feed on the dead carcasses of these animals that the vulture population has been virtually eliminated. Across India, vultures were an effective way to hygienically dispose of polluted and inedible meat, but this meat is now consumed instead by a growing population of rats and feral dogs, which spread disease. The Parsis can therefore no longer rely on vultures to consume the bodies of their dead, which become bloated and foul-smelling when left untouched. Finally, the rapid

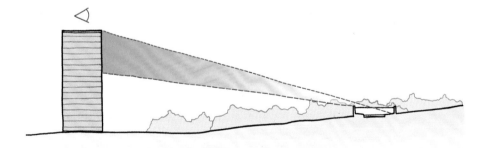

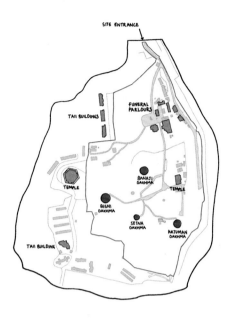

urbanization of Mumbai is creating another set of challenges. The Parsi burial site falls within the area of the city with the highest land values, equivalent to London's Mayfair. While the Towers of Silence were originally designed to be impossible to look into from the ground, people are increasingly able to peer down into them from the tower buildings that are springing up around the edges of the site, giving the residents of luxury penthouses an unwelcome view of decomposing corpses. Although this piece of land has been used in this way since the fifteenth century, there is growing pressure from property developers and local residents to discontinue the Parsi burial practices and redevelop the site, with potentially disastrous consequences for the community.

Since the future of the faith seemed to depend on helping the vultures to do the job of disposing of human remains, we were asked to look for ways to make an aviary around and over the Towers of Silence, to create a sanctuary in which to nurture a new vulture population, safe from contamination, as well as solving the problem of overlooking. Analysing how this aviary would be perceived, we found an unusual contradiction.

As the family bids farewell to a corpse before it is placed in the Tower of Silence, the tower itself plays no liturgical role in the funeral ceremony. Parsis do not need to be reminded that there is an aviary over their Towers of Silence, but at the same time other people in the city should not readily see something that makes them think about vultures eating dead bodies. Yet for the vultures to fly between the towers and have a good quality of life, this could well have to be the world's largest aviary. Although you might normally want to make a feature of such a structure, the need for discretion ruled out an extroverted building like the aviary in London Zoo, which has an expressive shape that can be seen for miles around. However, if you were a Parsi, you would want to know that your body would be left in a special place. Although it might be inconspicuous, it would still exist in your mind.

The aviary that we designed faces towards the sky, putting its entire focus upwards. Completely flat on top, it is based on a structure of tension cables and netting supported

by simple columns. Its shape derives from the layout of the Towers of Silence, its volume comes from the numbers of vultures it has to support and its height is defined by the need of the birds to be able to fly above the tree-tops. The sides that could be visible to surrounding tower buildings are planted with climbing plants to form natural camouflage screens, blending them into the wooded site.

This project has significance for the future of Mumbai's Parsi community, as well as providing a catalyst for the restoration of the wider site, which contains heritage buildings and other structures that are crumbling.

London Bus

*Can a London bus be better
and use 40 per cent less fuel?*

THE LAST BUS DESIGNED specifically for London was the famous Routemaster developed between 1947 and 1956, which had an open platform that allowed passengers to jump on and off when it was stuck in traffic. After production ceased in 1968 and London's bus routes were contracted out to private operating companies, new types of vehicle, without open platforms, were ordered from the catalogues of bus manufacturers. The only aesthetic criterion that the transport authorities applied was that the bus had to be red. However, as legislation imposed ever more requirements, the design of London's buses, particularly their interiors, became increasingly compromised and uncoordinated.

Dissatisfied with the city's buses, the Mayor of London decided to commission the first new bus for the capital in fifty years and the studio was excited to be asked to collaborate with the vehicle's manufacturer on its design.

Even though it had been much loved, the brief was not to replicate the Routemaster, which had been inaccessible to wheelchair-users and difficult for people with prams. The new bus had to be completely accessible as well as minimizing the time it would take at bus stops to load and unload passengers. To do this efficiently, it needed to have three doors and two staircases, making it almost 3 metres longer than a Routemaster. At the same time, it needed to substantially reduce its energy consumption by using 40 per cent less fossil fuel than existing buses, and, as the fleet would potentially number several hundred, it had to be affordable. TfL also specified that the New Routemaster should be cooled with roof-mounted chillers, and that to make this cooling system effective the bus windows would need to be fixed, unlike those of London's other buses.

The main similarity to the original Routemaster was that the bus would have an open platform, but, because a conductor would be on duty only during peak hours, it had to be possible for the platform to revert to an electronically operated opening and closing door for the rest of the time. The bus also had to comply with a vast body of new regulations, European laws and good practice guidelines. (One of the stranger requirements was to make it impossible for anyone to insert a sword through gaps in the protective screen around the driver.)

To meet the environmental performance target of using 40 per cent less energy, the team took two steps. The first was to develop a hybrid vehicle

powered by both electricity and diesel, and the second was to make the bus as lightweight and therefore as efficient as possible, which greatly affected the type and quantity of materials we could use in the design.

As the 11-metre vehicle would be longer than most double-decker buses currently in use on London's streets, it was given rounded corners and edges to reduce its perceived dimensions, notably the apparent size of its huge, flat sides. The bus would function asymmetrically, its three doors on one side creating an uneven flow of people inside, and we allowed this eccentricity to generate the geometry of the external design. The first ribbon of window begins next to the driver, where it forms the windscreen, then wraps around the bottom deck, enclosing the rear platform, before spiralling up the rear staircase to become the windows for one side of the top deck. The second strip of window angles up the front staircase to form the windows of the rest of the top deck. Running the windows up the staircases in this way makes passengers visible from the street and transforms the staircase from a dark, constricted shaft into a lighter and more generous space.

In recent years, bus interiors had grown increasingly chaotic, with their peculiar seating arrangements, fluorescent yellow handrails suggestive of radiation warning signs, protruding lumps of machinery encased in mysterious fibreglass housings, over-bright strip lighting that reflects harshly off the windows at night, and floors covered in the same brightly coloured sluice-downable vinyl that you see in the accident and emergency department of a hospital. Our priority was to

improve this environment for passengers by recalibrating the numerous separate design compromises that had accumulated over the years, trying to bring them together into an interior that felt as calm and coordinated as possible.

Using a simple palette of colours and materials, we developed a family of details that included new stairs, lighting and hand poles, as well as new stop buttons. Feeling that the individualized bucket seats now fitted to all buses make their interiors feel cluttered and untidy, we argued instead for a return to benches that two people could share. We then designed a new pattern of moquette, the tough woollen furnishing fabric traditionally used to upholster the seats of London's buses. Rather than a continuous, small, repeating pattern that could go on any piece of transport furniture, it has a pattern that is specific to this seat,

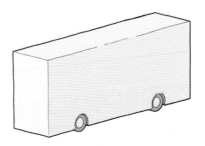
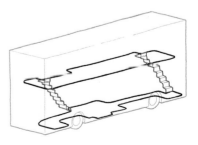

based on the contour lines that outline the form of a seated person.

In November 2010, a full-size prototype of the bus was unveiled and put on display in London's Transport Museum and a few months later, in the spring of 2011, a working test vehicle was successfully trialled at Millbrook Racecourse. London's transport authority has commissioned eight hundred vehicles to enter service by 2016, the first six of which were on the streets in time for the London 2012 Olympic Games.

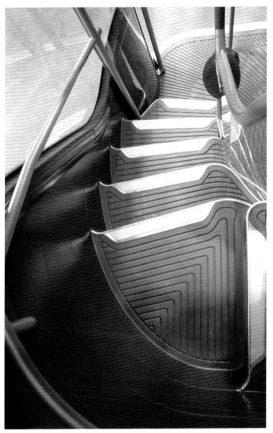

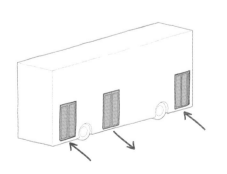

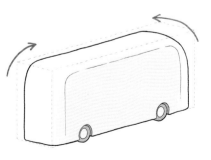

263

Christmas Card

Can a Christmas card be made from the postbox that it will be posted into?

THERE IS A MOMENT when a card or letter is pushed irreversibly into a postbox and begins its journey through the postal system. Our idea was to make a cast of the actual slot that your card will be posted through and make this our Christmas card.

The studio's cards are posted using the postbox near our building on Gray's Inn Road in King's Cross. For this card, members of the studio went out at four o'clock in the morning and took casts of the slot of this postbox. These casts were later used to make the cards from clear, glass-like silicon.

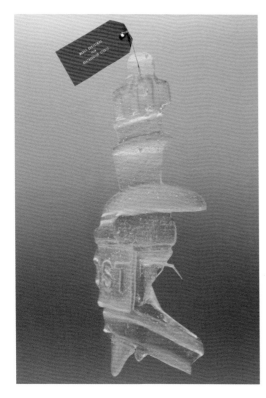

Large Span Rolling Bridge

Is it possible to make a rolling bridge long enough to span the River Thames?

AFTER BUILDING THE ROLLING BRIDGE (pages 436–41), which spanned a small section of London canal, the studio wanted to develop the idea by making a rolling bridge long enough to cross a large river. The City Bridge Trust, the six-hundred-year-old charity that maintains London's bridges, gave us the opportunity to work on this when it asked us to design a float for the Lord Mayor's Show. This annual procession through the streets of the City of London brings the City's livery companies, charities, emergency services, businesses, community organizations and marching bands together in a huge mobile exhibition about London life. Many of these organizations produce a float, which is an extravagant display mounted on a lorry or special trailer.

Our float, which was to symbolize the work of the City Bridge Trust, would be an 8-metre-long working model of the new Rolling Bridge. Opening and closing as it travelled through the streets, the model gave us a chance to test the idea.

As part of the project, the studio collaborated with the Hackney Building Exploratory, a charity that encourages young people to discover London's architecture, and began working with forty children from an east London primary school. When asked to suggest other ways in which bridges might get out of the way of boats, they had some very interesting ideas, including one that we particularly liked, for a bridge that vanished by submerging itself underwater.

The Large Span Rolling Bridge is simpler than its predecessor. Instead of multiple hydraulic rams, it uses cables, gravity and an electric winch. The winch reels in the cables, which make the bridge sections fold into each other, one by one, opening the bridge. When the cables are allowed to unwind again, the bridge sections open out under the force of gravity. Long enough to cross the River Thames in London, the 200-metre bridge consists of four of these rolling mechanisms, mounted on two pillars in the river. When the bridge opens and the four decks are rolled up, the bridge is transformed into two heart shapes, balancing on the columns.

The 8-metre model was built by our workshop team from machined aluminium and welded steel, and contained around two thousand parts, which we laser-cut from 2-millimetre-thick aluminium sheets. The model is powered by

The City Bridge Trust ♛ Celebrates 800 y... ...concept for a new opening bridge

turning a single handle, which operates a winch that pulls all four sets of cables, synchronized by a system of pulleys.

For the procession, the schoolchildren devised a dance inspired by the bridge. On the day of the show, the bridge withstood the bumping and lurching as it travelled through the streets on the back of its specially designed trailer, opening and closing all the way. Studio team members took turns to wind the handle while the schoolchildren walked next to the float, performing their Rolling Bridge dance moves. Thousands of Londoners cheered us on. By lunchtime it was pouring with rain and the children were sent home by their teachers. We found that the rain washed away the studio team's shyness and we all began dancing through the streets, beside our bridge, in the pouring rain.

This project demonstrated that the Large Span Rolling Bridge idea could work. Now it requires a home: a city somewhere in the world divided by a river that needs connecting together with a special bridge.

Extrusions

*Can you squeeze a chair out of
a machine, the way you squeeze
toothpaste out of a tube?*

WHEN I WAS CONSTRUCTING A PAVILION (pages 606–11) as a student at Manchester Polytechnic, the aluminium components I used were manufactured for me at the British Alcan factory in Banbury using an industrial process called extrusion. Commonly used in inexpensive, double-glazed window frame systems, extruded aluminium is made by heating a billet of metal and forcing it through a shaped hole in a steel plate, known as a die, which produces a straight length of aluminium with a cross-section determined by the shape of the die.

Watching this being done, I was surprised to find that this was not the rigid, clinical industrial process I had imagined. Even in this technologically advanced manufacturing process, warped imperfection was unavoidable. As the metal began to squeeze out of the machine, the first part of it caught unevenly on the surfaces of the die, contorting as it struggled to work out what shape it should be. After that, it straightened out and became perfect. Once the extruding process was complete, the straight parts were stretched with a special machine to make them even straighter and the imperfect beginning bits were chopped off and melted down. To me, though, these unwanted mutated sections were the best part, and I wondered if it was possible to produce warped lengths of extruded aluminium on a larger scale.

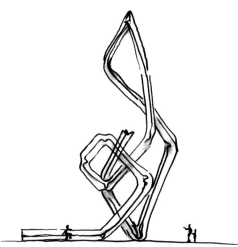

With so many new airports and stations being built around the world, there is a need for many linear kilometres of new seating. Could we use the extrusion process to create this seating? Furniture usually consists of numerous separate components. Instead, could we form a seat from a single component by squeezing it like toothpaste, in one go? As all you need to make a long bench is a seat and a back, could we extrude this as a consistent, elongated L-shape? Instead of attaching separate legs, the contorted ends of the profile could be twisted down to the ground to support the seat.

At the time I was studying at the Royal College of Art, and I telephoned every main aluminium manufacturer I could find, to see if there was a machine capable of producing an extrusion on this scale, but no such machine existed. Instead, I made a three-dimensional sketch of the form, a full-size, functional test piece, using hundreds of layers of laminated birch plywood as a substitute for the metal. In the studio, we continued to look for an extruding machine large enough to make the aluminium version. Sixteen years later, we learned that a new extruding machine had been built in the Far East that was the largest in the world. Capable of exerting 10,000 tonnes of pressure, it was being used to make rocket components for the aerospace industry. Its capacity was so great that it could extrude a shape to form not only the seat and back, but the legs as well. All we needed to do was to design a single cross-section from which the metal die would be made. As the machine was new and had not been tested to its full potential, the factory could not say if it would be possible to squeeze the metal into the fullest extents of what would be the largest extrusion die ever produced. However, we were determined to try. We travelled to the factory and watched the machine successfully realize our idea. Working with our gallery, Haunch of Venison, in London, we were able to produce a series of pieces, in which a straight, clean, extruded length is contrasted with its raw, contorted end.

Although the original idea was for infrastructural seating, we are currently exploring the use of large-scale extrusion in other architectural and furniture applications, such as building structures, load-bearing columns, cladding systems and bridges. We also plan to produce a 100-metre-long extrusion that is not only seating but contorts into a 20-metre-high structure.

Theoretically, there is no limit to the length of seat that this machine can extrude. If we decided to make a kilometre-long bench to seat 1,500 people, the factory could just open its doors and carry on squeezing. But because we could never transport a piece this long, the only alternative would be to carry on extruding until the extrusion reached around the planet to wherever it needed to go.

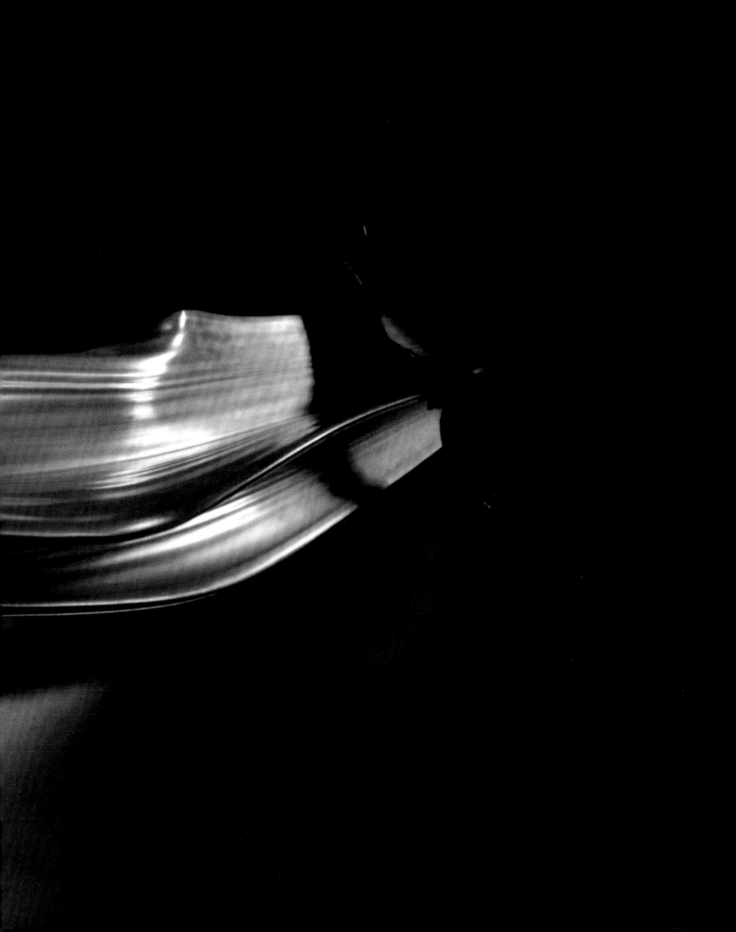

Worthing Swimming Pool

How can you give a building a specific relationship to its site?

AS PART OF A COLLABORATIVE TEAM that included experienced swimming pool designers Saville Jones, the studio was shortlisted in the competition to design a new swimming pool in Worthing, a seaside town on the south coast of England. The pool was to replace the Aquarena, where the British Olympic champion, Duncan Goodhew, used to train.

The local authority intended to sequentially redevelop the entire pool site, with its strategic position on the town's seafront promenade, by building the new pool next to the existing one, then knocking the old pool down and using that part of the site for a second development.

The team developed a simple master plan for the build-ing. Given the footprint of the site and the complex sequencing of the development, we felt that the optimal shape for the building was an uncomplicated rectangular shed. Its main entrance could be on the long side of the building, facing the new develop-ment, so that as the swimmers came in and out of the building, they would bring life and activity to the development. All the changing rooms were also in this side of the building, leaving unobstructed views out of the pools on the far side of the building towards the sea and the next-door park. For the materiality of the building, we were drawn to wood, rather than concrete or painted steel, as there seemed to be good precedents for using timber to make pool buildings because it deals very well with moisture and condensation.

While trying to develop an idea for this building that could be unique to Worthing, we remembered the Worthing wood slick. Four years earlier, a ship named *Ice Prince* had capsized close to the town in a storm and its cargo of wood was washed overboard. Astonishing quantities of shipwrecked timber were deposited on Worthing beach, tangled up in vast piles. For a brief moment, Worthing made world news with the powerful imagery of this wood slick. In subsequent years, the town found itself celebrating this strange occurrence with a week-long arts festival and the installation of a commemorative stained-glass window on the town pier.

The raw quality of the piles of wood deposited on Worthing's beaches made a connection in our minds between the rectangular box of our swimming

Worthing
Herald

Thursday, January 24, 2008   An edition of the Herald/Gazette series   www.worthingherald.co.uk   Price 40p

WOW!

**SOUVENIR
PULL-OUT
PACKED
WITH
PICTURES**

pool and the rectangular bundles of wood that had been broken apart by the sea. Our idea was for a building that was like one of these pallets that had burst apart. While maintaining a simple box-like configuration on the inside, the building would be very dynamic on the outside, its disordered external elements forming structural cross-bracing, and at the same time creating practical solar shading in front of the glass. Lit up by night, the pool would glow from within like a lantern.

While being relatively straightforward to build, the idea was strong and relevant: it would be hard to find an idea for a building that was more specific to Worthing and its wood slick.

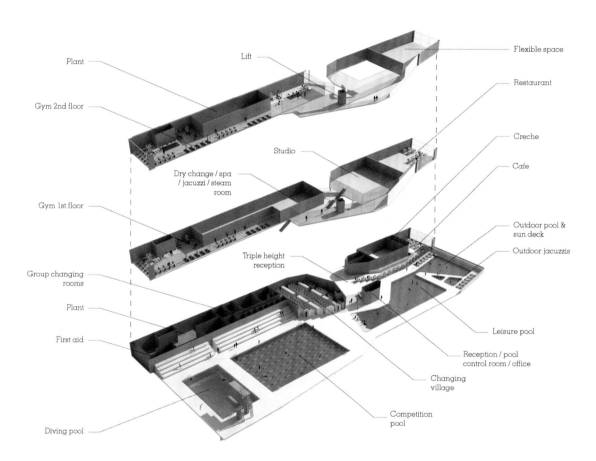

Masdar Mosque

What might a twenty-first-century mosque be like?

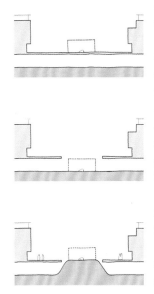

THE STUDIO WAS INVITED TO DESIGN a community mosque in Masdar, Abu Dhabi, a new city being master-planned by architects Fosters + Partners and conceived as the world's most sustainable city.

The plan for Masdar is to build the city two storeys up in the air, as if on a table, creating an underground service zone containing the transport system and all utilities. Removing cars from the streets and putting all transport below the raised ground allows buildings to be positioned closer together to create cooler, shadier streets that will never need to be dug up to mend cables or pipes. Because one of the main environmental issues in this climate is to reduce the energy used in air-conditioning systems, the city is laid out on a strict rectilinear grid that consists of tightly packed buildings, oriented to capture the cooling breezes that come off the desert by night and off the sea by day.

The mosque, however, breaks these rules because it has to be oriented to face Mecca, setting it at almost 45 degrees to the city's grid. We felt that this gave it permission to be different from the other buildings sitting on top of this table.

The Prophet proclaimed the whole earth to be a 'masjid' (mosque), meaning a place of prostration or prayer, so originally a mosque was simply a space where worshippers gathered to pray. A piece of open desert could be a mosque. There are now rules governing the layout and facilities of a mosque but there is nothing to say that it must have minarets and domes. Such features evolved out of pragmatic needs: before steel and concrete came into use, a dome was the only way to create a large, spanning roof to protect worshippers from the sun; before electronic amplification, the only way to enable people in the surrounding area to hear a call to prayer was to proclaim it from a minaret.

Muslims kneel and place their heads on the earth to pray, but the extraordinary thing in Masdar is that worshippers will be elevated above the ground, placing their heads on a tabletop 7 metres above the desert. As a mosque should be a particularly precious place, we felt that there was an opportunity to step off this futuristic slab of sustainable living and reconnect with the earth. If we made an opening in the surface of the tabletop and lifted the ground, then the worshipper could step through the opening and back on to the desert. Kneeling down to pray inside, he or she would be reconnecting with the earth.

Our idea was to take the flat plane of paving that supports the buildings of Masdar and raise it to become the enclosure of the mosque, introducing no new elements and making the building as pure and elemental as possible. Unlike the other buildings in Masdar, the mosque and the public space around it would not sit on top of the raised table but be constructed from it.

As well as covered walkways and planting, the public square around the mosque has paving that mutates into the skin of the religious building. The paving has a pattern of perforations, with optical fibres threaded through them that transmit daylight into the space below, softening the harsh glare of the sunlight. These optical fibres hang down inside and correlate with patterns in the carpet, letting worshippers know where to kneel and pray. The perforations in the paving have a second use: they demarcate spaces the size of prayer mats, so that if necessary worshippers can also pray outside the mosque.

The building design that we developed meets all the requirements of a mosque – the qiblah wall faces Mecca and there are separate entrances for women and men, ablution areas and a library – while also having a clear connection with the surrounding city. The design also takes advantage of the city's raised table level to draw in cool air from beneath.

The project did not go forward. However, we believe there is a place for mosques that do not pretend to be historic structures and which speak strongly to the world of a forward-looking faith.

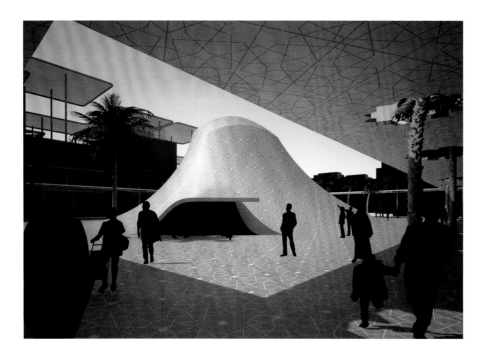

Christmas Card

*Can you turn somebody's name and
address into their Christmas card?*

THE IDEA FOR THIS CHRISTMAS CARD came from hand-writing the recipients' names and addresses on previous cards. We wrote out every name and address by hand, attached to its stamp and postmark. Then, thinking of the snowflakes that small children make by folding circles of paper into triangles and cutting into their folded edges with scissors, we turned each person's address into a snowflake by cutting away the empty space around, within and between all the letters.

What people received was just their own name and address, plus a stamp and postmark, cut into a folded piece of thin, white card. When they unfolded the card, it became a snowflake-like formation, which had the richness and detail of a piece of filigree lace. We made 350 cards and each one was unique, like a fingerprint or a DNA profile.

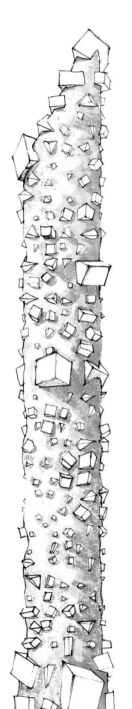

Sheung Wan Hotel

*How can a new building fit into
the atmosphere of a busy old district
of Hong Kong?*

A TEAM OF YOUNG PROPERTY DEVELOPERS asked the studio to design a new forty-storey tower, a hotel with three hundred rooms, in the Sheung Wan district of Hong Kong. This area is famous for its streets full of the texture and stinky richness of shops selling hundreds of types of dried fish, with unpackaged seafood hanging everywhere and piled in baskets. What concerned us was that the atmosphere of streets like these can be wiped out when a city block containing lots of small shops is replaced by a single flat, shiny building.

Some new hotels are just new interiors within existing buildings that were once offices, apartments or previous hotels, so that their design is often arbitrary and lacking any connection with the architecture of their exteriors. This project was unusual because it was being built from scratch, so it was an opportunity to conceive the inside and outside at the same time and build in a relationship between the two.

Typically, a hotel room contains a familiar set of objects – bed, window, mini-bar, safe and somewhere to keep the iron – which we interpreted as a series of boxes. This became the logic for our scheme, in which all the furniture and fittings for each room are formed out of boxes of four different sizes. These boxes are either open-ended and glazed to form windows or solid and enclosed to contain refreshments or valuables; the building's façade is composed of the outsides of these thousands of boxes. By varying how far the boxes protrude relative to their neighbours, we can give the façade an eroded, rugged feel, very different in texture from the smooth, shiny frontages that are normally seen on newly constructed buildings. Every room in the hotel is unique, giving guests different spatial experiences.

Hong Kong regulations encourage tall buildings to take the form of a tower set back on top of a podium building, an arrangement also seen in some British architecture of the 1960s, such as the British Telecom Tower in London, where the separation of the building into two distinct parts disrupts its relationship to the street. In an effort to avoid this, we pushed the tower component right to the front of its podium, so that from the street it appears cleanly and confidently as a single entity, rather than sitting back on a separate mass of podium.

The building is a concrete structure filled in with metal boxes, which are manufactured employing the same technology that is used to make air-conditioning ducts and water tanks. Sheet metal is folded, riveted or welded together and then painted and waterproofed. Inside the building, the metal boxes can be lined with bronze and sprayed directly with rigid insulation foam, a cost-effective and characterful technique that the studio has been developing in other projects, or upholstered to make beds and seats.

From the street, an elevator takes people up to the main lobby, which has a ceiling height of 7.5 metres. For coaches and cars, there is a loading bay that contains a turntable and a vehicle lift up to a car park.

Cloud Bridge

Can a strong structure look delicate?

THE STUDIO WAS INVITED to design a foot-bridge for the gardens of a stately home in the north of England, to replace a small wooden bridge in a historic rock garden that had a stream running through it.

Instead of a conventional bridge, constructed from two structural beams with a separate deck and balustrades added to it, our idea was to use a single structural substance and sculpt the entire bridge, including its deck and balustrades, out of it.

To create a bridge that was delicate and floating, rather than solid and heavy, we wondered if it would be possible to fuse hundreds of stainless steel discs to form a structure that resembled a fluttering swarm of butterflies. Although fragile looking, this mass of identical elements creates an efficient triangulated structure, although it does not look triangulated. The bridge would be made by welding together circular plates of metal and applying a glass bead-blasted finish. Rather than being shiny and reflective, each disc would take on a different diffused tone, depending on the angle at which it caught the light.

UK Pavilion

How can a building represent a nation?

IN 1851 THE FIRST WORLD'S FAIR was held in Hyde Park in London. It began a tradition for an event that is now called World Expo and takes place every few years in a different city. Nations of the world create government-sponsored pavilions that promote their country, economy, technology and culture. The 2010 World Expo, held in Shanghai, China, was the largest Expo ever, consisting of more than two hundred pavilions. With a team of collaborators, the studio won the competition to design the pavilion that would represent the United Kingdom.

As we were being briefed by the UK government, we could imagine governments of every country saying exactly the same things to their Expo designers: 'Show that our country has a strong economy... Show our splendid industry... Show that we are a good country for a holiday... Show our cultural diversity... Show that we are sustainable.' But in the final paragraph, the UK's brief changed tone and demanded that: 'When people vote for the best pavilion, make sure that you are in the top five!' This competitive order was useful to our design process because, having established that the objective was to win, we could work backwards to try to get to that outcome.

The brief posed another challenge. Like most of the other Western countries, the UK had been allocated a site the size of a football pitch. But even though our site was the same size as that of other nations, our budget was approximately half the size of theirs.

To meet the government's goal, the UK Pavilion would need to stand out from the hundreds of other pavilions. Like us, none of the other countries had designed their pavilion yet, but we tried to guess what they might do, in order to avoid doing the same. Working with our initial collaborators, Casson Mann, we imagined what it would be like to visit the Expo and go into every one of its 240 pavilions. If every pavilion competed for your attention in the same way, the effect would be overwhelming. At the end of this sensory bombardment, you might well be so over-stimulated and numbed that you could stand in front of something incredible, but your eyes would be too dazed to take it in. Our challenge was to do one powerful thing that had clarity.

While seventy million people would visit the Expo and many hundreds of millions would see the pavilion on television, on the internet or in the press, only a small proportion of those people would actually go inside it. This told us that the outside of the pavilion mattered most. To make a powerful impression, the exterior had not only to be striking by itself but also to communicate the essence of the interior.

In Expo pavilions that we had seen before, there seldom seemed to be a connection between the architecture of the pavilion building and the content of the exhibition inside it. Instead we decided to do everything we could to make our building a manifestation of its content, so that if you took away the building, there would be no content.

We were also contending with assumptions that the pavilion should contain interactive television screens, buttons to press, projected film and images, pre-recorded sound and colour-changing LEDs. Such things are already familiar to people, being so widely used in museums, exhibitions and even retail displays that they have become predictable and exhausting. We were determined that our pavilion should surprise visitors with its simplicity and absence of technological devices.

We understood, too, that every pavilion was an advertisement for its country. What, in that case, could we say about the UK, and how could we say it? Research showed that the perception of the UK in much of the world still carried lingering stereotypes of London smog, bowler hats, Marmite, double-decker buses, the Royal Family and red telephone boxes. How could we get away from these clichéd, old-fashioned stereotypes and better reflect the inventiveness and creativity of many people working in contemporary Britain?

With its slogan 'Better City, Better Life', the theme of the Expo was the future of cities. We decided to consider the relationship of cities to nature, an area in which the UK has made a unique contribution. For example, the world's first urban public park of modern times was in the UK and, for its size, London is the greenest city in the world, with its hundreds of parks, squares, trees and gardens. London is also home to the world's first major botanical institution, Kew Gardens. The subject of nature and cities also touches on the broader relationships between plant life and human health and the meaning of these for urban development, economic success and social change.

In developing a master plan, the budget forced us to be strategic and pragmatic. Most pavilions are as big as their football pitch-sized sites. As well as

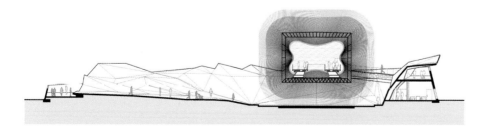

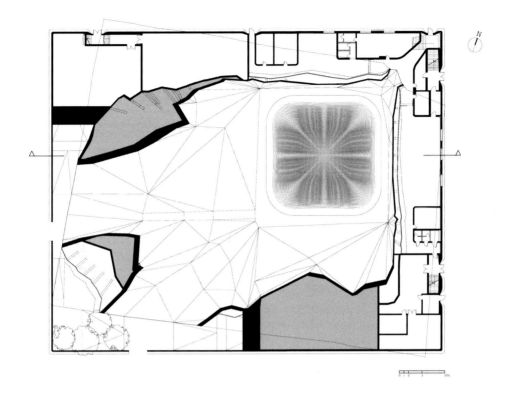

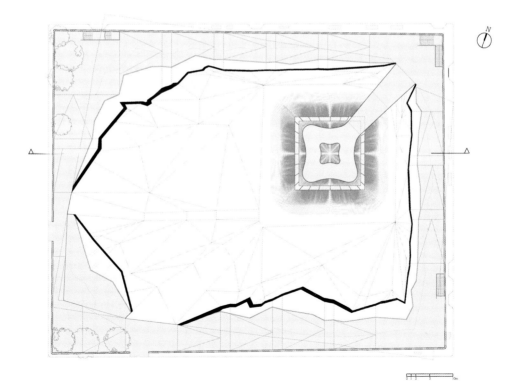

a public exhibition, they contain a large amount of space devoted to back-of-house functions, such as toilets, administrative facilities, hospitality spaces and storage. We felt that making all of this distinctive and extraordinary would be expensive and unnecessary.

We decided to break the UK Pavilion into two elements: a focal object, which we hoped would be unforgettable, and a broader architectural treatment housing the rest of the functional spaces, which did not need to be memorable. Instead of diluting the budget and spreading it across the whole of our site, we could concentrate our resources by making the focal object – the most expensive bit – take up only a fifth of the site. Its relatively small size would also mean that its internal space would require less energy to keep it cool than a larger pavilion. Then, within the other four-fifths of the site, the back-of-house requirements could be met separately in a quieter and more cost-effective way. We did this by building those facilities underneath a public space, on which our focal object would sit and in which visitors could sit down, draw breath and recover from Expo-exhaustion. This space also framed the focal object and separated it visually and physically from its chaotic surroundings. We also hoped that, by creating a large flexible space around the special object, we had built in the capacity to absorb any  compromises that might be forced on the project. If a new government minister suddenly insisted that the UK Pavilion must include a Formula One car or a waxwork of Sherlock Holmes, we would be able to find somewhere to put it on the rest of the site, without damaging the main story.

We imagined that many of the surrounding Expo buildings might follow the architectural trends in form-making. Instead we concentrated on exploring texture. Our starting point was the opening sequence of the 1985 film *Witness*, starring Harrison Ford, in which the camera pans across fields of grass buffeted into flowing patterns by the wind, like a beautiful kinetic sculpture. Was there any way to make the skin of a building behave like this? On the exposed Expo site, could we make a building façade move in the wind coming off the river?

Ten years earlier, we had put forward a proposal (pages 524–27) for treating a building like the Play-Doh plastic figure who grows hair and a beard when you squeeze coloured dough through holes in his head and chin. The idea is that the original object is lost inside the texture, but that the tips of the hairs can be conceived as forming an outward projection of its original shape. It seemed that if you magnified the texture of a building enough, there would come a point when the texture actually becomes its form. What was exciting to us was the idea of making the outside of the building so indefinite that you cannot draw a line between the building and the sky, because they merge into each other. This notion of texture gave us a way to relate to the pavilion's theme of nature and cities.

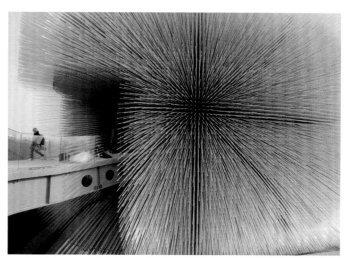

Most people find flowers, plants and trees beautiful, but seeds tend to be underappreciated, unceremoniously sold in garden centres in little paper packets. However, seeds are immensely significant for the ecology of the planet and fundamental to human nutrition and health. Wheat seeds and rice seeds feed nations; another seed could produce the plant that makes a drug enabling your elderly relative to live another fifteen years. For this future-gazing Expo, seeds seemed to be the ultimate symbol of unfulfilled potential and future promise.

For a number of years, Kew Gardens has been running a project called the Millennium Seed Bank, which is aiming to collect and preserve the seeds of 25 per cent of the world's wild plant species. Although it is well known, few people have seen this collection because it is based not at Kew Gardens but at a facility outside London near Gatwick Airport. Kew's seed collection gave us a way of connecting the texture of the building with its content. Our pavilion could be a cathedral to seeds.

The Seed Cathedral consists of a box, 15 metres wide and 10 metres high. Its 60,000 silvery, tingling hairs protrude from every surface, lifting it into the air to make a structure six storeys in height. The hairs are rods, identical 7.5-metre lengths of clear acrylic, which extend through the walls of the box into its interior. Inside the pavilion, the geometry of their tips forms a space described by a curvaceous undulating surface. Within this space, cast into the glass-like tips of all the hairs, are 250,000 seeds.

By day, the Seed Cathedral is lit only by the sunlight that is drawn into the cube along the length of each acrylic hair, in the same way that lightwaves travel along a fibre-optic cable. By night, tiny light sources concealed within the length of every rod illuminate both the seed ends inside the pavilion and the tips of the hairs on the outside. They appear as thousands of dancing points of light that sway and tingle in the breeze.

The Seed Cathedral sits on a landscape that is crumpled and folded like a giant sheet of paper, suggesting that the pavilion is a gift from the UK to China, still partly enclosed in its wrapping paper. Because it has inclined surfaces and lifted edges, the landscape creates a gentle amphitheatre that focuses on the Seed Cathedral. The form of the landscape is designed to guide people's experience of the Seed Cathedral in a particular way. Just as car advertisers know that a vehicle looks best from one of the front corners, rather than head or sideways on, the flow of visitors to the UK Pavilion is organized so that people's first glimpse of the Seed Cathedral is from a corner angle.

The entire surface is carpeted in silvery grey Astroturf, the artificial grass used for outdoor sports facilities, translating the softness of the Seed Cathedral into the landscape under your feet. An atmosphere of intimacy is created by the possibility that you can sit down anywhere and the suggestion that you might even lie

down or roll down the slopes. The effect of the angled floor plane is to turn people into spectators and performers, generating an atmosphere of theatricality. It also means that people do not obstruct each other's view of the building.

In order to protect visitors from the rain and sun as they go up the ramped walkways into the Seed Cathedral, as well as to exhibit interpretive material exploring the theme of nature in British cities, we placed the walkways underneath the edges of the sheet of landscape and then integrated a series of artistic installations into the walls, designed by Troika.

There was also a requirement for 1,500 square metres of space to accommodate a VIP suite, hospitality facilities, press and administrative offices, changing rooms, storage and toilets. All these functions are incorporated into space underneath the three-dimensional landscape. Though these spaces were simple and low-cost, their windows were developed with a particular detail that blended wall and glass, echoing the blurred silhouette of the Seed Cathedral.

The critical moment in the early stages of realizing the pavilion was when the director of Kew Gardens' Millennium Seed Bank agreed to provide us with 250,000 seeds, in collaboration with Kew's partner organization in China, the Kunming Institute of Botany. It then took many weeks to design and calculate the geometry of the pavilion's hairs, based on a set of rules we had drawn up: that the rods had to be identical in length; they had to point to a single spot in the centre of the pavilion; and their tips had to be evenly spaced on both the outside and the inside and not spread out or crush together as they went around corners. We worked with structural engineers Adams Kara Taylor to define a spacing density that avoided revealing too much of the central cube and giving the building bald patches. Outside, the Seed Cathedral had a specific quirk that we had designed into its geometry, which meant that, from whatever angle you looked at it, the image of the British flag, the Union Jack, appeared within the hairs of the pavilion.

Building the Seed Cathedral took a year. It was constructed in Shanghai by a Chinese contractor, using materials sourced locally. The central cube was built from red-coloured plywood, drilled with 60,000 holes to accommodate all the acrylic rods. As all the hairs pointed towards a single spot, every one passed through the walls at a different angle, which meant that every hole had its own unique drilling angle. In addition to holding the rods in place, an extra challenge was to waterproof a building with 60,000 holes in it. The detail that we engineered involved threading each rod through two aluminium sleeves, slotted one inside the other, and securing every join with rubber waterproofing rings, before attaching the tiny light sources that would illuminate each hair.

To develop the vast piece of carpeting for the landscape, we worked with a specialist manufacturer of outdoor sports pitch surfaces to formulate a version of Astroturf that has a red base and silvery grey hair, like the Seed Cathedral itself. Like shot silk, the red colour hidden in the depths of this surface came through as you moved your head.

Inside the finished Seed Cathedral, the space was like a cool, dimly lit cave filled with glowing jewels. As it silhouetted the seeds, the light had a calm, passive quality, like the light from stained glass, and the space was silent and serious. As the hours of the day went by, you could track the movement of the sun from inside by changes in the light coming from the seed ends, and pick out the shadows of passing clouds and birds flying overhead. The light would be strongest from the hairs that happened to be pointing directly towards you, wherever you were standing, so that it also changed as you moved around, becoming brighter towards the centre of the space. The UK Pavilion had no flashy electronics: just daylight illuminating the 250,000 seeds from the myriad hair ends. Inside the Seed Cathedral, you were at the most biodiverse point in Shanghai.

Apart from a programme of events and performances that took place daily on the pavilion landscape, the purpose of the outdoor space was deliberately ambiguous, giving people the freedom to treat it almost like a village green. This little piece of Britain, with people sitting all over it and children rolling down the slopes, was designed to reflect the UK's record as a pioneer of the modern urban public park and the part this played in the UK's legacy to the design of the world's cities.

In a national competition to find a Chinese nickname for the Seed Cathedral, the winning name was Dandelion. The association with blowing a dandelion and making a wish was a good symbol for this temporary building, resonating with our plan to distribute the seed ends among Chinese and UK schools and botanical institutions after the project was dismantled.

The Shanghai Expo lasted six months, during which more than eight million people – including the Chinese premier, Wen Jiabao – went inside the Seed Cathedral, making it the UK's most visited tourist attraction, nearly 10,000 kilometres (6,000 miles) from the UK. Two weeks before the end of the Expo, a state ceremony was held, at which it was officially announced that the UK Pavilion had won the event's top prize, the gold medal for Pavilion Design.

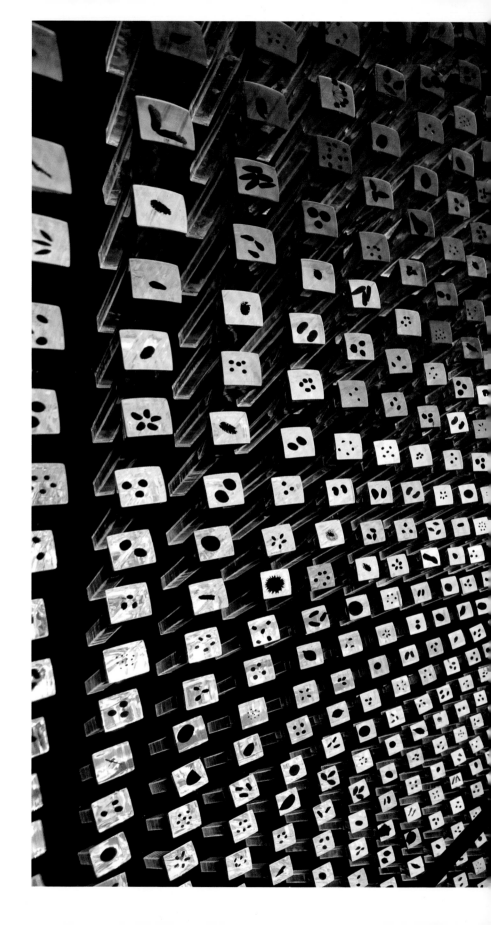

322

Spun

*Can a rotationally symmetrical
form make a comfortable chair?*

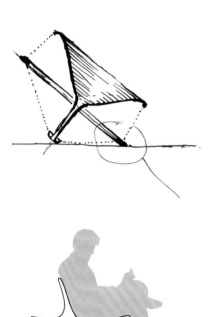

THIS PROJECT CAME ABOUT from wondering if it was possible to create something to sit on using the process of metal spinning, which is used to make objects such as lampshades and timpani drums. This traditional technique involves pressing flat sheets of metal against a shaped former while they both rotate, gradually forcing the sheet to take the shape of the former. If it was possible to make large drums from spun metal, was it possible to make a whole chair? And if it was, would it be comfortable to sit in?

This object would have to be a completely symmetrical rotational form and be able to work as a chair whichever way round it was rotated. So, the seat would have to be capable of serving as a back support, and the back support would also need to be comfortable to sit on. And how would it rest on the ground? When you sat on it, would it not fall over?

To understand the geometry and the ergonomics, we experimented with making full-size models that we could sit on. The most useful model was made from wood, MDF and a large amount of squashed Plasticine modelling clay, which we used to build up a seat shape. Spending many weeks making one subtle tweak after another, we felt as if we might be trying to force a functional idea on to a geometrical one. There seemed to be an endless trade-off; you either had a comfortable seat with an uncomfortable back or the other way round. But there was a moment when it suddenly seemed that we had found the optimum shape.

We translated the shape of this maquette into a set of drawings and asked a metal spinner to make a full-size prototype in aluminium. Before doing so, he had to fabricate the set of formers on which to shape the metal. The finished piece was not only comfortable but surprisingly enjoyable to sit on, with its capacity to rotate and rock in three dimensions.

We produced the spun chair as both a craft object and an object of mass production. At Manchester Polytechnic I had been taught by a silversmith who used big sheets of silver to make large goblets and trophies, and together with our gallery, Haunch of Venison, we produced a series of highly finished pieces in different metals. Each chair was composed of six spun metal pieces fused together, with a leather detail protecting the metal where the chair touches the ground.

We also collaborated with the Italian furniture manufacturer Magis to develop a version made with a different kind of rotational process: rotation-moulded polypropylene. In this process, pellets of polypropylene plastic are placed into a metal mould that is heated and rotated until the inner surfaces of the mould are evenly coated with plastic before the finished object is released from the mould. Unlike our smooth metal versions of the chair, the plastic one is covered

with a detail of fine ridges, like the grooves on an old vinyl record, which reinforce the rotational shape of the form and give it the appearance of a clay pot that has been thrown on a wheel that still bears the marks of the potter's fingers.

Notting Hill Residential Tower

*Can you make a new building
without knocking the old one down?*

THE STUDIO WAS GIVEN THE TASK of transforming a thirteen-storey concrete office block in Notting Hill Gate in west London into a high-value residential tower. The existing tower, constructed in the 1960s, was in a prestigious residential area close to major London parks and was an unpopular feature of the skyline, regarded by some as a blight on the streets around it. But from the property developer's point of view, demolishing the tower was not an option, as the local planning authority was unlikely to grant permission to rebuild to the same height. This meant that the challenge was to revitalize the building, retaining its concrete frame and increasing the existing floor area to create more space within it.

Our outline proposal was to reduce the perceived squatness of the single tower by breaking it into two interlocked towers and to add four storeys of penthouses with substantial gardens on to the building. Our intention was to stop the building feeling as if it was sitting on a podium by bringing the tower to the ground at street level and configuring a better public space around it.

Looking for a way to make the building special, our first thought was to enliven the façade by allowing it to express the organization of the building's internal spaces. However, for this type of luxury development, the interiors of the apartments had to be arranged in a relatively conventional orthogonal manner so that they produced an ordinary-looking exterior, with regular repetition of rectilinear windows, framed by horizontal and vertical elements.

It was by imagining these elements around the windows as strips or ribbons that we developed an idea of weaving them over and under each other to contain the building in a woven surface, like an architectural basket. Formed from Portland stone pieces, some of

335

 the ribbons could be pulled out of this composition to become balconies and gardens for the penthouses, giving the apartments outdoor spaces held within the woven façade.

Rather than a fixed design, we proposed a system for the building's skin that did not conflict with the squareness of its underlying architecture and arrangement of its windows. The three-dimensional composition of animated interrelated elements would give the structure a cohesive façade, stitching together and softening a building that was formerly hard and rectangular. Instead of demolishing the whole tower, the project would be added on to the structure of the old building.

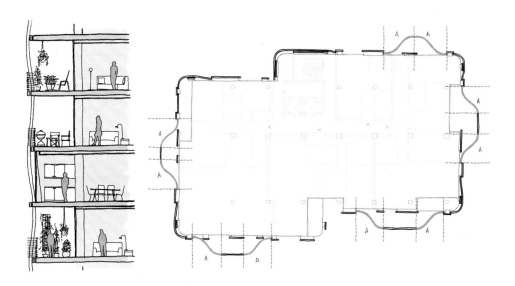

Christmas Card

What happens if the perforated edge of a postage stamp is allowed to grow?

THE IDEA FOR THIS CARD came from looking at the tiny stumps of paper around the edge of a stamp, made by the perforations that enable a stamp to be torn apart from its neighbour. Taking our cue from the shapes of these edges, we decided to try letting the stamp abandon its crew cut and become a long-haired hippy.

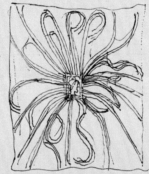

The final card design has strands that flow outwards from the postage stamp, like long hair floating across the water when someone lies down in the bath. The extruded perforations spell out the words 'Happy Christmas'. However, of the three hundred people we sent the card to, only one noticed the message in the hairs.

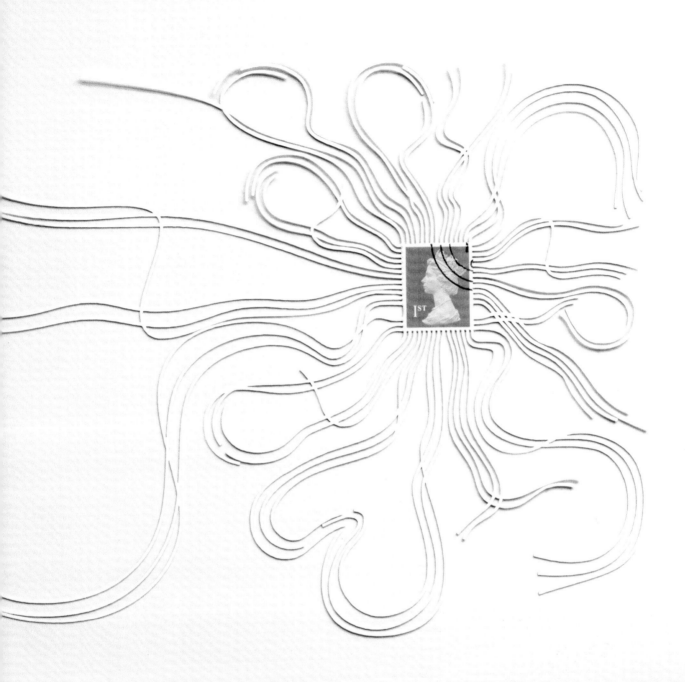

Baku Monument

How might people interact with a monument?

THE STUDIO WAS INVITED TO PROPOSE a monument for one of the highest points in the city of Baku, Azerbaijan. Although it had a spectacular view over Baku to the Caspian Sea, the site was a park that was run-down and neglected. On this spot there had once been a large statue, demolished when the country gained independence from the Soviet Union.

Instead of a monument that people would just look at, we wanted the structure to give them a monumental and engaging experience, by allowing people to go up it. Topographically, the elevated site was already very special, but lifting visitors up another 70 metres would make the view truly remarkable. Feeling that the hard work of climbing would make the experience still more rewarding, and liking the idea of creating a greater sense of engagement, we conceived of this monument as a heroic staircase. It would give people stories to tell, such as the first time their child had walked up by herself or the time that, having made it to the top, a young man went down on one knee and made a proposal of marriage.

As there were other vertical structures behind our site, including a telecommunications mast, which was taller than our structure would be, the monument needed to be eye-catching without competing to be the highest. To differentiate this structure, we determined that it should not rise straight upwards, putting its emphasis on a single destination point at the top, but instead move from side to side and contain a number of destination points.

Our idea is for a grand helical staircase that rises 70 metres into the sky out from a circular performance space, surrounded by stepped seating. Suggesting growth and continuity, this is a branching form that reaches up and out in various directions, with several different summit points or stopping places on the way, so that the top is not the only place that matters. As well as the 450 steps to walk up, there is an elevator within the structure and a slide offering a quick route down.

The concept included the renovation and reinvigoration of this neglected ex-Soviet landscape. Built into the underside of the outdoor performance space is a gallery and museum space, and the stairs of the structure also create seats from which to watch performances. During festivals and holidays the structure could draw many thousands of people and any visitor to Baku would feel obliged to go up it, pausing at the tea stalls and kiosks on the landings. The end points are the perfect size for a pair of lovers to sit in.

Engineered in a shipyard in Turkey, using shipbuilding techniques and huge sheets of welded steel plate, the structure would in effect be an enormous, curling cantilever.

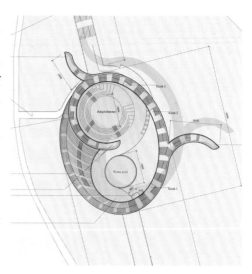

STEFANY TOMALIN
7 DOUGLAS COURT
QUEX ROAD
LONDON
NW6 4PT

Best wishes from
Heatherwick studio
Love Thomas & Maisie
xxxx

Christmas Card

How can you turn a postmark into the main ingredient of a Christmas card?

AS OUR CHRISTMAS CARDS had increasingly dealt with the processes of sending and receiving cards, the studio began to think about using the circular postmark that the Post Office prints on a postage stamp to prevent people from using it again. It is normally printed in the top right-hand corner of the envelope, overlapping the corner of the stamp, but we thought it might be interesting to cut around the postmark, leaving a piece of paper that was the exact shape of the stamp and its postmark. We could then break the postage charge down into many low-value stamps and treat each stamp and postmark pair as a link in a chain.

Working with the Post Office, we found a method of producing invisible joins in each postage stamp link, allowing us to form charm bracelets of stamps.

Pacific Place

How do you deliver a £166 million programme of improvements to a shopping centre while keeping it open for business?

THE STUDIO WAS INVITED by the chairman of Swire Properties, one of the largest property development companies in Hong Kong, to propose ways to improve one of its most valuable and profitable holdings: the 5.2-million-square-foot, mixed-use complex in the centre of Hong Kong, called Pacific Place. Completed in 1990, it had been the company's first major retail project and its location and extraordinary success had made it one of the most valuable pieces of real estate in the world.

Like a small town, Pacific Place is a self-contained entity. It consists of a four-storey shopping mall housing 130 shops and restaurants that forms a podium for four fifty-storey towers sitting on top of it, occupied by offices, serviced apartments and four hotels. With its subway station, bridges into neighbouring developments and principal routes to Hong Kong Park and key government buildings, up to 130,000 people pass through Pacific Place every day. As well as shopping there, working there and staying in its hotels, people go there to see films, have clothes cleaned and mended, attend conferences, swim and use the banks.

Even though it was considerably older than some of its competitors, the generous scale of its spaces and a consistent use of materials gave Pacific Place an atmosphere of relative calm. But there was scope for substantial improvement. Within the mall, the sightlines between the open floors were obstructed by the edge detail of the floor plates, partly obscuring the shop fronts on other floors. The lifts and escalators did not go to all floors and the functionality of some of the public spaces was poor. Also, the rigid angularity and shiny surfaces felt outdated.

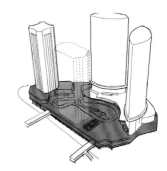

Since Pacific Place opened twenty years ago, its style and format had been widely imitated and our commissioner feared that it would one day be overtaken in its position as a market leader. Also, changes in the economic and political realities of Hong

349

Kong in the previous decades had created the potential for Pacific Place to function better and to become more profitable. However, the value of the development and its profitability precluded the possibility of knocking it down and starting again. Instead, the strategic decision was taken to spend £166 million on a project to bring the structure up to date in such a way that it could survive the next twenty years of changing fashions in an intensely competitive market. From the beginning we were also convinced that it was important to maintain confidence in Pacific Place's original vision. In an effort to redevelop and modernize, it seemed easy to erode the authenticity of a building or city and eradicate what made it unique and valuable in the first place.

Instead of designing a single large new building, our work at Pacific Place was the equivalent of designing and building fifteen separate but interrelated projects, making this a complex piece of construction management. The transformation had to be carried out without disrupting trade and the flow of rental income by keeping the highly profitable retail outlets, office spaces and hotels open for business throughout the project.

In a programme of changes to Pacific Place, we improved circulation by introducing new escalators and lifts, and also transformed the signage and way-finding systems. We modified and enhanced the sightlines inside the  mall, increased the quantity of natural light and upgraded its environmental performance by reducing energy use. We designed new restaurant and café buildings and the exterior of a new hotel, created a large amount of public space and gardens and designed a pedestrian bridge.

As the project was not a rebuild, it became an exercise in detailing on a massive scale. Our task was to use these details assertively and consistently throughout the environment so that they accumulated and worked together to exude the confidence of the original design but at the same time communicate a new identity. We employed principally wood and stone, relying on their natural imperfections to bring life and warmth to the environment, and the details we devised were intended to create greater integration between elements within the space. For example, where the handrails of the balustrades met the moving handrails of the escalators, we made them meet with the same curve, rather than

colliding arbitrarily. The detailing work extended to using our workshop in London to produce the casting patterns for the sand-cast bronze lift buttons and other metal elements.

Another unique detail we developed for the project was the toilet door hinge. Instead of putting box-like cubicles around the toilets, we chose to enclose them with a single undulating surface made of wood. It seemed to go against the spirit of this curving wall to break it by inserting doors with ordinary hinges. How could we make the doors open in a curved way, and eliminate the hinges completely? After extensive experimentation we found a means of making a wooden wall that bent on both the inside and outside without any visible hinge or line. To evaluate it, we developed a test rig that opened and shut a prototype door thousands of times using an electronic motor, which we constructed in our workshop in London. The device was shipped to Hong Kong and installed in the corner of the project office, where it operated continuously for two weeks to simulate twenty years of use, profoundly irritating the project team with its repetitive thwacking.

The greatest physical transformation was achieved by our work on Level Four of Pacific Place, which is the outdoor area on top of the podium that forms the base of the four towers. Dominated by the road that formed drop-off points, delivery access and turning circles for the hotels, this open space was barely accessible. The many glass pyramid-shaped skylights set within large raised planting containers let daylight into the mall below, but formed barriers within the space. For anyone arriving by car or taxi, this was the front door to Pacific Place, but it felt more like a service entrance.

We replaced the skylights with dramatic and substantial areas of flat glass, set into the podium surface, which could be walked on. This involved developing a special glass detail with a non-slip surface that also prevented people in the mall below looking up the skirts or trouser legs of others walking across it. In order to be strong enough for lorries to drive over and to achieve the accredited fire rating,

the surface had to be made up of seven layers of glass. Taking advantage of these multiple layers, we found a way to obscure the glass without blocking the light or hiding the sky. We put roughened dots on the top surface of the glass, making it non-slip, and then etched different-sized rings on each subsequent layer of glass, which accumulated to describe three-dimensional pebble-like forms within the layers. These one hundred walkable skylights both transformed the previously dead area on Level Four into a significant public space and increased the quantity of daylight in the mall below.

In addition, we designed and constructed a new café building and a stand-alone restaurant with a roof structure made in a Chinese shipyard from ribbons of steel. We also re-clad and unified all the surrounding façades with surfaces of shaped, cut Bedonia stone, which form flowing, curtain-like shapes around the buildings and the new hotel entrance we designed. On this landscape, there are now areas of plants and greenery in containers made with the same stone as the façades, and the paving incorporates many special details, such as a sculpturally carved stone dropped-kerb detail, which has a contorted twisting form as the kerb squashes downwards to meet the road surface. With Level Four transformed into a new front door for Pacific Place, the shopping centre's most prestigious retailers have taken additional new units facing on to the space.

The project will be completed by the reconfiguration of all the office entrance spaces on Level Four and the construction of a hundred-metre-long footbridge across the road in front of the complex, which will incorporate garden spaces along its length.

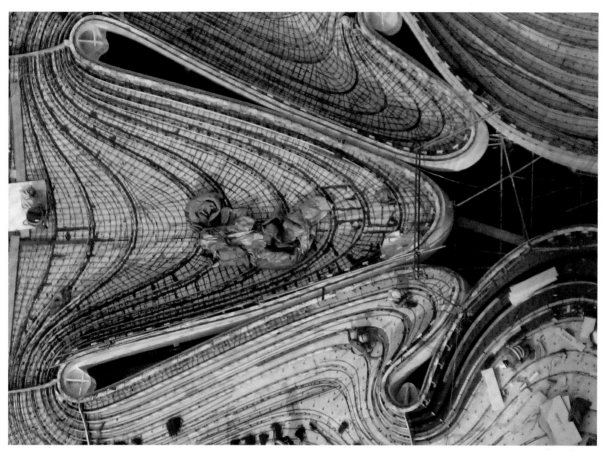

Konstam

*How do you make a new restaurant
in an old London pub?*

CHEF AND CAFÉ OWNER Oliver Rowe asked the studio to help him turn a run-down pub in King's Cross, London, into a restaurant. There was growing interest in the idea that, to reduce the energy used to transport food, it should be seasonal and locally sourced, and Rowe planned to obtain all the food ingredients for his restaurant from within London. His television series *The Urban Chef* showed him searching out mushrooms grown under the M25 motorway, honey made in hives on top of tower blocks and mackerel fished from the River Thames. Instead of hiding Rowe and his kitchen away in the basement, our first move was to place the kitchen in the middle of the new restaurant, where people could see him at work.

With its tiled exterior and small multiple window panes, there was no denying the identity of the space as an Edwardian pub. Because it seemed to have become a cliché in the world of restaurants to take an old pub, strip out the brown carpet, put hearty food on big white plates and call it a gastropub, we wanted to look for a different approach. Rather than imposing an aesthetic that fought with the character of the space, we looked for a way to acknowledge it.

The space had about fifty panes of window glass and, at the same time, the new restaurant needed to seat around fifty people, which led us to the intuitive idea of making an umbilical connection between every window and the light that would illuminate each table.

By putting a fringe of fine metal chain around every window pane and drawing these chains into the room in bunches, as if capturing the light from the window, we could then sling the bundles over hooks in

the ceiling, and let them hang down to form a beam of light over every table. Using only chains and gravity, we could make extraordinary, void-like forms smeared out of the window frames.

The finished project used 110 kilometres of nickel and stainless steel chain that crossed the ceiling in swathes, like ponytails or cobwebs, held in place over each table by square, clear acrylic frames. The rest of the restaurant – floor, walls, ceiling, window frames and chairs – is painted in a rich, dark turquoise to make a relaxed low level of light within which the small pools of light can stand out. Inside, you can play with the chains, running your fingers through the bunches. Daylight shines in through the windows but the area outside, known for its takeaway food shops and massage parlours, is filtered by curtains of beaded chain.

Aberystwyth Artists' Studios

How do you give individuality to the skin of inexpensive buildings?

THE ROYAL INSTITUTE OF BRITISH ARCHITECTS ran a competition to design artists' studios in Aberystwyth, a seaside town on the west coast of Wales. The competition was held on behalf of the Aberystwyth Arts Centre, which is part of the University of Aberystwyth. The university is known for the excellence of its arts courses and the gallery in the arts centre provides students and practitioners opportunities to exhibit their work. However, the lack of affordable workspaces was driving creative people away from the town to establish their working lives in Birmingham, London or other big cities. The arts centre wanted to create an incentive for creative people to stay in Aberystwyth by constructing eighteen new workspaces for rental at affordable rates to artists and creative sector businesses. The budget was extremely low, but the aspiration was to show that a low-cost project could still be special.

A site was identified on the university campus, close to the halls of residence and the arts centre building on a steep slope, covered in trees. Our first thought was that this woodland was precious and that placing a big campus building here would mean clearing away all the trees. We wondered if there was a way that the project could sit among the trees instead.

Rather than one big building, we decided to make nine smaller buildings, placed between the trees and connected by a path. Each building could house two units of workspace on a single floor. We liked the idea of making this a community, like a village, rather than a single unit accommodating everyone. It also better suited our limited budget. It would cost less than a single building with two or three floors, because we wouldn't need to spend money on lifts, stairs and corridors, and the separation of the buildings was a cheap and practical way to insulate them for sound.

The studios needed to feel special but not overshadow the creativity of the people using them and they needed to be flexible, functional spaces in which creative people could do whatever they wanted. We decided to keep the form of each building simple and to concentrate on making the skin of the buildings special.

Normally, inexpensive buildings are clad with industry-standard panel systems, selected from catalogues such as the Barber Index. Although these

products meet the building codes and come with guarantees and warranties, to us they often appear flat and dull. Instead, we decided to make the buildings feel fundamentally different by inventing a cladding material with its own life.

This material had to be long-lived, and the most phenomenally long-lasting material is stainless steel. However, conventional stainless steel cladding, which is more than a millimetre thick, would be far too expensive for our budget. We had also noticed that buildings clad in steel of this thickness tended to look slightly crinkled because the material dents easily during construction, making the building look as if there hasn't been enough money to buy sufficiently thick metal.

If we could learn to love crinkles, rather than trying to avoid them, a metal that was much less than 1 millimetre thick could make an effective and affordable cladding material. We asked ourselves if very thin stainless steel sheet could be used like cling film or Sellotape and wound around a building to create a skin that would be tough, waterproof and corrosion-resistant and would not degrade in ultraviolet light.

After much searching, we found a manufacturer in Finland who produced stainless steel sheet that was one tenth of a millimetre thick. To our astonishment,

this metal was priced by weight, so it was one tenth of the price of standard stainless steel sheet. Once we got samples into our workshop we found that there was no way to stop it crinkling but that, as we let it crinkle, it turned into something mesmerizing to look at. This excited us because we felt that the way a building feels has as much to do with the texture encountered at the human scale, as with the overall form of the building. A building that has dead, flat, sterile surfaces conveys a physical coldness, but if it has a richness of detail, such as the crinkles that this sheet made all by itself, your eyes touch a surface that is both unexpected and absorbing, as well as three-dimensional.

Also, when we held the crinkled metal next to trees outdoors, it was as if we had crinkled a mirror. The crinkles were the size and scale of leaves and their surfaces took on the colours of leaves and sky.

To be a viable cladding material, this had to be rigid enough to withstand damage, and also have insulating properties. In the East Beach Café project (pages 378–87), we sprayed the interior of a steel-shelled building with an insulation foam originally developed for use in pig sheds, which sets so hard that the animals cannot chew through it. So we sprayed the back  of the crinkled steel with this foam. This combination of materials gave us a cladding system to use in the project that was lightweight, inexpensive and durable but also soulful.

The proposal was to create a family of nine small buildings, connected by a footpath, set in woodland. They are arranged in a curve, so that although the design of all the buildings is identical, each one sits in the landscape and relates to its neighbour in a different way. As the site is a hillside, they stand on stilts where the ground slopes downwards. Each building is divided into two independent workspaces, making eighteen units in all. The buildings are simple, pitch-roofed, timber-framed structures that have been split down the middle and pulled apart to make space for skylights, an entrance, ventilation and toilets. The building is clad with the custom-made crinkled metal cladding.

For the competition, we made a full-sized piece of the building, using steel we had crinkled in the studio and insulating foam from a builders' merchant. We hid the prototype in the woods and asked the judges to come outside during the interview to see it there, reflecting the trees and sky.

To build the project, the studio became the contractor for the skin of the building and invented a special crinkling machine, a giant mangle with nodules on the rollers, turned by a big handle. Feeding the stainless steel, which came on rolls a metre wide, through the knobbly rollers to manipulate it into a 10-metre length of uniformly crinkled metal made a thunderous noise.

As the long panels were much longer than normal cladding panels, we reduced the number of the joints that needed waterproofing; however, the lengths still had to be tailored together at the corners and edges. The process of crinkling the strips of metal seemed raw and rough but the detail was finely crafted, precise to a millimetre, so that each piece could be folded over to meet its neighbouring piece and become a waterproof sealed joint.

For each building, a timber frame was constructed and the metal skin was fixed on to it. Then the inside of the skin was sprayed with insulating foam. This was followed by the fit-out, which included flooring, boarding, electrics and plumbing.

All the workspaces were rented out before construction was finished. There are now sculptors, painters, textile artists, web designers and a theatre company working in the buildings.

377

East Beach Café

*How can a seaside building
relate to the sea?*

WITH THE INVENTION OF SEASIDE HOLIDAYS in the nineteenth century, British resorts like Blackpool, Brighton and Scarborough and smaller seaside towns such as Littlehampton were visited by thousands of holidaymakers and day-trippers. Consequently, there was investment in hotels, attractions and amusements and these towns prospered and grew; but in recent decades, when it has been fashionable and affordable to take holidays abroad, they have gone into decline. It was in Littlehampton, on England's south coast, that the studio was commissioned to design a café building to replace a kiosk that sold chips and burgers, as well as £100,000 worth of extruded ice-cream from its Mr Whippy machine every year.

The site was a long, narrow strip of land, layered between the seafront promenade in front of it (where a pretend train pulled carriages full of visitors up and down all summer) and a high-pressure sewage line behind it (which could not be built over), so the building was forced to take on the proportions of a cigarette.

The site was also bleak and exposed, causing a tension between the urge to shelter and protect people and the desire to give them a fantastic view of the sea. Our idea was to resolve this contradiction and create a place of both refuge and prospect by making a building that is solid behind you and transparent in front of you as you looked out to sea.

But how could we ensure that the back of the building, without windows, was not a flat, dead façade? Also, how could we protect 40 metres of glass along the front of the building from vandalism and weather?

It seemed to us that modern seaside buildings have tended to conform to a ubiquitous architectural approach, an aesthetic based on white sails and yachts, which seems to romanticize a bygone era of Art Deco steamships. However, in our view, the British seaside did not conjure up experiences of golden sand, blue skies and twinkling sea, but of stumbling around on damp brown shingle, spotting all the objects the sea has abraded and offered up: slimy pebbles, matted seaweed, lumps of polystyrene, old shoes, fragments of wood, and frayed and tangled rope. Rather than reference sun, sea and sailing boats, we were inclined to create a connection with this texture and richness of a British beach.

It was also in our minds that British architecture has for many years been burdened by the idea that new buildings must be in keeping with any surrounding old buildings. In Littlehampton, the first row of houses, a Georgian terrace, is set back a long way from the sea. The café being closer to the sea than to any of these buildings, we felt it could be more 'in keeping' with the beach than with the Georgian houses 100 metres away. The building could sit in the shingle like any other interesting seaside object.

Unexpectedly, the most critical influence on the design of the building was the roller shutters, which were the affordable way to protect the windows on the front of the building. We had ideas for buildings next to the sea, but ran into problems as soon as we tried sticking large metal boxes containing shutter mechanisms like big eyelids above the windows. In desperation, we wondered what would happen if we made the whole building out of steel shutter boxes.

We found we could use long, undulating ribbons of steel, the width of shutter mechanism boxes, and wrap them around a space to form both roof and walls, making a raw steel building sitting on the beach. By day, the roller shutters on the front could be hidden inside the building without looking like unhappy additions. Angling the geometry of the box ribbons across the building

from the back to the front articulated the otherwise flat façades, giving the building greater three-dimensional sophistication. The welded metal skin of the building could also be its structure, acting as a monocoque like the shell of an aeroplane. It also happened that our friends in Littlehampton, the steelwork company who had fabricated the Rolling Bridge (pages 436–41), were enthusiastic about the prospect of making the project.

Obtaining planning permission for the project could have been difficult; but our client had a talent for communicating her vision. While serving ice-creams and burgers from the existing kiosk, she would show people the drawings over the ketchup and vinegar, explaining the project and why it would be good for Littlehampton. She invited us to give windswept presentations on the beach to whoever would

listen and was so good at exciting people and stimulating their aspirations for the development of their town that planning permission was granted with not a single letter of objection, only letters of support.

The entire metal structure was welded by just two men. The building was longer than the factory, so they had to fabricate it in sections. To ensure that the sections fitted together, they would finish a section, slice off the end they were still working on, take the rest away to site and then carry on welding the next section, starting with the sliced-off end. The outside of the steel building was left as raw metal and the interior was finished with a rigid insulating foam, sprayed directly on to the inside of the steel shell.

East Beach Café is open and there are nearly always queues to get in. As well as serving a loyal local clientele, the high-quality modern cooking draws people to Littlehampton from all over England.

387

Christmas Card

*How do you make saliva
an important ingredient of
a Christmas card?*

IT SEEMS STRANGE THAT PEOPLE are willing to lick postage stamps and envelopes with their tongues, with no concern about hygiene or the taste of the glue. Given the amount of saliva involved in sending things by post, we explored the idea of sticking these tiny, lickable pieces of postal stationery to each other, rather than to paper or card.

We wanted to make a three-dimensional object using only the twenty-five one-penny stamps needed to cover the cost of posting a first-class letter. We developed an object that had the scale of a pine cone, stuck together using the stamps' own adhesive and dipped in transparent resin to make it hard enough to send by post. Strung on racks in our workshop while the resin cured, these hundreds of cards looked like sleeping bats hanging upside down.

MERRY CHRISTMAS
FROM
THOMAS HEATHERWICK
STUDIO

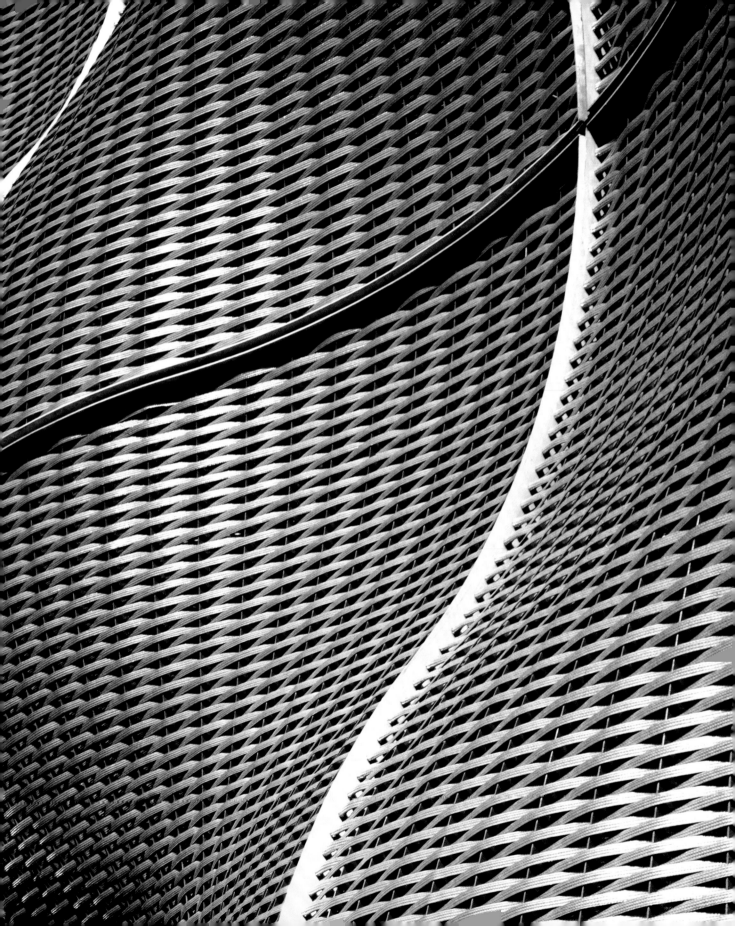

Guy's Hospital

*How do you turn the back door
of a hospital into its front door?*

BRITAIN'S HOSPITALS ARE KNOWN to be some of the worst public environments in this country, partly because they have a tendency to accrete more and
more uncoordinated buildings as needs change, funding becomes available and
new facilities are added. At Guy's Hospital, a teaching hospital in central London,
this process had resulted in a confusing and ugly campus.

This project was initiated because the hospital's grand entrance, built
in the 1970s, had fallen into disuse, and the back door had become the main
entrance instead. Not only was it hard to find the way into the hospital but staff
and visitors were forced to cross a chaotic car park to reach it. The main landmark
on the way to this back door was the hospital's concrete boilerhouse. Its concrete
was beginning to crumble, the equipment inside it overheated in summer. And
staff had voted it the worst building on the site.

Rather than looking at just this one building, we worked in consultation
with the hospital to look at the larger problems of the site, including the main
entrance and all the approach spaces. We started by analysing the traffic. The car
park was mayhem, with three routes in or out, and the main route into the hospital was jammed with parked cars. If you were taking an elderly relative to hospital,
you would arrive at the entrance with the pavement on the driver's side and they
would have to get out of the car into the traffic. Our first moves were to enlarge
the pavements, improve the parking system and reorganize the traffic so that it
became safe and easy to drop off a passenger. We also provided the hospital with
a new shop in a better location and new cycle parking facilities.

The heart of the project seemed to be to transform perception of the
entrance to the hospital so that it seemed like a proper front door. The boilerhouse
next to it disorientated visitors because it did not look like the kind of building you
would expect to see near a main entrance. As well as stopping it from overheating
– which we did by ventilating it with a breathable skin and shading its southwest-
facing windows – our task was to make the boilerhouse into the signpost that
visually communicated the way to the main entrance.

In the rectilinear housing blocks and office buildings of the 1950s influenced by architects such as Le Corbusier and Lubetkin, you sometimes find a
panel of sculptural concrete or ceramic tiles near the entrance, a gesture of

specialness that adds three-dimensional richness and complexity as you enter an otherwise flat, undecorated building. The tiles in these panels, maybe 30 centimetres square, are so small that from a distance their sculpted tiled surface appears virtually flat. The starting point for the design of the boilerhouse was to imagine what might happen if you enlarged these tiles.

We designed a system of square tiles, 2.5 metres across, which can be demounted to allow the replacement of boiler equipment. The panels are woven, their permeability allowing air to move freely in and out of the building and their highly textured surfaces discouraging graffiti. Four of these tiles, rotated relative to each other and arranged in a square, unify to make what looks like a single tile 5 metres by 5 metres. This four-tile form can be repeated to constitute even larger shapes, making the texture of the tessellated panels accumulate into a large, three-dimensional pattern that appears to ripple across the building surface. When you look at the finished boilerhouse, the texture is so large that it has almost become the form of the building.

We gave the project multiple layers of texture at different scales for the eye to read: from a distance, you see that the building is composed of a large pattern of undulations; as you get closer, you understand that each of these panels is made of steel ribbons woven on to a steel frame that acts as a loom; close up, it becomes clear that the ribbons are braided from hundreds of fine steel wires. The only colour is a very dark purple on the sides of the vertical steel ribs and the door and window openings.

Longchamp Store

How do you make customers overcome their inertia and walk up flights of stairs?

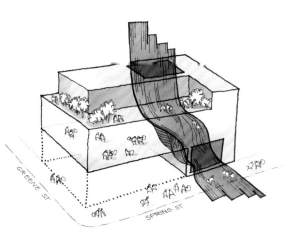

FOLLOWING THE SUCCESS OF THE ZIP BAG that the studio had designed for French luxury goods company Longchamp (pages 502–7), we were commissioned to design its flagship shop in New York.

The site was a building on a corner in SoHo, a district of downtown Manhattan known for its muscular, iron-fronted, industrial buildings. It was a two-storey structure, built in the 1930s, which had been given a new brick façade in the 1980s.

The problem was that the main retail space was not where it needed to be. Although it was large, it was upstairs, on the first floor. Its only connection to the street was a tiny space on the ground floor and its shop window appeared to be shared with the chocolate shop next door. Far from the eye-catching street frontage that is so valuable in retail, our site had almost no impact on the street. The challenge was to scoop people in off the street and make them go upstairs. A design solution that focused on the aesthetic character of the space alone would not do this.

The brief asked for a wholesale showroom as well as a retail space, but there did not seem to be enough room for both. Instead of chopping away the retail space to fit in the showroom, we proposed adding another storey to the building, in which to create both a showroom and a garden terrace. This would be an unusual space to hold events and a place for the staff to relax.

The first part of our proposal was to draw people in using daylight, by cutting a hole down through the entire building. Normally, it is the window display at the front of a shop that seems illuminated and when you stand outside, the interior of the shop seems dark by comparison. The hole brought daylight down through the building to the back of the shop, which was previously constricted and dark, giving it a sense of space and drawing the eye upwards. Instead of people feeling that they were going up to a level above the ground, it would give them the impression that they were below ground and needed to make their way to the surface.

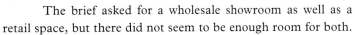

Our problem was still how to get people upstairs because, if you are worn out after a day's shopping and weighed down with shopping bags, a flight of stairs is an obstacle to be avoided. To counteract such reluctance, we needed to get away from the idea of a conventional staircase, and instead began to think about this as a piece of hillside. Recruiting the small ground floor area into the campaign to drive people upwards, we made a landscape stair device that reached right through the building from the window at the front of the shop to the giant skylight three storeys above. While the light well acts as the organizational device for the functions of the building, the landscape stair is the symbolic architectural element that stitches the three storeys together: the ground floor, the first-floor retail space and the wholesale showroom. Nothing is separated and it is possible to sense the activity going on throughout the building.

Working within the strict New York building code requirements, we used a series of ribbons, the width of steps, to make a landscape that flows in two directions. Starting at the front door of the shop, the ribbons flow up through the building, pulling apart to form steppable surfaces you can walk up, travelling on upwards past the second-floor showroom and out of the skylight. There is also the sense of a downward flow, like a waterfall falling from the skylight, dropping through the storeys, bouncing over, its big, generous, curved surfaces becoming stairs and landings and more stairs. Streets in New York are sometimes paved with giant sheets of thick steel. The landscape stair, which weighs 60 tonnes, was made with great precision from substantial, one-inch-thick steel plate, with strips of coloured rubber set into its surfaces.

The staircase had to have a handrail and balustrade, the kind of details that could easily ruin an idea like this. A balustrade would have to cut across the flowing energy of the ribbons and the sightlines of the space. The usual approach to making an inconspicuous balustrade is to construct it out of sheets of flat glass, which are transparent but to us felt rigid and opposed to the flowing ribbons. Window panes in London's nineteenth-century houses, which pre-date the industrialization of glass production, tend to have slight undulations and ripples that warp what you are looking at and give off reflections that are alive and magical. In contrast, modern glass is so perfect that it appears sterile and blade-like. The triumph of modern glass manufacturing techniques is that even the cheapest piece of contemporary glass is too clinically perfect. There is also an assumption that this kind of glass is totally transparent, but much of what you experience is its cold, hard, mirror-like reflections. It is also ubiquitous: whether you are in a Walmart store or the Museum of Modern Art in New York, the glass balustrades look and feel the same.

Instead, we imagined the landscape stair as a ski slope that had poles stuck into it, with a transparent fabric slung between them. We felt that something that draped would compete less with the flow of the ribbons than rigid panels. After a lot of experimentation, we found that we could make transparent panels behave like fabric by heating the material to the point at which it began to relax and drape under the force of gravity, and then letting it harden. The reflections from these draped pieces were dramatically different from the cold, dead reflections from flat glass; there was a soulfulness and vitality in the way that they caught the light, turning everything they reflected into gorgeous shapes.

The pieces for the project were manufactured by a company that also fabricated windscreens for aeroplanes and cars. A giant toaster was specially made for the project, in which big sheets of PETG, a transparent polymer, were heated until they softened and sagged under their own weight. Every panel was unique, formed not by a mould but by allowing gravity to shape it into sculptural forms.

Needing to design furnishings for the shop, we thought about the way in which this upstairs space might be perceived from the street below. To someone looking up into a first-floor space from outdoors, what they predominantly see is the ceiling of that space. As the challenge was to draw people upstairs into the shop, it would help if the ceiling was special. For this reason, we tried to use the ceiling to make the furnishings of the shop, in a way that also related to the ribbons of the landscape stair. However, in retail environments, the ubiquitous solution is to install a suspended ceiling, although this reduces the height of a space and can feel like a way of concealing the problems of a building rather than solving them. The design we developed was a plywood ceiling that was sliced open and peeled down, the layers of wood delaminating to form sets of shelves for the bags. To create display spaces within the steel staircase, we were able to use industrial magnets to

attach removable lights and display shelves directly to the steel, without having to drill holes in it to attach fittings and brackets.

Finally, using a display system made from a single, continuous picture frame that mitres its way around images, sink, shelf and mirror, we made the staff toilet into a micro-museum of Longchamp, displaying photographic archive material from the company's history, including the leather-covered pipe that they had made for Elvis Presley.

Salviati Glass Furniture

Can blown glass be structural?

FOR AN EXHIBITION IN LONDON, the studio was invited to work with the artisan glassblowers of Murano, near Venice in Italy. We visited several times, working with the craftsmen in their workshop to develop ideas.

Glassblowing is almost always associated with making vases, but we wanted to try making something else. What was the largest possible scale of glassblowing? Could blown glass be strong enough to support not just water and flowers but the weight of a human being? Could we construct the seat, back and base of a chair entirely from bubbles of blown glass?

The size of a piece of blown glass is limited by the weight of glass that a glassblower can lift and by the dimensions of the door to the furnace that keeps the glass hot as the craftsmen work on it. With the glassblowers, we made separate pieces, which were then bonded together with ultra-violet adhesive to make chairs. As part of the project, we also created a free-standing table piece, a multiple cluster of blown bubble objects bonded together that serves as a container, and a design for a side table.

Having started out determined not to make a vase, we found that, because our chair consisted of open-ended bubbles, the back was a perfect vessel for flowers and water, so we had unwittingly made a vase anyway.

Colindale Tower

*Does a skyscraper have
to be monolithic?*

A PROPERTY DEVELOPER APPROACHED THE STUDIO to design a twenty-storey tower of residential apartments in Colindale, a suburb of north London, next to an Underground station. Despite the existence of the station, there was no identifiable town centre or any sense of being the hub of a neighbourhood, as several main roads into the capital passed some distance away. There seemed to be a need for not only a tower, but also a public space that could give the neighbourhood a heart.

Although the brief was for a single tall structure, we wanted it to have a more human scale and more variety than a straight tower. Having seen a man on a beach in San Francisco constructing sculptural piles of carefully balanced rocks, we developed the idea of stacking three separate building objects on top of each other and skewering them together like a shish kebab. A straight shaft containing the lifts, staircases and services would pass through the entire building and hold the three elements together.

The building's rounded, interconnected forms are built up in horizontal, one-storey layers of varied shapes, so that each floor feels different, and terraces

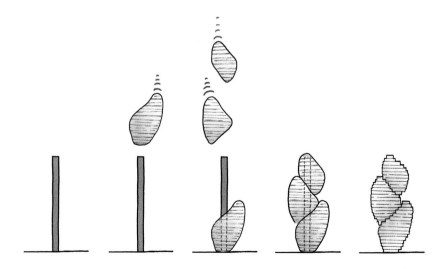

and balconies are created on the surfaces that are exposed as the layers step backwards. The building sits on a new public square over the train platforms, with shop units at ground-floor level. The lower element is a public building that is part of the local university, while the two upper elements, which consist of apartments, each have their own distinct identity.

Because the asymmetrical, sculptural form of the tower looks different from every angle, people at a distance can orientate themselves in relation to the new town centre. And since the tower is visible from the nearby M1 motorway as it enters London from the north of England, it can act as a landmark that signals to travellers their arrival at the edge of the city.

Christmas Card

What is underneath the Queen's head?

WE GAVE OURSELVES THE TASK of making a Christmas card that had no envelope but would not allow the postman to read the greeting. To do this we decided to hide the message under the postage stamps, and this meant that the stamps would have to move out of the way.

The card consists of a small wooden box with a transparent front and four stamps inside. Below the name and address etched on the back is a small silver star hanging on a cord, with the instruction, 'Pull gently'. As you do, the inner corners of the stamps peel open, revealing the studio's Christmas message written underneath. To make the stamps peel open and spring back, we manufactured micro-mechanisms, using fine wires that were so fiddly that they could only be handled with tweezers.

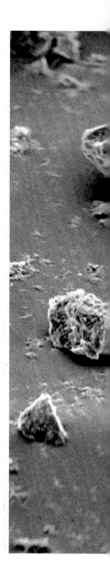

Grange-over-Sands Café and Bridge

*How can an electron microscope
help to design a building?*

GRANGE-OVER-SANDS IN CUMBRIA, northern England, is a small coastal town set in a beautiful and distinctive landscape, with a shoreline consisting of vast expanses of sand, where the incoming tide is notoriously dangerous. The brief for the competition we entered, in collaboration with a landscape architect, specified both a new bridge over the railway lines, connecting the town to the seafront promenade, and a new pavilion containing a café and flexible space for exhibitions and events, on the site of the old lido.

Because the tides pose a risk to people venturing out onto the sand, we felt that a new bridge should not only get people over the railway lines, but also give them a way to admire the landscape safely. Our proposal was to lengthen the footbridge into a significant cantilever that extends 60 metres out over the sands after crossing the railway. Starting at 4 metres, the width of the deck gradually tapers to 1 metre, so that the tip resembles the prow of a ship. The bridge would be constructed in a shipyard from welded steel plate, finished with a marine-grade paint system and brought to site in sections and assembled.

For the design of the café, we began by working out the optimum functional arrangement of spaces within the building and searched for a form that would be particular to this site. Taking sand from the shoreline and magnifying it under the electron microscope of a university near our studio in London gave us the idea of generating the form for our building from a single grain of real sand. The actual grain that we chose was broken into halves, which sat well with our proposal to put the café in one side of a building and flexible event spaces in the other, with stairs between them at the site of the split. We proposed constructing the building out of alternating layers of glass and stone to express the minuscule natural strata we found within our grain of sand.

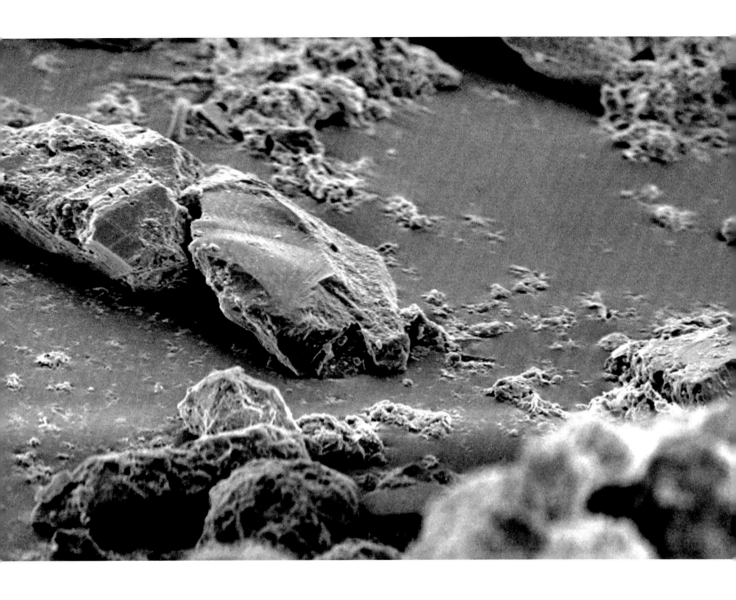

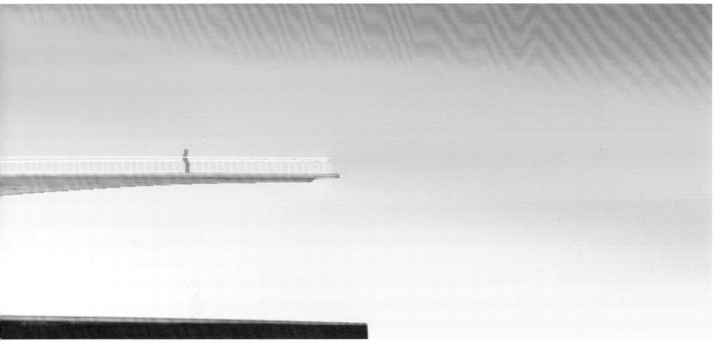

417

Kagoshima Carpet

*Can a construction drawing
become a carpet?*

AS PART OF THE CELEBRATIONS of its fortieth year, the Aram Gallery in London invited the studio to design a limited edition carpet. Basing the design on the plan of our Kagoshima temple in Japan (pages 480–85), we made a carpet that was the same shape as the building and which exactly reproduced the lines of the black-and-white drawing with tufts of wool.

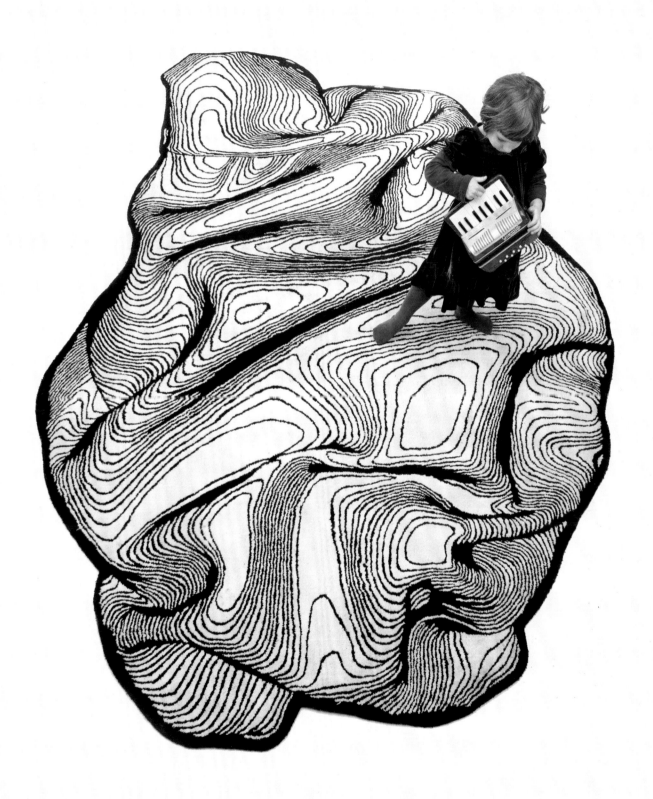

Glass Bridge

*Is it possible to make
a bridge out of glass?*

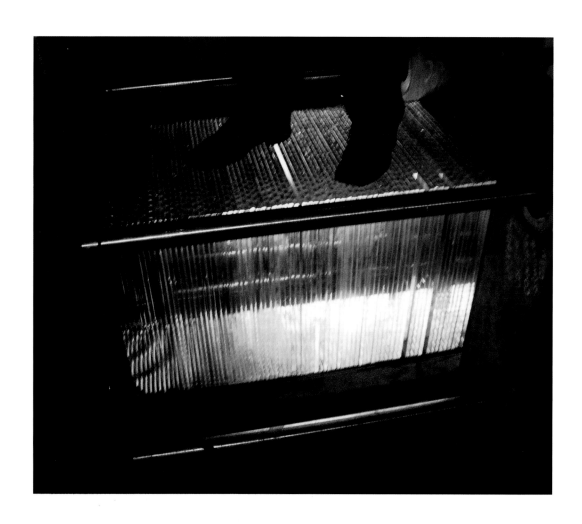

DURING THE 1990S, glass was increasingly used as a structural material in architecture. Structures appeared that were described as glass walkways or glass staircases or glass roofs. Although they contained glass used in a structural way, they relied on metal bars, bolts or tension cables to do much of the work. At a smaller scale, in contrast to the architectural trend for minimalistic glass structures, artists and craftspeople seemed more prepared to take pleasure in this extraordinary material and use it more expressively.

The idea that the studio conceived in 1995 was to build a bridge across water that both celebrates the optical qualities of glass and uses it as its structural material, without resorting to steel fixings, cables or structures to support the span, in the same way that a medieval bridge builder might have used rock. The potential for lighting an object like this at night seemed fantastic. Although architectural structures are normally lit by shining lights around the outside, to illuminate an all-glass bridge you would need only to put lights in each end for the light to be transmitted inside the glass and make the bridge glow from within.

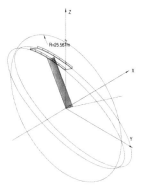

BASIC GEOMETRY ISOMETRIC VIEW

The initial design used pieces of glass layered together in the direction of the bridge. Instead of specially shaped pieces of cast glass, which would have been expensive to produce, it employed identically shaped sheets of standardized float glass. Because we were also interested in making a form that altered the typical symmetry common in bridge design, it had a tilted, longitudinal geometry, which gave it directionality. Crossing the bridge from one end, the deck and its balustrade are coming towards you, while in the other direction, they appear to be flowing along with you. As this approach was dependent on adhesives that were not sufficiently tried and tested, we looked for a different way to make a glass bridge.

The new structural idea came out of analysing the Millennium Bridge over the River Thames in London. This entire structure is extremely slim because the cables that support the deck are held in high tension. The extraordinary tension in this bridge gave us the idea of using the opposite principle: could we use extraordinary compression? Instead of making two river banks pull on the ends of the cables, could you make two river banks squeeze together so hard that they create enough friction to hold hundreds of pieces of glass between them?

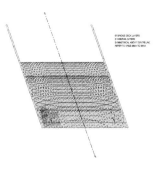

FRONT ELEVATION 1:2

When you are moving books around on shelves, you find you can lift a whole shelf-full at once by squeezing the stack of books from both sides between your hands. Instead of books, could we use pieces of glass? And instead of using the strength of your arms, could we apply a vast mechanical force?

Our design proposal is to take 1,200 pieces of glass, weighing 140 tonnes, and arrange them perpendicular to the direction of a bridge to form a beam by squeezing them tightly together. With their stone arches made of wedge-shaped elements, traditional stone bridges relied on gravity for their compressive

force. Instead this structure would squeeze the pieces horizontally with 1,100 tonnes of lateral pressure. When we were considering how such pressure could be exerted, we imagined that it would require a powered mechanism or motorized hydraulic system, which would be costly and need constant maintenance. Our engineers developed a method that employed only weights and levers, using gravity to power a cam to transmit the pressure from 800 tonnes of weight suspended in shafts adjacent to the bridge. One mechanism would be sufficient, but placing a second mechanism at the other end of the bridge would create a failsafe system that allowed you to lock down one side and carry out maintenance work

on it while the other one continued to apply enough pressure to hold the bridge in place.

The bridge is made from 1,200 layers of glass, each layer given a U-shaped profile to make the balustrade, handrail and bridge deck as a single form. The profiles of the pieces alter progressively across the span, in order to use the glass efficiently and to give the bridge its distinctive form that changes along its length. We used glass with an especially low iron content, to avoid the green tint that gives normal glass its dark edges. To prevent the deck from being slippery to walk on, the finish is raw and crystalline. Being pre-chipped, it makes the bridge less tempting to vandalize and absorbs inevitable minor surface damage, in the same way that the carpets in cinemas are sometimes designed with a pattern that looks as if they already have popcorn all over them.

The feasibility of the glass bridge concept has been tested in collaboration with leading engineering experts in bridge design and glass technology using a series of scale models and prototypes. At Imperial College London, full-size test rigs were constructed in a large underground facility for the testing of industrial prototypes. One test proved the strength of the compressed glass beam, allowing a person to stand on it, suspended in mid-air. The glass performed so well when its compressive strength was being measured that it broke the laboratory's testing machinery. We also measured the potential slipperiness of the bridge deck, how it might respond to cracking, how it would be built and maintained and the costs of construction.

The project is a romantic, powerful idea that has evolved with sponsorship, the prize money from a glass award and our own investment in research and development. It now needs a patron to give it a river to cross.

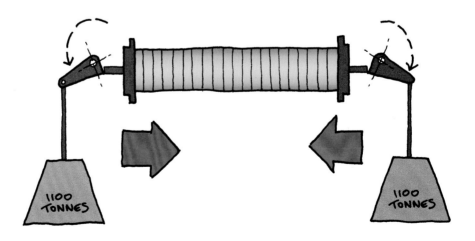

Christmas Card

How can a postage stamp become a star?

WONDERING WHAT WOULD HAPPEN if the tiny perforations around the edge of a postage stamp mutated into something else, we had an idea for a Christmas card that initially appears to be a rectangular block of white cardboard with an address and a stamp on it. Pushing the Queen's head with your thumb causes the stamp to pop out through the back of the card, exposing a three-dimensional object in the form of an abstracted star, which has been produced by the progressive distortion of the stamp's perforated edges. Once the card has been broken open, the negative form of the stamp star can be seen embedded in the remaining block. The stamp looks like any other but turns out to be just the top surface of an extroverted object submerged in the card, which is revealed under pressure.

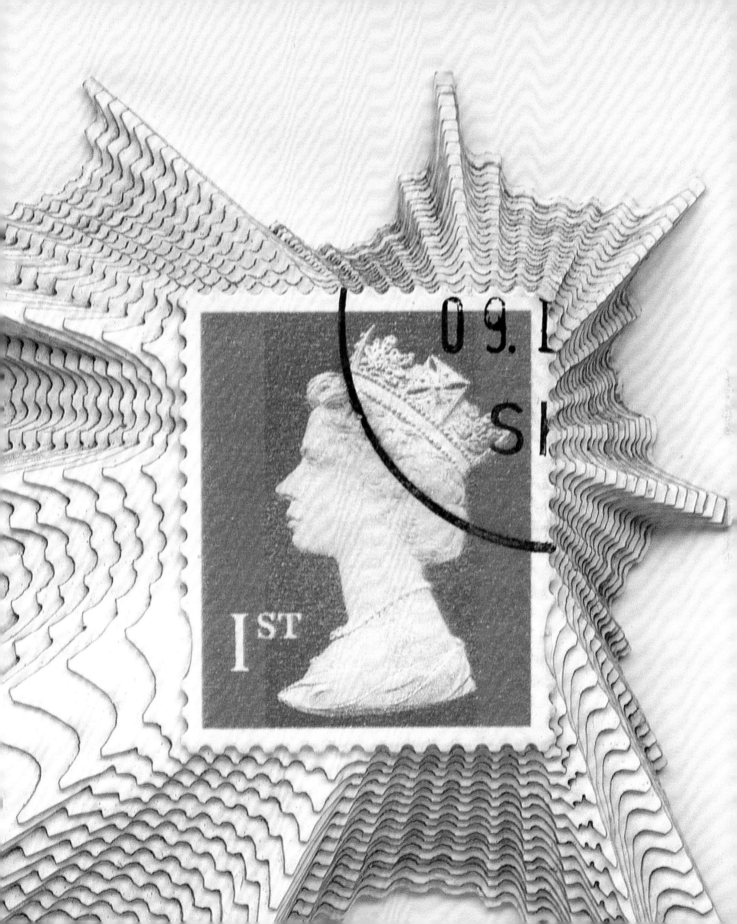

press firmly

helpline:020 7833 0000

LONDON SW
A
09. 02
SMC

FRITH KERR AND AMELIA NOBLE
STUDIO 53
PENNYBANK CHAMBERS
33-35 ST JOHN'S SQUARE

LONDON EC1M 4DS

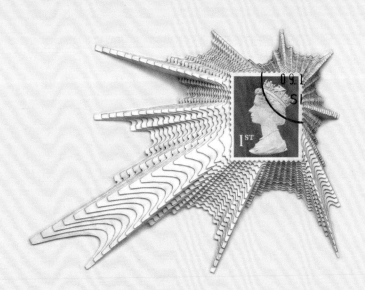

Merry Christmas
from
Thomas Heatherwick Studio

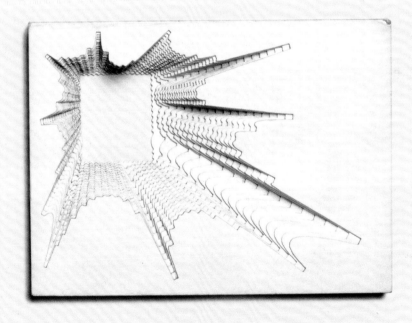

BMW Pavilion

*Is it possible to design a building
in less than a minute?*

BMW WAS LAUNCHING A NEW CAR and the studio was invited to design a pavilion to promote it. Instead of the usual television and billboard campaign, the strategy was to create a temporary pavilion in which to exhibit the car in a prominent location in London and, without carrying any branding on the outside, let the manufacturer become known as the company behind this special project.

The first decision was not the design of the pavilion but its placement, and finding a suitable place was surprisingly difficult. Most of London's public spaces are either obstructed by benches or railings or have a sculpture, a column or fountains in the middle. Others are already well known for temporary installations or loaded with associations. It showed the value of flexible unprogrammed space in the city – and how little there is of it in London.

Our choice of location was the space around the well-known landmark Marble Arch. As a site, it was unique in London: a large, open public space, a highly visible hub and meeting point of four major routes through the city. It also had greater relevance to cars than a space in a park or next to the river and although its identity is world-famous, it was an underexploited location that offered few people an excuse to actually go there.

Asking ourselves what kind of object could sit next to this classical structure, we decided on making a confident contrast. Our idea was to take a sheet of material the size of the open space and wrap up the car to form an enclosure. We imagined it to be an entire building, taller than Marble Arch, made out of a single sheet of architectural wrapping paper. It was a development of the studio's interest in translating spontaneity into building structures and came from experimenting with crushing sheets of paper with our hands. It intrigued us that, instead of designing a building in a normal way, painstakingly working through every detail, we adopted the role of a midwife, helping a material to take on a useful form while it underwent a spontaneous and uncontrolled transformation.

To develop the design into a final form, we had to invent a special kind of thin paper laminated with aluminium foil, which was able to hold the crinkles. We carried out hundreds of tests, looking for a piece that made an extraordinary internal space as well as a sophisticated external form. Although the act of crushing this paper was a spontaneous gesture, it had to be done carefully because

if the paper was fiddled with or over-manipulated, it lost any special quality and began to look bullied. In our search for the form, we covered every surface of our workshop with test pieces of carefully laminated, crumpled paper. We came in one morning to find that the studio's cleaner had thrown away every single carefully crumpled test piece.

We finally found a piece that seemed to meet the project's architectural needs and used a 3D scanning arm to turn all the folded corners and edges into exactly replicated data points. We then translated the digital information from this delicate object into a proposal for a welded structure made from nine hundred uniquely shaped pieces of laser-cut steel. If the pieces were laid out flat, they would form a sheet of steel the shape and size of the open space at Marble Arch.

The client was enthusiastic and Westminster City Council wanted the project to go forward. We fabricated test pieces and negotiated costings and a programme for delivering the project but an unexpected slump in the sales of luxury cars prevented the project from going ahead.

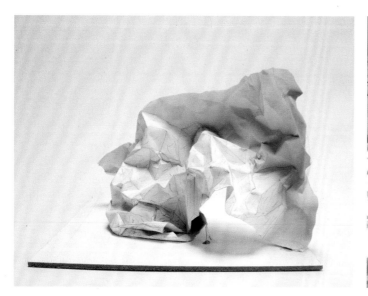

433

434

Rolling Bridge

Can an opening bridge open without breaking?

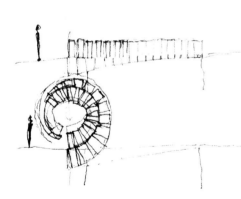

AS PART OF THE REDEVELOPMENT of Paddington Basin in London into a landscaped enclave of housing, shops and offices, the property development company Chelsfield decided to commission three new pedestrian bridges. The studio was invited to design one of them. The brief was for a pedestrian bridge to span an inlet off the main canal basin. It had to be possible to open the bridge to let boats through.

From the Industrial Revolution to the present day, Britain has acquired a wonderful heritage of opening bridge structures, from Tower Bridge with its decks that flap up like pinball flippers, to the opening bridges of Newcastle, which swing round or tilt over. People seem to love the spectacle of these pieces of civil engineering, even though the motion of a big, clunking element moving out of the way on a giant hinge is often crude. To us, it seemed that opening bridges tended to 'break' as they opened to let boats through. We couldn't get the image out of our heads of a newspaper picture that showed a football player who had been going for a tackle when another player accidentally stamped on his knee as he reached for the ball; his leg badly broken, bent at the wrong angle like a snapped-open half of Tower Bridge.

Rather than considering how to make a bridge 'open', which suggested that it needed to break, we began to think about how to make a bridge 'get out of the way', and looked for a softer, less crude mechanism. Could we make a bridge that got out of the way by transforming itself – by mutating rather than fracturing?

We began thinking about the animatronic creatures made for films such as *Jurassic Park*, in particular the dinosaur called Apatosaurus, which had a tail longer than our bridge. Using steel mechanisms covered in silicon rubber to simulate the animal's flesh, the animators had given their dinosaur a bendy tail that moved fluidly. We wondered if we could do the same with a bridge, imagining a simple form bending in a smooth, animal-like way, its mechanism sheathed in silicon, but then we realized that this confused the idea. It would be perceived as a 'rubber bridge', even though the rubber had nothing

437

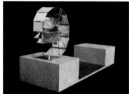

to do with the way it opened. The silicon material would also be both expensive and heavy.

The final idea was for a bridge that rolls up until the two ends join together to make a circle. It is a simple, self-contained object, fixed to one bank, with no ramps or platforms on the other side, so that when it rolls up on to one bank, it leaves nothing on the other side, where the end was resting. To allow the emphasis to be on the theatrical effect of watching it open, rather than on what it looked like, we chose architectural materials that allowed the bridge to blend into its environment, a deliberately uncontroversial palette of familiar architectural elements: grey-painted mild steel, stainless steel cables, timber decking and aluminium treads.

The deck of the bridge, which people walk on, is made in eight sections. There are seven pairs of hydraulic rams set within the balustrades, which correspond with the joints between each deck section. Most of the time, the bridge is down and the hydraulic rams just look like the posts that hold up the handrail. But these rams are powerful extending mechanisms and, as they lengthen, they

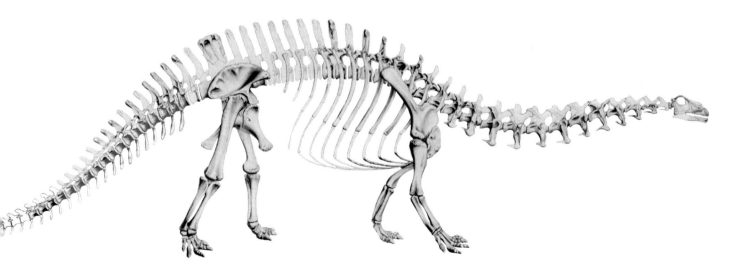

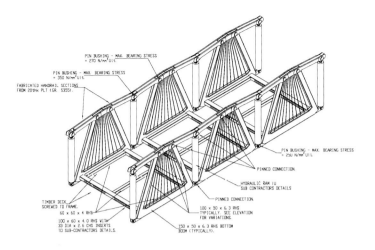

PIN BUSHING - MAX. BEARING STRESS
= 270 N/mm²Ult.

PIN BUSHING - MAX. BEARING STRESS
= 350 N/mm²Ult.

FABRICATED HANDRAIL SECTIONS
FROM 20thk PLT (GR. S355).

PIN BUSHING - MAX. BEARING STRESS
= 250 N/mm²Ult.

PINNED CONNECTION

HYDRAULIC RAM TO
SUB CONTRACTORS DETAILS

PINNED CONNECTION

TIMBER DECK
SCREWED TO FRAME.
60 × 60 × 4 RHS

100 × 60 × 4.0 RHS WITH
33 DIA × 2.6 CHS INSERTS
TO SUB-CONTRACTORS DETAILS.

100 × 50 × 6.3 RHS
TYPICALLY. SEE ELEVATION
FOR VARIATIONS.

150 × 50 × 6.3 RHS BOTTOM
BOOM (TYPICALLY).

push upwards on the handrail, causing it to fold. Folding of the handrail folds the deck sections in on themselves and makes the bridge roll up. The fourteen rams are powered by one mechanism, a single, large ram, which is set in an underground box next to the bridge.

Most of the time it is an unremarkable footbridge across the water, but when it rolls up until the two ends kiss, it mutates into a free-standing sculptural object that looks nothing like a bridge. We imagined that the bridge would be noisy as it opened but, because it is powered by hydraulic fluid, the mechanism is so quiet it is almost spooky.

The project was built in Littlehampton on the south coast of England and the studio worked closely with the fabricator to develop the details of the design, as well as with the hydraulic power experts who helped to engineer the mechanism.

Although the Rolling Bridge rarely needs to open for a boat to pass through, it is operated regularly for visitors and tourists.

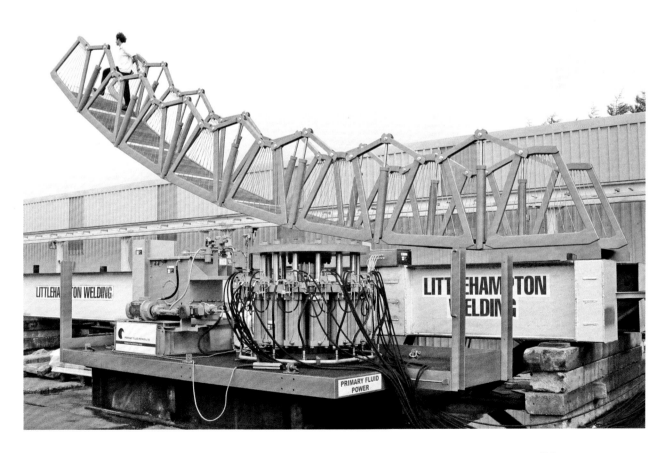

Bleigiessen

Can a giant sculpture fit through a letterbox?

THE WELLCOME TRUST, the charitable organization known for funding bio-medical research, commissioned the studio to design a sculpture to go above a pool of water in the seven-storey atrium of their new headquarters building in London.

Even though this new building had been designed to accommodate a large object, the only way to bring anything inside was through a smallish, domestic-sized front door. We found that we were uncomfortable with the idea of making a huge object out of door-sized pieces and bolting them back together once they were inside the building, with connection lines that would always be there to tell you how it had been made.

This was a large sculpture in a prominent location for a well-established organization, which might well be in place for a hundred years. It would not be enough to make an extraordinary shape; the project had to have depth and complexity and meaning. How could we find a shape sophisticated enough to justify a long-lasting presence in the building?

The tall, shaft-like proportions of the 30-metre-high space reminded us of a gigantic gravity chamber and this, combined with the pool of water at the bottom, gave us the idea of experimenting with falling liquids. As water falls, it does not form simple teardrops but tumbles and contorts into surprising sculptural forms. It seemed that a form with a complexity determined by natural forces might be appropriate for this project, rather than a form sculpted by hand in clay, for example.

To harness this idea, we experimented with a number of approaches, including photographing falling liquids and pouring hot wax into the snow that had fallen in London that week. We found that the best way of capturing the form of falling liquid was to pour molten metal into

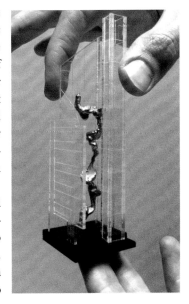

cold water. This produced extraordinary unique and tiny objects in a fraction of a second, the metal squealing explosively as it made contact with the water.

While the process itself was quick, it took a long time to analyse each test piece to see if, enlarged to 30 metres, its proportions and detail would fit the building. We had little control over the process and had to make more than four hundred pieces before we got one, 50 millimetres high, that fitted the proportions of the building. The form of the giant sculpture that would be there for a hundred years had been created in a hundredth of a second. But in the absence of any drawing or sculpting, who was its designer? Was it us, or were we just curating or choosing?

The piece we finally chose was not the most obviously beautiful object produced in the course of our experiments but it was the one that had the best sculptural personality and changing diet of detail throughout its length. It was a shape that your brain could never have thought up and your hands would never have formed from clay.

The piece was three-dimensionally scanned, so that we could enlarge the form to 30 metres, scaling up its every idiosyncrasy and contortion. But, given the modest size of the doors, how could we bring such a large and complex object into the building? If we could not bring the sculpture in through the door, why not bring it in through the letterbox?

I remembered that many years ago my mother, who is an authority on beads and threading, had been commissioned to make a large bead curtain with coloured beads arranged on hanging strands to produce an abstract image. Thinking of this, it occurred to us that we could make this piece out of bead-like elements. Within this 30-metre-high form, each bead would be a three-dimensional pixel (or, to be precise, a voxel) that would fit easily through a letterbox. By suspending thousands of wires from the top of the atrium, we could make a grid in three-dimensional space, within which we could make an object, defining its volume by locating beads at different points on these wires. But if beads were the main ingredient, what would make them special?

We commissioned two British glass artists, who work under the name of Flux Glass, to make us samples of handmade beads the size of golf balls, in different colours, but we were reluctant to choose any one colour. They then showed us a prototype of a glass sphere with an unusual iridescent quality, made from bonding colour-changing dichroic film between two glass hemispheres. These acted as lenses, which magnified the colour changes within the sphere depending on the angle of the light and the position of the viewer. Unlike a clear glass bead, this had warmth and life and its coloration changed constantly.

Our next challenge was to find the most effective way to arrange beads on wires so that they would form a dense enough skin for an object. When the beads were arranged in a grid pattern, the effect was stripy and full of gaps. Researching how to organize spheres in space, we found a body of scientific literature on the subject, including studies of the most efficient way to pack oranges.

At this point we had a sculptural form and a way of constructing it, but it was almost impossible to produce an accurate representation of what the finished piece would look like. On the computer, the thousands of fine vertical wires turned the screen black, and the most powerful machine in the studio crashed when it attempted to render the 150,000 colour-changing beads.

The final piece was made from just under a million metres of stainless steel wire and 15 tonnes of glass beads. The colour-changing beads were made in two stages. A spectacle lenses factory in Poland manufactured 300,000 half-spheres of glass, while a company that usually makes bottles for perfume and cosmetics bonded them together in London, inserting a layer of dichroic film between each pair.

To put the sculpture together, the beads were hung on the wires suspended from a specially made frame, which cantilevered out from the building's uppermost floor plate. On every wire there were 600 points at which a bead could be placed to create the form, so there were 16,000,000 potential locations for beads. With each of the 27,000 wires programmed differently – some wires holding one bead but others having dozens – this project became all about data management and a system of manufacturing that resembled a factory production line. A team of thirty people assembled the piece on the seventh floor of the empty new building. They worked in three shifts, twenty-four hours a day, for four months. There was a data sheet for each set of ten wires, listing the coordinates for every bead that was positioned by hand and crimped in place on the wire. We made plywood tables 35 metres long to use as jigs, with egg-cup-like

indentations for the beads. These tables acted as tracks for specially made trolleys that rolled up and down them carrying the beads and data for each set. Everything had to be done extremely slowly and carefully. It was a huge problem if the wires tangled as we hung them in the atrium; this happened frequently and there was no solution other than to cut them down and start again.

It was not until we were halfway through installation that we began to see our object emerge. The wires accumulated into a shimmering cloud, and with every set of wires that was carefully unrolled down into the space, the floating object became more and more apparent. The beads define the surface of the sculpture – the form is hollow – and while the shapes were still emerging, before the form was complete, you could look into the hollow pieces as they appeared. The holes were unintentionally so sensual and sculptural that we were faced with a dilemma as to whether to stop there and leave the form unfinished, but we took photographs and decided to let this be the project's secret.

When my German-born grandmother saw what we were working on, she immediately said: 'This is Bleigiessen.' Bleigiessen means 'lead pouring' in German, and is an Eastern European tradition. On New Year's Eve, people melt pieces of lead in saucepans on their cookers. Then they pour the melted lead into water and interpret the unusual shapes it makes to predict their fortune for the coming year. Without realizing it, we were making an object that symbolized the future of an organization in its new building, using an old custom about telling the future.

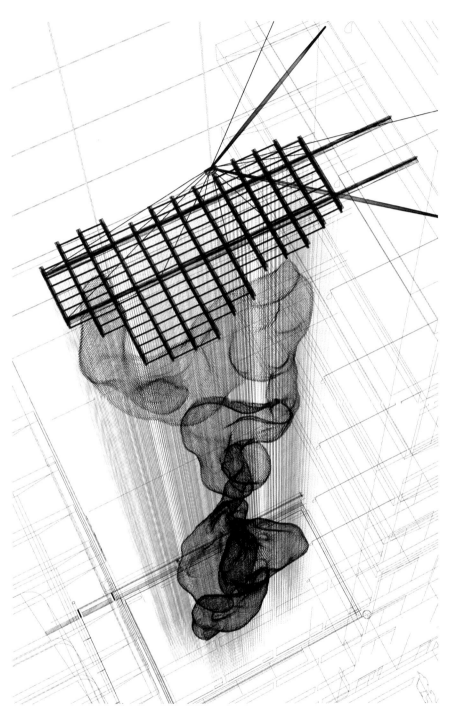

447

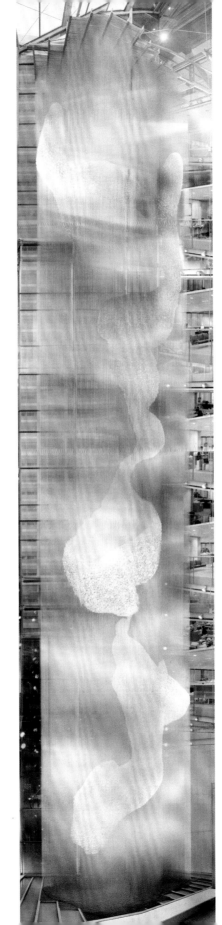

Eden Project Exhibition Buildings

How can you put one building next to another one but not see them both at the same time?

THE EDEN PROJECT IN CORNWALL, England, transformed a vast hole in the ground, once an open clay mine, into an educational visitor attraction by creating exotic gardens in vast, climate-controlled glasshouses known as biomes. The studio was commissioned to design new spaces on the site that could be used for temporary exhibitions.

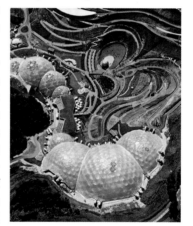

Arriving at the Eden Project, you get your first spectacular view when you look down over the precipice on the south edge of the pit at the glasshouses, the heroes of the site, which are built into the opposite side of the pit. However, with huge numbers of visitors to cater for, many temporary structures have been added to the site and the space in front of the biomes has become littered with yurts, tents, stages and kiosks. Being reluctant to add to this clutter or to compromise the visual impact of the biomes, we decided to design something that could not be seen when you first looked at the biomes. To do this, we would need to build into the slope opposite the biomes, below this first viewing point, so that when you first looked into the pit you would look over the tops of the new structures without realizing they were there.

Our proposal was to prise the contours of the ground apart and wedge the giant slabs of land open by inserting simple, rectangular buildings. This would create two kinds of space, both different from the biomes. The enclosed buildings provided controllable indoor space, suitable for exhibitions, while the sheltering eaves of the lifted slabs of land made cave-like spaces that could act as semi-outdoor rest areas for visitors walking up the steep pathways out of the pit.

These small buildings, inserted into the landscape between the site's zigzag paths, posed no visual challenge to the biomes, since the two structures could not obscure each other or even be photographed together.

A woodcarver who had been involved in the renovation of St Paul's Cathedral in London helped us to make the wooden model of the proposal that we presented to the Eden Project team.

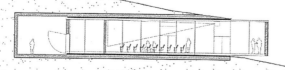

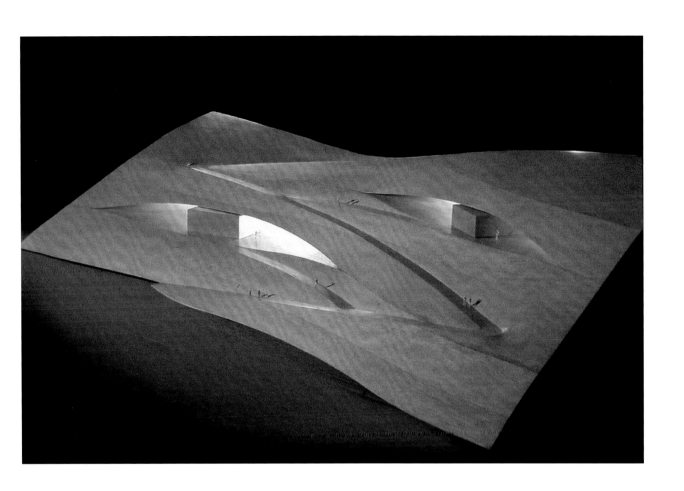

Paper House

How can you make a newspaper stand quicker to set up?

THE DEPUTY LEADER of the Royal Borough of Kensington and Chelsea in west London approached the studio with the idea of replacing some of the borough's existing newspaper kiosks. Watching traditional newspaper sellers at work, we saw that setting up a stall in the morning, often in the freezing cold or pouring rain, could take more than an hour. It was strenuous work, shifting heavy piles of newspapers and magazines to rebuild the display taken down the night before. By night, when a kiosk is closed, it becomes a dead, uninteresting object. It needs shutters to protect it from vandalism and theft but these flat surfaces force the

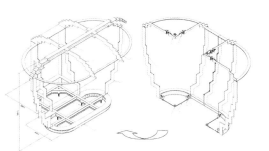

kiosk into the shape of a box and perversely seem to invite people to put graffiti or stickers on them. Also, kiosks tend to be made from fibreglass and plastic; cheap, lifeless materials that get grimy, scratched and faded with age.

We set ourselves the task of designing a newspaper kiosk that could be set up in ten minutes instead of an hour. Even when closed, we wanted the kiosk to be a positive presence on the street and we looked for a way to make it secure without using conventional flat shutters or hinged panels.

The shape of our kiosk comes from the stepped tiers of shelving inside that hold the magazines. The steps on the outside of the building are the height of the magazine shelves inside. Instead of an obvious door or shutter, the curved walls at each end of the kiosk rotate open, sliding round each other, with the magazines in place. The magazines can be left on the shelves overnight and the vendor can simply roll open the doors in the morning. At the uppermost tier of the kiosk, a window brings in daylight and at night, when lit, the little building feels like a nightlight for the street. The kiosk's rounded plan comes from its opening mechanism and the point at which the structure connects with the pavement is recessed so that any urban grime has less impact.

Two of these kiosks were installed in the Royal Borough, but newspaper vending in London is a dying trade, with vendors increasingly reliant on selling sweets, drinks and cigarettes.

B of the Bang

*What shape should a monument
make against the sky?*

IN 2002, THE COMMONWEALTH GAMES were staged in the city of Manchester in northwest England. The studio won the competition to design a commemorative sculpture to be placed outside the Games' main stadium, which was to become the home ground of Manchester City Football Club. The project was part of a strategy to regenerate this rundown area of the city.

The initial concern was how to site a sculptural object within a landscape of low-quality housing, industrial buildings and large empty spaces with roads passing through them. Other than the stadium, which sat in an open space, the closest building was Europe's biggest supermarket. Most of the time there were few people around and the area was occupied by passing cars, buses and lorries.

Since the site was so flat and open, we felt that whatever we built should be on a similar scale to the stadium. To establish a relationship with people inside the passing vehicles, we needed to pull the sculpture away from the stadium towards the road and, to engage with the intermittent match crowds, we decided to make it form a gateway that straddled the path into the stadium, rather than being a conventional statue on a plinth.

We wondered how to represent or connect with the Commonwealth Games that had taken place there. The monuments we had seen commemorating international sporting events all seemed to be celebrating international cooperation and harmony. While this spoke of sport as an arena in which nations compete in peace, the athletes' determination and ability to channel intense energy for fractions of a second seemed anything but peaceful.

Whether an athlete is a pole-vaulter about to jump in an Olympic final or a sprinter aiming to run faster than any other human being, he or she has to be utterly determined to win during those fleeting instants. This explosion of passion and energy seemed

worthy of a monument and we decided that our sculpture should be as dynamic-looking as possible.

We began to think about the silhouette that a large sculpture creates against the sky and how we might use this silhouette to express extreme dynamism. Instead of a singular smooth entity, we chose to splice the object and the sky together. By giving it texture on such a gigantic scale, we formed a shape with a vast perimeter, creating fingers that stretched out into the sky and in turn allowed fingers of sky to extend back into the form.

We turned to the technology used to make the steel lampposts that are seen in their thousands along British motorways. We took these long, tapering tubes and pointed them outwards from an exact point in space above the ground. Although the arrangement of the spikes initially appears random, the structure has a sub-geometry, which, like the organization of the florets in a head of broccoli, subdivides them into smaller conical groupings. As you walk around the structure, looking into its core, you find yourself in the beam of a floret, as if a firework is exploding towards you. There are twenty-four of these groups, each consisting of three, five or seven spikes. Fabricated by rolling flat metal sheet into tapered cones, the columns we used varied in length from 5 to 35 metres.

The entire structure was made from weathering steel or COR-TEN, which develops a protective rust-like coating that stops the metal corroding without the need for paint. A model of the sculpture underwent wind tunnel tests to assess its performance under wind-loading. To support a structure 56 metres tall (almost eighteen storeys) and inclined by 30 degrees, concrete foundation piles had to be sunk 20 metres (six storeys) into the ground.

The core, where these elements met in the middle, held this 180-tonne sculpture together. In the 1980s and early 1990s there had been an architectural fashion for structures made from steel tubes, in which the nodes where tubes joined became an important detail. The centre of our structure was an exceedingly complex node, where 180 tubes, of all different sizes, came together with an irregular geometry.

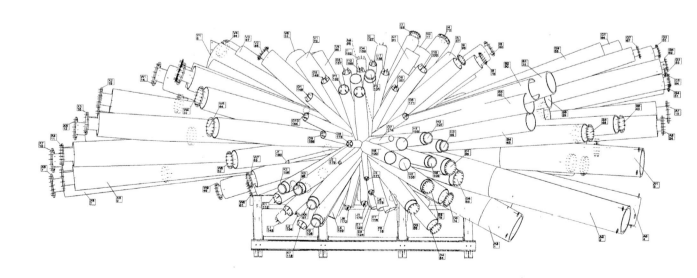

 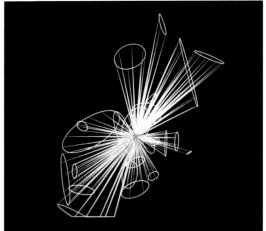

The construction of this core became an extraordinary work of craftsmanship. The welding was built up in stages, until the core eventually contained 11 tonnes of welding material alone. As the tubes were at narrow angles to each other, the welders had to get themselves into deep crevices like cavers. It was so awkward that we required the services of both left- and right-handed welders, since many welds could be reached only by one or the other.

We named the project B of the Bang, a phrase used by the British runner Linford Christie when explaining that fellow athlete Kriss Akabusi had trained him to leave the starting blocks on the 'B' of the bang from the starter's pistol and not to wait for the 'G'.

It was devastating when the project developed a technical problem and was taken down in 2009, four years after its completion, by Manchester City Council.

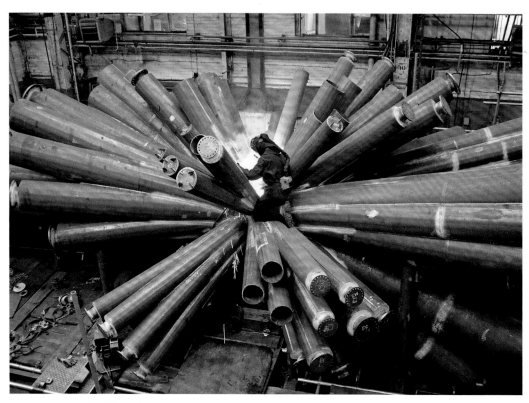

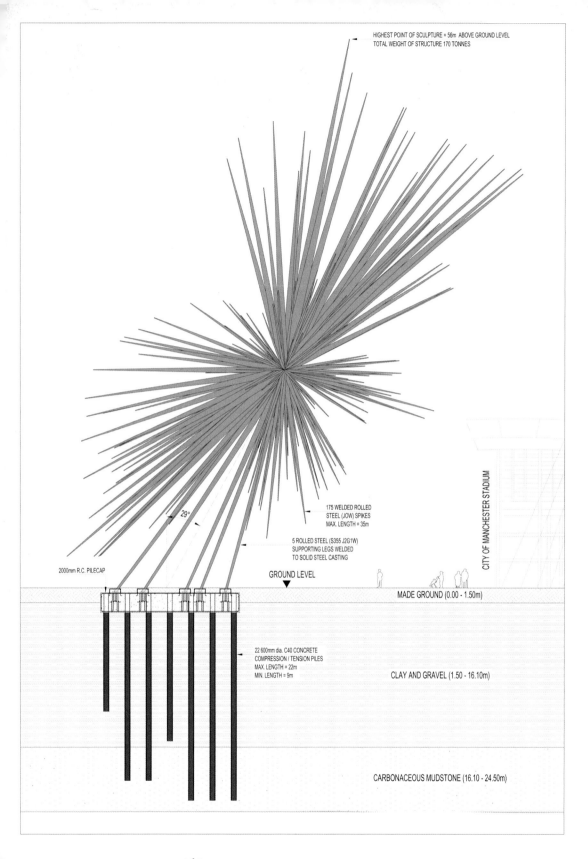

HIGHEST POINT OF SCULPTURE = 56m ABOVE GROUND LEVEL
TOTAL WEIGHT OF STRUCTURE 170 TONNES

CITY OF MANCHESTER STADIUM

29°

175 WELDED ROLLED
STEEL (JOW) SPIKES
MAX. LENGTH = 35m

5 ROLLED STEEL (S355 J2G1W)
SUPPORTING LEGS WELDED
TO SOLID STEEL CASTING

GROUND LEVEL ▼

MADE GROUND (0.00 - 1.50m)

2000mm R.C. PILECAP

22 600mm dia. C40 CONCRETE
COMPRESSION / TENSION PILES
MAX. LENGTH = 22m
MIN. LENGTH = 9m

CLAY AND GRAVEL (1.50 - 16.10m)

CARBONACEOUS MUDSTONE (16.10 - 24.50m)

464

Christmas Card

Can you steal the picture from a postage stamp and use it as the festive image on your Christmas card?

THINKING ABOUT THE DESIGN of that year's Christmas card, we wondered what was the absolute minimum that we could send through the British postal service. Whatever it was, we could not get away without paying the postal charge and the way to do that was with a stamp.

The finished card was nothing more than a single stamp and its postmark, floating within a piece of clear resin. On the back of each stamp, in tiny writing, we put the person's name and address and a Merry Christmas message.

For our previous cards, we had always chosen ordinary stamps depicting the Queen's head but this year we used the cheesy, special edition Christmas stamp showing a smiling Father Christmas, because it was slightly bigger, giving us more space for the details on the back.

Manufacturing the cards in our workshop, with the friendly advice and cooperation of Post Office staff, we found a way of making the postmark float in the resin and calculated the exact size that the block would need to be, so as not to exceed the weight limit for normal first-class post. We posted them off as they were, with no envelope.

Brian Ham
Director Enterprise & Environment
Civic Centre
Newcastle Upon Tyne
NE1 8QN

Merry Christmas from
Thomas Heatherwick Studio

Conran Foundation Collection

*How many ideas can you buy
for £30,000?*

Slicing, grating, pouring, brushing, baking, drinking, feeding, planting, freshening, cleaning, exfoliating, grooming, combing, funnelling, gouging, freezing, drying, organizing, space-saving, separating, bonding, tying, wrapping, binding, holding, clamping, turning, driving, spreading, writing, painting, daubing, papering, castrating, harvesting, attacking, trapping, killing, shooting, learning, teaching, drilling, running, jumping, throwing, catching, reminding, remembering, counting, measuring, testing, checking, locking, folding, erasing, playing, loving, marrying, praying, deceiving, protecting, concealing, spying, sacrificing, worshipping, embalming, enforcing and comforting.

EVERY YEAR FROM 1993 TO 2004, Terence Conran, the founder of London's Design Museum, invited a different person to spend £30,000 on a selection of designed objects, which was made into a small exhibition at the museum and then archived. The studio was invited to curate the eleventh and final collection.

bread roll
restaurant, Bolona, Italy free

At that time, museums of design seemed to have a preoccupation with familiar pieces of expensive furniture and domestic objects and to neglect designed objects from other areas of human life. Curious about different kinds of ingenuity and innovation and objects from areas rarely

glue for making caucasian-style creases in japanese eyelids
department store, Tokyo, Japan £4.30

represented in such museums, we took the invitation as an opportunity to collate an exhibition about ideas, by looking for examples of problem-solving in other worlds, such as food, farming, medicine, science, religious worship or paint-balling.

In the studio's experience, it was immensely difficult to get any new idea manufactured and into the shops. To us, the fact that somebody managed to do this seemed worthy of celebration in a museum of design, whether or not the item could be considered beautiful, stylish or tasteful enough.

In the story of every silent object, a clever idea is only the beginning. After that, a manufacturer must be convinced to produce it, a wholesaler persuaded to stock it and a retailer given the confidence to put it on to their shelves. Everything depends on being able to manufacture the product at a low enough cost for everyone

udder bucket
agriculture supplier, UK £6.90

fifteen meters of sausage skin in a roll
made by Devro, Glasgow, UK

to make a profit, without pushing the selling price up too far or compromising quality. As well as navigating the patent process and complying with safety legislation, the product needs to be easy to package, distribute and display, while its name, brand identity, style, colours and materials have to appeal to current tastes. A person who comes up with an original concept, method or object has to be phenomenally determined and creative to see it through. We wanted this exhibition to celebrate the inventive thoughts that have managed to get through this obstacle course of a process.

Instead of reinforcing the idea that £30,000 doesn't go very far in the world of design by choosing a small number of high-cost objects, we set ourselves the task of squeezing the maximum value out of the budget, by focusing on ideas instead of design objects. The challenge was to collect a thousand ideas, spending an average of £30 on each object and turning

untomatoey coloured ketchup
made by Heinz UK £1.50

fruit that has been grown inside the bottle
duty free, Heathrow, UK £80

decorative thread packaging
market, Berlin, Germany £1.00

this collection into a major exhibition that would occupy the museum's main gallery, instead of a small part of its top floor. It meant collecting five objects every working day for a year, obsessively filling every spare moment in scouring shops, warehouses and mail-order businesses and interrogating everybody we met, in case a conversation about someone's obscure hobby or secret specialism might yield up another suitable object. The evolving collection became a snapshot of things that you could buy in the world at that time. Mostly, we gathered objects in person – from China, Japan, Poland, Italy, Nepal, Turkey, Germany, the USA, Australia and Mexico, as well as the UK.

Whereas a major show in the museum might normally contain up to two hundred artefacts, this show would have five times that number to source and display. As the collection grew larger and sub-collections began to emerge within it, there was an urge to count, categorize and seek order in the mayhem, but with limited time available, we stuck to the simple curatorial principle of displaying the thousand objects in a thousand boxes, in the order in which we found them. We wrote a brief caption for each object, trying to explain what it was and why we had chosen it, in no more than ten words, trusting viewers to make up the rest of the story for themselves.

Some of the objects we collected happened to be very beautiful and appealing. Others might be regarded as superficial, even repellent, flawed or undesirable. In themselves they could be unfashionable, imperfectly resolved or compromised by the inevitable difficulties of getting them into production but our aim was to celebrate innovation and human ingenuity, not to debate whether a particular problem was worth solving or even if the solution was the best possible one.

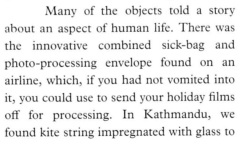
buried ceramic signage for underground cables
building site, London free

nappy-like bag for pizza boxes
made by Saeko, UK free

Many of the objects told a story about an aspect of human life. There was the innovative combined sick-bag and photo-processing envelope found on an airline, which, if you had not vomited into it, you could use to send your holiday films off for processing. In Kathmandu, we found kite string impregnated with glass to enable you to cut the strings of your opponent's kite in their fiercely contested traditional kite battles. Then there was the glue that Japanese girls use to create Caucasian-style creases in their naturally smooth eyelids, which spoke of a bizarre form of interracial envy; the mirrors with little lacy covers that you could put over

brush with handle made entirely from bristle
brush shop, Beijing, China £9.17

donor kebab meat catcher
cookware shop, UK £63.71

the glass to improve the feng shui of your room; the Chinese children's crotchless trousers, a response to deal with the country's lack of nappies; and the budgie feeder with built-in mirror that allowed lonely birds to dine in the company of their own reflections. We also included the two versions of prosthetic dog testicles: one is for surgically placing inside the empty scrotum of a neutered dog and the other, a jewellery version, for hanging around the human neck, to enable the owner to sympathize with their castrated pet.

We uncovered a world of innovation in objects that had been grown. In Japan, we found square bamboo produced by forcing the stalks to grow through wooden formers, increasing the numbers of ways that this light, strong wood can be used in furniture making, and square watermelons, grown in clear Perspex boxes, which stacked more effectively for transport and display. Next to the Great Wall of China we found souvenir pumpkins for sale, with text that had been carved into their rinds when young so as to heal and scar into engraved lettering as they grew. And in Beijing we found apples with albino writing marked within the coloration of their peel, made possible by a sticker that blocked the light, like a stencil. In Shanghai people had worked out how to grow a good-health message inside the shell of a pearl oyster by embedding a small, plastic, letter-shaped form inside the shell, which the oyster then coated with nacre.

As the collection developed, it would suddenly go off in a new direction. At one time we had a rush of objects from the trade in supplying mortuary and embalming equipment, which yielded the spiky pieces of injection-moulded plastic that are placed under the eyelids of a dead body to hold them closed while it is in an open casket, and the stand that allows the angle of the cadaver's head to be adjusted. In the farming industry, we found a device that places elastic bands around the testicles of a

jar with a handle
supermarket, Datong, China 31p

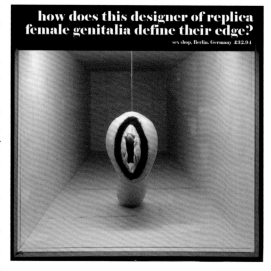

how does this designer of replica female genitalia define their edge?
sex shop, Berlin, Germany £32.04

young bull, cutting off the circulation so that they drop off after a while; a bucket for feeding milk to calves, which looks like a mutated builder's bucket with three nipple-like teats coming out of it; and a spiked nose ring to discourage nanny goats from drinking their own milk. From the world of espionage came the glasses that allow you to look behind you to check if you are being followed and a bottle of water designed for concealing secrets in your fridge. From the first aid industry we found training devices such as the rubbery birthing mannequin with no legs and the gory, three-dimensional wound-recognition kit.

good health message grown into pearl oyster's shell
pearl shop, Shanghai, China £21.48

For some reason, perhaps because of the primal curiosity we have about mutated life forms, we were drawn to objects that embodied unusual kinds of repetition. As well as double-ended pens, double-headed brushes and a double tap, there were the scissors for cutting up bait worms that were like normal scissors, but with multiple blades. The double umbrella for a couple was one of the most appealing objects in the exhibition. Beverage-making seemed to be an area in which repetition had been employed in interesting ways, with a double coffee pot that is turned upside-down when the coffee is brewed and the teapot with two spouts, one pouring tea and the other dispensing hot water.

coiled candle with holder that limits burning time
candle shop Stockholm, Sweden £40

Our quest brought us into contact with the inventors of some of the objects, such as Shaun Mooney, the designer of a plastic bag specifically for carrying pizza boxes flat, which looked like a nappy for a four-legged baby, with four holes for the corners of the pizza box to stick out of, and a young man called Adam Stuart, who, aged sixteen, had invented and marketed a very simple device for helping people to improve their golf swing.

bare-minimum socks
craft shop, Tokyo, Japan £4.74

cups for keeping the eyes of dead body closed
mortuary supplier, US £8.51

We could only hint at the stories behind the objects and, without the resources to find out the designers of everything in the show, the emphasis was on the things themselves. We included the body bag with a window in it, to enable someone to look at a body without opening the bag and allowing the terrible smell to escape. Somebody else had had the astonishing idea of car hubcaps that carry on spinning once the car has come to stop, so that at traffic lights it looks as though

welding masks with character
welding supplier, UK from £69.99

the wheels are still going round, and another had come up with under-car lighting that illuminates the road beneath the vehicle with bright blue light. Then there was the white plastic stick that is sold with a helium balloon to make it easier to hold on to and the tiny plastic table that stops a pizza box lid sticking to the pizza.

Some objects spoke of a deeply felt tradition, such as the colourful Chinese cardboard replicas of clothes, shoes and consumer goods, which are burnt as a way of despatching them to the deceased, the beautiful Indian wedding garlands made of paper banknotes and the thin plastic trousers sold to shorts-wearing visitors to the Vatican to cover their legs. There was also a kit used in the Eastern European tradition of bleigiessen, in which pieces of lead are melted in a saucepan or spoon over a flame and poured into cold water to form complex shapes that are then interpreted for signs of what the coming year will bring; and the sinister Turkish wedding ring that is a complex, three-dimensional puzzle, which comes apart if it is taken off during an extramarital liaison. The mosque alarm clock, featuring the muezzin's call to prayer, gave the exhibition a haunting sound-track.

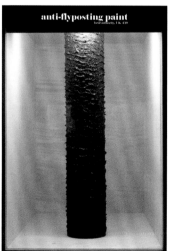

We were astonished by how much human ingenuity had been applied to hygiene. As well as a wealth of products designed to allow a woman to pee standing up, there were tiny, triangular sanitary towels to wear with G-strings and black towels to match black knickers. Ecological feminine hygiene products were represented by the washable, reusable sanitary towel and the Mooncup, a small silicon vessel that is worn internally to collect the menstrual flow. The collected blood can then be used to fertilize your roses. Dental hygiene was another area that had received a disproportionate amount of original thought, with flossing devices that meant you no longer had to wrap dental floss around your fingers, cutting off the circulation and turning them blue, and an assortment of tongue scrapers. Meanwhile, a Berlin sex shop turned out to be a hotbed of innovation, yielding the penis expander, the vibrating vagina with a puzzling hair-do and the puncture repair kit for an inflatable sex doll, for which the inventor's 'eureka' moment was particularly difficult to imagine.

Some objects we chose for being aesthetically innovative forms, such as the plaited cigar, the plaited bread and the plaited Jewish Havdalah candle. There was also a paintbrush

476

syringe for injecting jam into doughnuts
cookware shop, UK £28.88

drip-catching bottle
airport, Fucino, Italy £30

made from the entire wing of a bird, an instrument made from a complete shell and the glycerine enema from Shanghai, which was an uncannily pure form, like a translucent teardrop. Placed in a museum of design and lit well, items of sanitary ware took on a graphic visual appeal, such as the horseshoe-shaped toilet seats used in junior schools, with a section taken out of the front to avoid dribbles, and the hairdresser's sink shaped to fit your neck. The doner kebab catcher, a frying pan with a piece missing so that it fits around the doner meat, also took on a strange beauty.

receipt in shape of service provided
taxi, London free

Food was an area of prolific innovation that was not usually represented in a museum of design preoccupied with furniture, lighting and domestic tableware. Among the first objects we chose was the round tea bag, which acknowledged that a mug bottom was not square, and the Pop-Tart, because it was an inventive new way to use a toaster to make a hot cake. We liked the ketchup produced in colours other than red and the pickle lifter, a small plastic device inside a jar of gherkins that enables you to bring the last pickles up through the vinegar to the surface. It seemed brilliant to spot that problem, come up with that solution and manage to get it produced, even if realistically it is probably not going to make people buy more pickles. We also included the stuffed-crust pizza, the industrial bread-butterer and the machine that puts jam into doughnuts. Sausage skins turned out to be extraordinary objects packaged into short, concertina-ed lengths that pull out to a crumpled, papery length of nearly 5 metres. And we could not believe that someone had thought of calling a product 'I Can't Believe It's Not Butter'.

detects if parcels have been turned upside-down in the post
made by LPS Industries, US free

crotchless trousers for toddlers without nappies
supermarket, Shanghai, China £1.75

It was exciting to see the bigger objects in a museum of design, such as the dustbins with no base that builders

kettle for separate spouts for tea and water
cookware shop, Istanbul, Turkey £5.37

connect together to form waste chutes, the large sheathing device that allows market traders to put tight netting over Christmas trees and the machine that uses a piece of orange-lit flapping cloth to simulate flames. Our largest object was the circular hay bale, but it was the machine that made it that was the real invention, permitting bales of hay to be produced not in rectangular blocks but in gigantic rolls and changing forever the rural landscapes of Europe and North America.

streamer for magicians to pull from mouth
craft shop, Tokyo, Japan £6.46

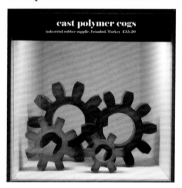

cast polymer cogs
industrial rubber supplier, Istanbul, Turkey £55.20

In some cases, the idea was in the packaging. We found dusters sold in cardboard sleeves printed with figures that seemed to have hair on their heads and chests thanks to the way in which the duster stuck out. What was appealing was that there were two versions of the packaging, male and female, which showed that someone had made the decision to give men AND women hairy, feather-duster chests.

In the area of protective clothing some surprisingly humorous inventions emerged, such as the construction helmet in the shape of a hardened Stetson, presumably for use by cowboy builders, and fully functioning welding masks shaped as the

glycerine enema
pharmacy, Beijing, China 75p

faces of cartoon characters. There was a fantastically shiny silver fireman's suit from Turkey and a phenomenally shaggy hunting suit that provided all-over, three-dimensional camouflage. We also included fishermen's waders that covered the whole body.

crayon strapped to rams' crotches to mark impregnated ewes
agricultural supplier, UK £25.15

478

pickle lifter from a jar of pickles
supermarket, London free

Within the thousand, one object was a fake. I had heard as a child about a chemical used in German swimming pools that makes the water change colour if people urinate in it. We spent months trying to find it, only to discover that the product was an urban myth. Doing our bit to promote this myth, we mocked up a bottle containing a blue chemical called Blurinate, which we put in the show and nobody questioned.

The exhibition was one of the largest shows staged at the Design Museum and attracted high visitor numbers. Having been displayed for six weeks, the objects are now archived.

stick-on stencil for apples that forms writing on the growing skin
supermarket, Datong, China 49p

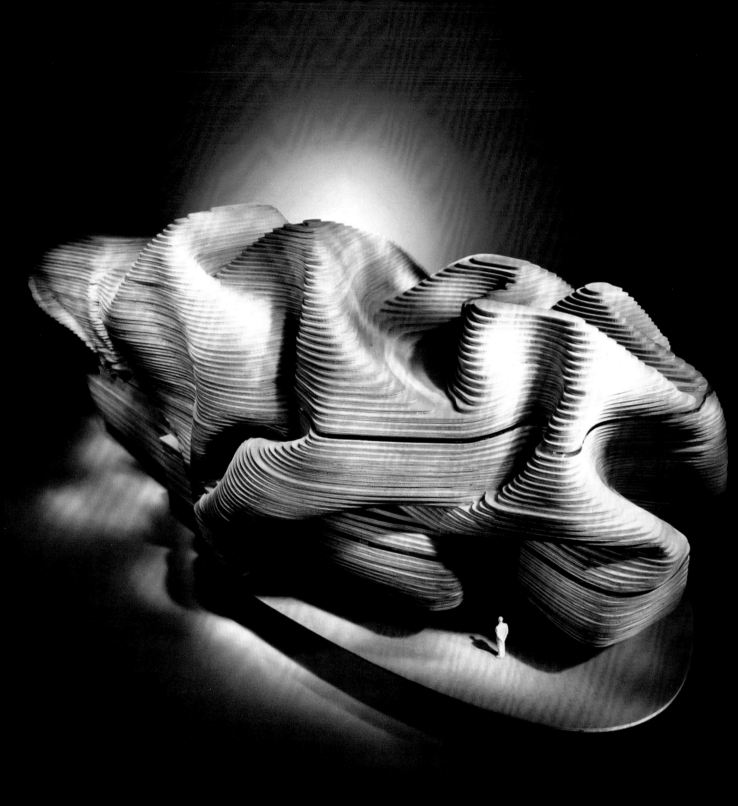

Temple

*Can the complex programmatic
needs of a spiritual building be
brought together with a single idea?*

EARLY IN THE STUDIO'S DEVELOPMENT, we were approached to design a Buddhist temple on the outskirts of Kagoshima, a city on the southernmost tip of Japan. The client was a priest of the Buddhist Shingon-shu sect. The temple site was on a mountainside looking over the city towards Mount Sakurajima, an active volcano famous in Japan. Kagoshima is also famous as the place where the forces of Saigo Takamori, the last samurai, were defeated by the imperial army in 1877. Saigo and twenty thousand soldiers and warriors died in these hills outside the town and the new temple was to be dedicated to him, as it is thought that he perished on this site.

As well as a place of worship, the temple was to serve as a depository for cremated remains. In this still traditional region of southern Japan, honouring the dead remains an important aspect of family life. Unlike in Great Britain, almost every grave in their cemeteries has fresh flowers on it. There is also a tradition of storing the cremated remains of family members in specially dedicated buildings. Ceramic urns containing ashes are placed in individual family altars, which are stacked up to form rows of tall cabinets. Visitors bring a ladder, with which to climb up to their altar to pay their respects. It is common for people to buy space for their family and make monthly financial contributions for its upkeep. This temple was intended to hold the cremated remains of 2,400 people, and this part of the temple would fund its construction. The priest's project managers were alarmingly modern in their thinking, suggesting an automated retrieval system, rather than the traditional rows of altars. You would enter the repository, swipe your identity card and the urn would be delivered to you automatically, like a vending machine. We suggested that it might be more dignified for an urn to be brought out by a young monk.

Visiting Japan was a powerful experience. In Kyoto we were taken to the old Buddhist temples and became anxious that the priest was hoping for something similar and had mistakenly thought us the right people to do this. However, they made it clear that they wanted us to understand the old temples but not to copy them.

Our starting point was to decide which part of the site to build on and how to configure the arrival sequence so that you felt as if you were leaving the rest of the world behind. It was important that you shouldn't be able to see the temple straight away. Putting it as far back on the site as possible, we could build a sense of anticipation and make the temple feel like a discovery.

In programming the building, we had to reconcile requirements for the placement of ceremonial elements. The large effigy of Buddha can face south or east, while the altars must face south. Using coloured wooden blocks, we developed a model of how this building might work but still needed an idea of what the temple might look like. We wanted a way to hold the building together, unifying all its separate functions.

Experimenting with shaping and sculpting forms in clay, based on the block model, we kept producing awkward, ugly shapes that didn't make any sense. The clay was allowing us too much control of the form. We suddenly found ourselves wondering if fabric, with its ability to fall into naturally sophisticated shapes, might give us the combination of cohesion and complexity that we were looking for.

In historical portraits, there may be a superb rendering of someone's head, but I am often captivated by the part of the painting that depicts clothing or textiles in rich drapes and folds. We had never seen a building that took its form from the way fabric moves and falls. Thinking of the stiff silk robes worn by our Buddhist priest, we were trying to achieve the kind of folds of fabric you see in Old Master paintings. We tried different fabrics, including a very expensive silk, and finally found a thin, rubberized foam material similar to that used to make wetsuits. The material could fold and crease and undulate and make fantastic forms by itself but it could also rationally define spaces, such as escape stairs, monks' cells or teaching rooms. Rather than actively defining how it folded, we allowed the single sheet of fabric to manipulate itself into a temple. After he had seen the design, the priest pointed out that our building made him think of the soft cushion on which the Buddha sits.

It had only recently become possible to scan a three-dimensional object to capture its exact form and turn it into data for use in a computer. The Royal National Throat, Nose and Ear Hospital, close to our studio in King's Cross, had bought a scanning machine that was used to assess the swellings on children's faces before and after operations and they allowed us to use this to scan our models. The form was reproduced exactly, even the drawing pins that fixed the fabric in place, which we didn't want to try to hide or smooth away.

We used multiple layers of steps to translate this complex, three-dimensional surface into a buildable form, building the temple up in horizontal layers that were

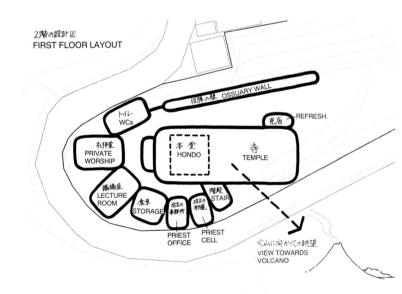

2階の設計図
FIRST FLOOR LAYOUT

但牌の壁 OSSUARY WALL

トイレ
WCs

売店
REFRESH.

礼拝堂
PRIVATE WORSHIP

本堂
HONDO

寺
TEMPLE

議室
LECTURE ROOM

倉庫
STORAGE

事務所

納骨堂

階段
STAIR

PRIEST OFFICE

PRIEST CELL

火山に向かっての眺望
VIEW TOWARDS VOLCANO

each the height of a step in a staircase. Constructed from plywood secured to a steel armature and coated with a waterproof membrane, the thick wooden layers also formed the interior of the temple. Extending the layers out of the walls, we could form staircases and furniture. We could also insert layers of glazing to give it windows.

To show what the temple would look like, at a time when the use of computer-rendered visualizations was not yet widespread, we commissioned an architectural illustrator to make watercolour paintings of the proposed building.

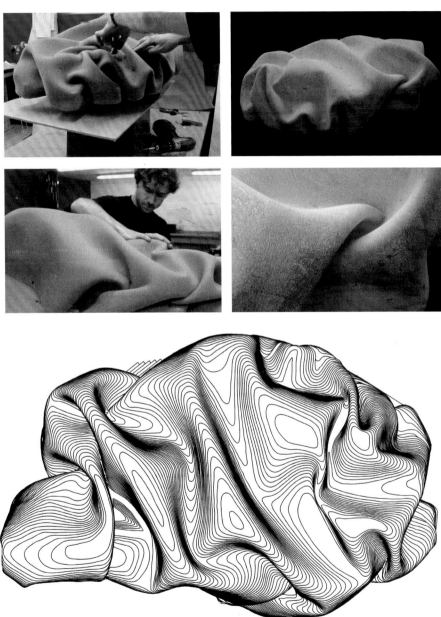

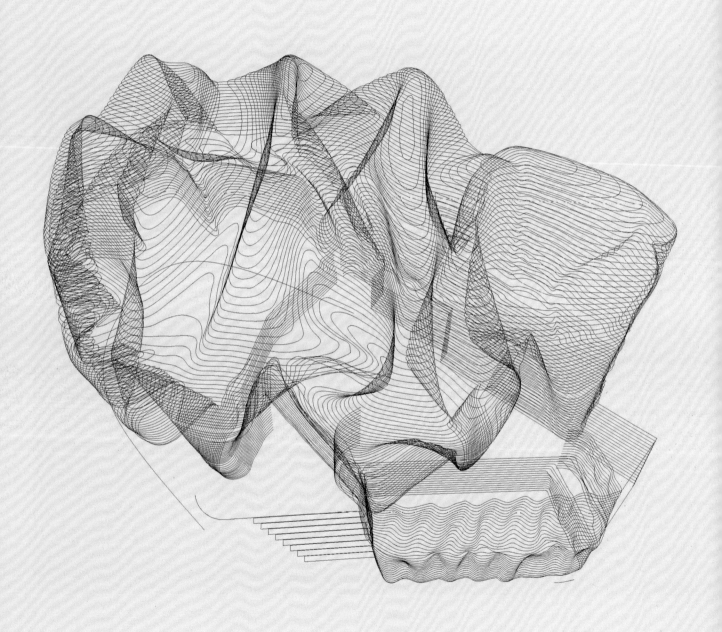

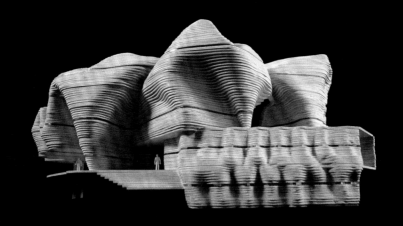

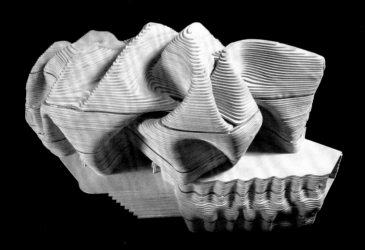

Turning Trees

*What could be more sculptural
than a tree?*

THE STUDIO WAS ASKED to develop an idea for an artwork to sit in the public space in front of a new office tower in Tokyo, Japan. As there was already a plan to plant mature trees into the space, we wondered if the trees themselves could become sculptures, instead of making a separate piece of public art. We recalled a British television programme called *Take Hart*, screened in the 1970s, in which sculptures that had been created during the programme were displayed on revolving tables to show their full beauty from every side.

Our proposal was to transplant large trees into the space and make them rotate within the pavement, so that they silently and almost imperceptibly turned on the spot like slow-motion ballerinas. The trees would be carefully selected for the sculptural quality of their branch structure, like the exquisite asymmetrical specimens in Japanese gardens.

Our idea was that the project would at first be barely noticeable. You could walk past it many times before noticing anything strange. But, after sitting for a time on one of the benches that encircle the trees, you might find yourself facing in a different direction, or suddenly notice the trees' shifting shadows. The only things that turn are the tree, the tree grille that surrounds it and the circular seat. The detailing of these and the stone paving in which they are set are of the highest quality, appropriate to the landscape design of a prestigious urban site.

With the help of a tree specialist, we developed a method of planting our trees into substantial circular containers that would hold all the soil, moisture and nutrients needed to sustain them. Below ground, these containers are set within devices similar to the turntables used to turn train engines and military tanks. It seemed that the trees would benefit from being rotated because they would be more evenly exposed to the sunlight, just as houseplants on a windowsill grow better if they are regularly turned around.

To communicate the idea, we made a wind-up musical box with miniature trees that rotated gently to the tinkling tune of *Für Elise* when the lid was opened.

Yorkshire Sound Barrier

*What is the large-scale equivalent
of an egg box?*

THE STUDIO ENTERED a competition to design a 2-kilometre-long sound
barrier for a motorway in the north of England, to dampen the impact of traffic
noise on a nearby residential area. Knowing that music recording studios sometimes had egg boxes glued to their walls to dampen the sound, we decided to
replicate the geometry and acoustic performance of this surface on an architectural scale, using the iconic orange plastic traffic cone. We proposed a
4-metre-high wall, 2 kilometres long, consisting of 32,000 cones mounted on a
simple steel frame. The barrier would be economical to build because its main
ingredient was a cheap, ready-made component.

Paternoster Vents

How can energy infrastructure be integrated into a public space?

AT PATERNOSTER SQUARE, next to St Paul's Cathedral in London, a new office development was being built. Below one of its public spaces was an underground electricity substation, which needed a system for cooling its transformers, a substantial structure consisting of two main elements: air inlet vents that enable cool air to be drawn down from above and air outlet vents that let warmed air escape upwards through a cooling tower. Our task was to design and configure this cooling system.

The commissioner had been exploring options that involved creating a single structure that housed both inlet vents and outlet vents. It made a large bulky object that dominated the public square around it, reducing it to little more than a corridor. As this was a sensitive location, close to St Paul's, we decided to make it our priority to shrink the visible mass of the vent structure to a minimum.

Since the substation itself is below ground, we worked with the project's engineers to find out if more of its cooling equipment could also be located underground. We learned that the ducts that brought cool air in to the substation did not in fact need to be accommodated within the tower structure, but could instead take the form of steel grilles set flush into the pavement, which would allow us to drastically reduce the size of the tower element. We also discovered that the warm air outlet vent could be divided in two, enabling us to break down the mass of the structure even more. Instead of a single, squat, fat object that would force you to walk around it, there could be two slim objects with a pathway between them. These moves opened up the space, transforming it by creating a composition of two objects that had a chemistry between them. It also made room around them for a viable public space.

The final form for this project came from experiments I had done as a student in Manchester, when I had explored the possibilities of making structures with textiles. Experimenting with folding heavily starched canvas into multiple pleats using an industrial iron had made the fabric behave like structural origami, twisting to make a strangely gorgeous geometrical form. Later, I found

490

that I could reproduce this form by folding a single piece of A4-size paper into identical isosceles triangles.

There was a moment when we looked at one of these folded shapes lying on a shelf in the studio and realized that it might give us the form for the two warm air outlet vents. The final towers are two of these forms, scaled up to a height of 11 metres, with exactly the proportions that came from folding a sheet of A4 paper. We tried using sheets of paper of various proportions, but the form looked best when it was made from an A4 sheet.

Rather than an identical pair, the towers are mirror images, each made from sixty-three identical isosceles triangles, cut from 8-millimetre-thick stainless steel plate, welded together. The steel is glass-bead-blasted, a long-lasting finish more commonly used for small components than for building-scale structures. Unlike a blasted finish using sand, which can feel rough to touch, firing tiny glass beads at sheet steel gives it a soft, silky look as if it has been finely pummelled by millions of tiny, rounded hammers. Because the metal triangles are set at angles to each other, the light reflecting differently from the angled facets gives the impression that they are made from different materials, like a harlequin's costume.

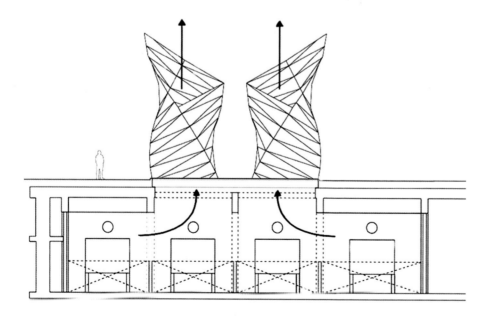

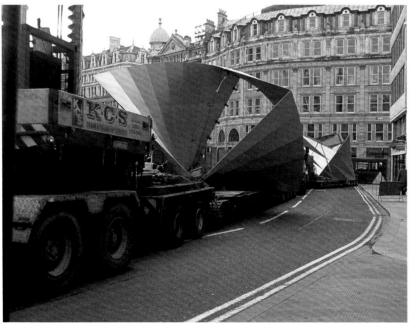

Guastavino's

*Can you flat-pack a
10-metre-high sculpture?*

THE BRITISH DESIGNER AND ENTREPRENEUR Terence Conran was opening a new restaurant under the arches of the Queensboro Bridge in New York, in a spectacular space with granite walls and a high, vaulted ceiling lined with white ceramic tiles. The studio was asked to design a sculpture for the wall that would face diners as they entered the restaurant.

Because the project did not have a high budget, it was clear that it would not be possible to do much construction in New York. Instead, we had to make something in London that could be packed flat in a box, like a shelving unit, shipped across the Atlantic and assembled on-site.

At first we found it hard to justify putting anything on the wall. There was no problem to solve. We could make anything we wanted. Rather than hanging something on the front of the wall, we wanted to anchor an idea into the wall in a more fundamental way. The wall was constructed from giant raw granite blocks, with spaces in between them, filled with grout. We began to think about squeezing material out of these gaps between the blocks. Something squeezed out of a slot of this shape would take the form of a ribbon and, if that ribbon was springy enough to hold its shape, we could make it twist and leap from slot to slot, across the wall.

The final idea for the sculpture was to stitch the wall together with ribbons of plywood. Each ribbon extrudes from the spaces between the stones, twists over and then tucks back into the wall. Like a tapestry kit, in which a fabric mesh is a guide to placing the stitches, the wall is a matrix, a grid composed of all the gaps between the blocks. The wooden ribbons are restrained at each end, where they emerge from the wall, and are held under their own tension by gravity.

To do this, the plywood had to be 7 metres long and thin enough to push into the gaps between the blocks, as well as light, strong and particularly resilient along its length, in order to hold its shape and not hang down limply. Existing plywood products did not meet these requirements, nor did they feel precious enough. For this reason we decided to make our own laminated wood for the pieces.

In standard, commercially sold plywood, the direction of the wood grain changes in alternate layers to make the material equally strong in all directions, but for our plywood we organized the layers so that more of the grain ran the length of the material. This made it springier along its length than across its width. Even different adhesives affected this characteristic of the plywood. To stop the wood tearing as it twisted, we worked with our structural engineer to develop a way of strengthening each piece by laminating strips of thin stainless steel foil into its edges. We also created a special fixing to mechanically anchor the pieces between the stone blocks.

After much prototyping and testing, we glued together the final plywood pieces in our studio in London and loaded them into a slim container and shipped them to America. Once they had arrived, we followed them to New York, where we transformed these flat elements into dramatic three-dimensional forms.

Zip Bag

Can you make objects out of long pieces of zipper?

DISCOVERING THAT IT WAS possible to buy, on a roll, a single 200-metre length of zip, I began researching ways to use it, not just as an opening device in a garment but as a main material in its own right.

Experimenting with sewing together spirals of zip ribbon by stitching the coil of the zip on to itself, we made three-dimensional objects that could vanish into a pile of zip when they were unzipped and re-form when zipped back up. We made many different kinds of bags and vessels and even a dress out of very long lengths, but it seemed that the bag, made with a single length of zip, was the best use of this idea.

After approaching the French luxury goods company Longchamp, we collaborated on a new version of the design that incorporated strips of fabric between the toothed edges of the zip so that the bag could open

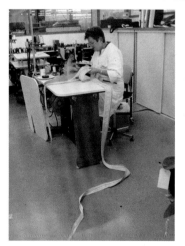

up and double its size. Our structural engineer had the task of carrying out surprisingly complex calculations to find a geometry for the bag that would allow it to do this without twisting. Having originated as a student experiment in 1993, the resulting product was manufactured and put on sale worldwide in 2004 and became a bestseller for Longchamp.

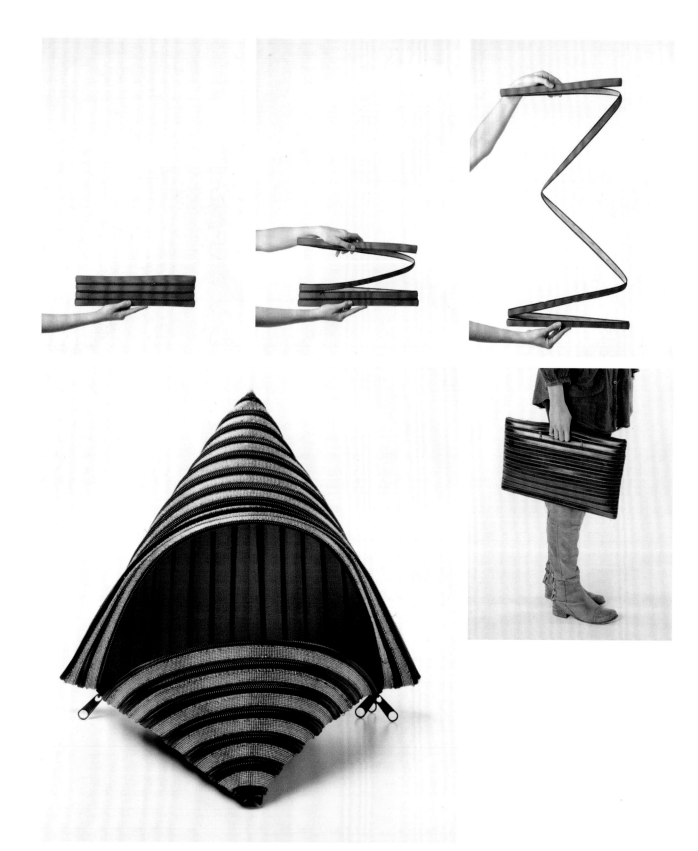

Barnards Farm Sitooterie

*How can a small building have
four thousand windows?*

THE TEMPORARY SITOOTERIE AT BELSAY HALL (pages 518–21) led to a commission for a permanent version, built with a new specification, for a public sculpture garden in Essex. To make this sitooterie into a permanent structure, we used anodized aluminium plate for the main box, instead of plywood, and hollow, square-section, aluminium tubes for the staves, instead of ash wood. The choice of aluminium tubes transformed the project from the original experiment with structure and visual texture into a building that also possessed an optical quality, with its four thousand staves that protrude from the central cube acting as four thousand windows. Each one is individually glazed with a tiny orange, transparent window that keeps out rain but allows warm-coloured light to pass through to the internal space.

The permanent sitooterie also has a different geometry from the first one: its staves point to an imaginary point at the centre of the cube, instead of projecting outwards perpendicular to the surfaces of the box. This means that every hole in the box is drilled at its own unique angle, giving it a distinctive geometry

and creating beautiful patterns on the walls, floor and ceiling, from the rows of angled, circular holes. Another effect is that if you stand inside the completed building with your head in the absolute centre, all the windows point in your direction and the daylight suddenly hits you at this optical sweet spot.

The central cube was not constructed by a conventional building contractor, but by an engineering company that specializes in milling aluminium for the aerospace industry, so the structure was made to tolerances normally reserved for small machine components, not buildings. Inside the sitooterie, this level of precision feels extraordinary. No mechanical fixings and no welding went into the construction, but instead the pieces were bonded together with adhesive. As in the Belsay structure, some staves extend inwards from the cube to form furniture and are machined to support seats made from thick aluminium plate, the same machined plate also being used for the door and window shutters.

By night, a single powerful light bulb, hanging at the exact centre of the space, throws light out through the thousands of glazed hollow aluminium staves. At the opening event, after it grew dark, a member of the studio went inside the sitooterie with her baby daughter and started walking around the central light, lifting the baby up and down. From outside, their figures appeared silhouetted in the dots of light at the end of the staves. Shrinking and growing as they moved nearer or further from the light bulb, the figures turned the sitooterie into a live, low-tech, computer-like display screen.

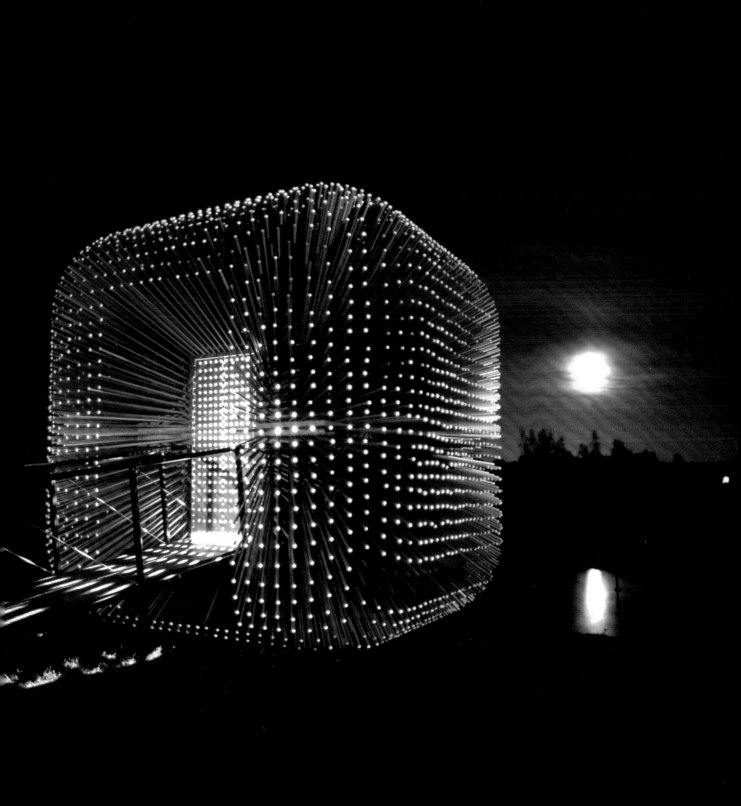

Street Chandelier

*Can conventional street furniture
be used to furnish a street in an
unconventional way?*

A BOROUGH COUNCIL IN SOUTH LONDON wanted to demarcate its boundary with neighbouring boroughs by installing gateway structures on two of the main roads into the borough. As London's streets are already littered with objects such as safety barriers, bollards, lamp columns, traffic notices, signposts and utility boxes, we began thinking about how we might use the street furniture that existed already, instead of adding to the clutter. The proposal we developed was to use ordinary street lamp columns – the biggest item that local authorities customarily install – to celebrate the gateway.

On the first site, a road junction with a central traffic island, we planned to set up a circle of leaning lampposts that had the combined effect of a giant decorative lighting feature, a grand version of the chandeliers that had become

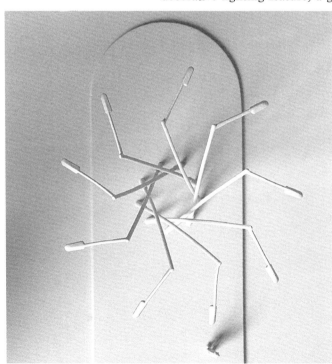

fashionable in domestic interiors. This chandelier would be made not from crystal but from ordinary street lighting components.

The second gateway, which was for a straight section of busy road, was to consist of a line of normal street lights on each side of the road, with the lamps on one side of the road leaning one way and those on the other side leaning the other way, so that they formed a dynamic relationship across the road without building over it, in a way that suggested a gateway.

The two compositions are very affordable to build because they use ordinary grey lamp columns that can be erected by the normal contractors, the only difference being in the angle and geometry of their placement.

Belsay Sitooterie

*Can a building stand on
the architectural equivalent
of matchsticks?*

ENGLISH HERITAGE APPROACHED THE STUDIO to build a pavilion at Belsay Hall in Northumberland, one of twelve temporary 'sitooteries', a Scottish term for a garden structure in which to 'sit oot'. Folly, gazebo and sitooterie form a category of buildings that fascinated well-to-do Victorians, who had these special structures built in the grounds of their country homes. It was a surprising commission to come from an organization better known for conserving old buildings than creating new ones.

Although the budget for each sitooterie was small, it was an opportunity for the studio to try out an unbuilt idea for a hairy building (pages 524–27), as 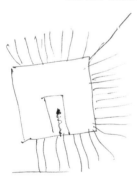 well as exploring a different way of making a building structure. An individual bristle of a scrubbing brush has little strength, but a whole brush is remarkably strong when you push down on it. Could we make a building stand on the architectural equivalent of bristles, a multiplication of single, delicate structural elements?

New buildings are generally smooth boxes, but this project experimented with the silhouette of a building against the sky. How far was it possible to splice building and sky together and blur the edges of a building? It was an exploration of texture on an architectural scale – taking a box, applying a texture to it and magnifying that texture to a point where it changes your perception of the form. We also felt that large building objects tended to be flat and textureless, their interest spread thinly over their form; yet smaller objects, like jewellery or clothing, often exhibit a rich concentration of detail. Could we apply this level of intricacy on an architectural scale?

The building is a cube with hairs embedded in every surface, like hundreds of thin legs, holding it raised above the ground. Individually, each leg is delicate and easily snapped in two, but together the legs combine to carry the weight of the structure.

The Sitooterie consists of a steel and plywood box, 2.4 metres square, perforated with 5,100 holes, with 1-metre-long ash wood staves fixed into each one. The staves project perpendicularly from every face of the central box, but

radiate around the corners. The rounded ends of the staves protrude slightly into the box, giving the interior a dotted texture, like tactile paving. Some are allowed to protrude further into the space to support seating.

The Sitooterie was in place throughout the summer, when Belsay Hall received record numbers of visitors, and was dismantled in the autumn.

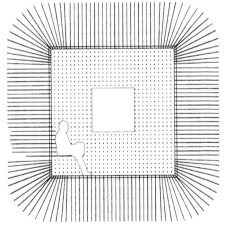

Electric Cinema Façade

Can a window make different kinds of reflections?

AS PART OF THE RESTORATION of a historic cinema in Portobello Road in London, the studio was asked to design the façade of the new building that was being constructed next door to act as the cinema's bar, café and meeting place.

Our proposal, developed in collaboration with a glass artist who specializes in making glass baths, was for a transparent curtain walling system consisting of shaped glass panels. These square tiles, 1 metre across, share an identical, three-dimensional form; when rotated relative to each other and repeated in sets of

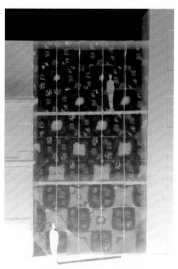

four, they tessellate to create a larger undulating surface that ripples across the building.

The panels are formed with a process known as heat slumping, which involves heating flat glass sheets in a kiln until they deform against a mould. They are then bonded to a structure of vertical glass blades to produce a glass façade with no metal fixings.

Hairy Building

When asked to put a sculpture next to an ugly building, how do you respond?

WITH THEIR SEVERE SILHOUETTES and ageing concrete, the buildings constructed at Notting Hill Gate in west London in the 1960s were considered by many local people to be cold and alienating. A group formed to look at ways to improve the area and invited the studio to propose a work of art, to be placed on or near a prominent building with shops on the ground floor and offices above.

We felt that the real problem was the poor quality of the buildings and the unpleasant spaces around them and that sticking unrelated pieces of art next to bad buildings would only accentuate how awful they were. To us, the only way to improve the public environment was to treat whole buildings. The question we wrestled with was how to transform a tired-looking rectilinear shape, without pretending that the underlying four-storey building was not there.

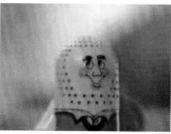

The legacy of the postwar building boom was an architecture of soulless boxes – the ubiquitous building objects of my childhood – and architectural fashion at that time appeared to have polarized into either jettisoning all ornamentation or retreating into a pastiche of historical building styles. The studio wanted to sidestep this aversion to ornamentation and had been exploring alternatives that relied on craftsmanship and materials and experimenting with texture on an architectural scale.

Our approach to this project was to engineer the greatest possible contrast with the rigid, hard-surfaced texture of the existing brick and concrete building. Our idea was to embed thousands of protruding hair-like elements in the façade, which would sway in the wind like a field of tall grass. In the same way that hair does not grow from mouths and eyeballs, the hair on this building grows only from its blank façade panels and not from the windows and doors. We liked the idea of thousands of hair-like elements growing from the building, shivering and trembling as a bus swept past.

Though highly textured, the surface remains a direct manifestation of the building underneath, just as the tips of someone's hair are an approximate projection of the form of their scalp. The idea was influenced by the Play-Doh barber shop toy, a hollow plastic man that 'grows' hair when you wind a handle by

extruding coloured putty out of holes in his bald plastic head. The form of his new hair is the shape of his head, projected outwards. On a square building, the protruding hairs would soften its sharp corners and, at night, tiny light sources at their tips would create a shimmering ghost of the façade beneath.

To realize the project, we worked with engineers to formulate a framework of prefabricated steel panels that could be brought to the site by lorry, lifted up and attached to the existing building. Six thousand hairs, made of fibreglass tubes with a fibre-optic core, could then be connected to the pre-prepared fixings.

The scheme did not go forward, but in later projects the studio got the chance to put into practice these ideas about texture in relation to buildings.

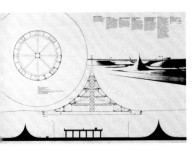

Twin Roundabouts

Roadwork or artwork?

THE STUDIO WON A COMPETITION to design an artwork to be installed on the A13, the main road that goes out of London to the east, passing through Barking and Dagenham. The work was to be sited on a new roundabout, with the A13 passing above, but, having seen sculptures stuck on the suburban roundabouts of many towns in many countries, we were wary of the disconnection that can occur between a roundabout and an artwork when the roundabout is treated as an empty plinth for the artwork.

Instead of making an individualized, isolated artefact, we chose to think of it as a special piece of road-building, an integral part of the road improvement scheme. To avoid making a distinction between the craft of road-building and the making of artworks, we wanted it to be made by the highway contractor, using the language and materials of highway design: tarmac, kerb and paving slabs. We also looked at integrating into the scheme a second new roundabout on the other side of the A13, so that the two roundabouts would create a gateway for the road passing between them.

Thinking about the millions of cars that would circle the roundabouts over the years, gradually wearing away the ground and carving out pinnacles of tarmac, like rock formations eroded by the sea, we imagined our roundabout structures taking similar carved-out forms.

With its height equal to its radius, the geometrical form of each roundabout structure is pure. The structures are made from concrete sprayed over tensile stainless steel mesh cones supported on steel posts. Inside each one is a large space that no one will ever go inside, like a sealed pyramid. In construction, with their mesh partially sprayed with concrete, these interior spaces provided an unusual optical experience. Where the concrete faded out, solidity gave way to transparency in a way that was unlike the sudden transition between walls and windows that we are used to. This led to the design of windows for the pavilion that the studio built for the World Expo in Shanghai (pages 308–25).

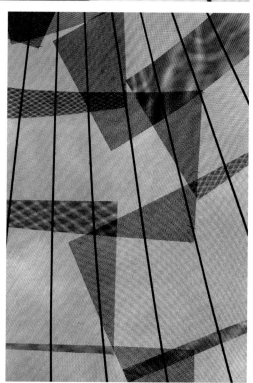

1999 Blackburn Emergency Platform

Can a wall shelter you from the rain?

THE STUDIO BECAME INVOLVED in a project to improve a railway station in the north of England. Three elements – a windbreak, a rain canopy and an artwork – were being separately commissioned for the station's emergency platform, where trains stop when the other platforms are in use. Our challenge was to fuse the three elements into a single proposal.

The rain canopy would stop rain running down the ramp into the tunnel that connected the emergency platform with the rest of the station; the windbreak was to shelter the station from the wind sweeping across the main platforms. We felt that if we could solve these functional requirements in a distinctive way, there would be no need for any additional artwork.

Our idea was to take the windbreak, which was a 140-metre-long wall along the length of the platform, and twist the entire structure above the entrance to the ramp through 180 degrees, to become a canopy. As the vertical element twists, it forms a horizontal surface that shelters the ramp.

In collaboration with engineers, we developed a structural solution based on aeroplane wing technology, which used a catenary structure of internal steel tension cables within a metal-clad form.

534

Christmas Card

*Can a Christmas card be
bigger than its envelope?*

THE IDEA FOR THIS CARD came from feeling sorry for the envelope that normally gets thrown away as soon as someone has taken the Christmas card out of it. We wondered if the envelope could avoid its usual fate by being the card itself.

You receive what looks like an ordinary white, sealed envelope, lined with green tissue. When you open it, you find a second smaller envelope inside. Inside that is a third envelope, which is even smaller, and inside that a fourth one, a miniature envelope that contains a tiny chocolate Father Christmas. The telescoping, green, tissue-lined envelopes are connected to each other with pieces of ribbon, so that when you hang them up, they dangle one below the other and form a surprisingly large Christmas tree.

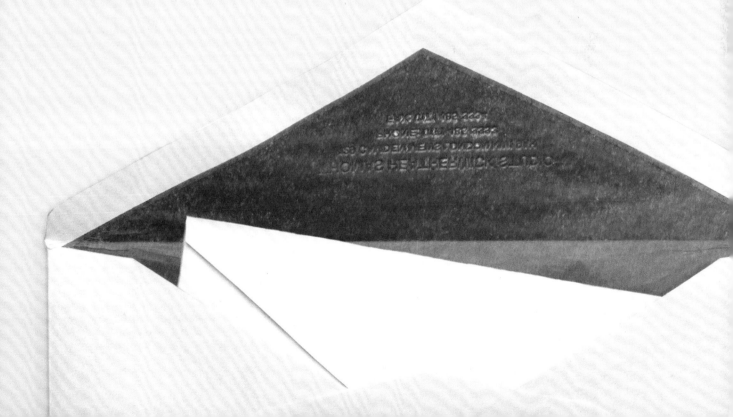

Installation

How much three-dimensional form can you give to flat boards?

THE STUDIO WAS ASKED TO DESIGN an installation that would be in place for one night at a party to celebrate the work of D&AD, an organization that champions the creative industries. They wanted to show text and pictures that would be displayed on computer monitors but felt that, to encourage people to look at the screens, they needed to do more than put computers on tables.

Using the largest available wooden sheets, 3 metres high and 50 millimetres thick, we constructed a series of small buildings to house the screens by cutting hundreds of concentric, radiating circular shapes, which turned the flat sheets into vast contoured forms when they were telescoped outwards. By leaning them against each other, we transformed these manipulated sheets into structures that you could enter, with surfaces suspended inside for the computers to sit on.

Having pre-cut hundreds of metres of curving lines into the heavy boards with jigsaws, we loaded the flat pieces on to a lorry. Once at the venue, they were pulled out into shape to make the three-dimensional sculptural objects.

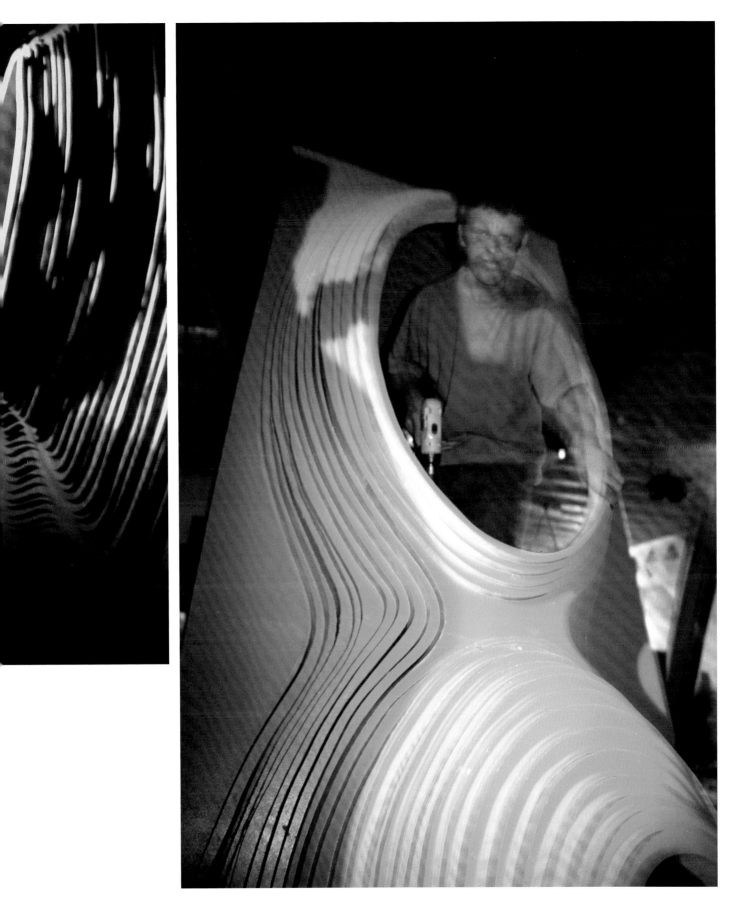

Materials House

*How do you engineer a structure
using 213 materials without giving
any one greater importance?*

THE SCIENCE MUSEUM IN LONDON commissioned the studio to produce an exhibit called the Materials House for a new gallery about materials. The brief was to design a structure that would show everything that anything can be made of.

At first, we wondered what to make this house out of. The implication was that we would choose one main material to build the house and stick all the other materials on to it. But we did not want to give one material a more important role than any of the others.

Studying design at Manchester Polytechnic, I was able to go into the college's material stores and see piles of copper sheeting, racks of different kinds of glass with exotic finishes and different textures, bundles and reels of nickel-plated wire and stacks of wooden planks. In some ways it was depressing to go into the stores, because these materials were already gorgeous. They seemed to be defying you to do something with them that made them more beautiful than they already were.

When the Science Museum sent us the box full of the materials that we were to use, it was disappointing. They resembled manufacturers' free samples, each one the size of a small tile, and seemed inconsequential, even pathetic. With materials capable of such phenomenal things as conducting electricity or protecting spacecraft, the challenge was to find a way to do justice to their capabilities.

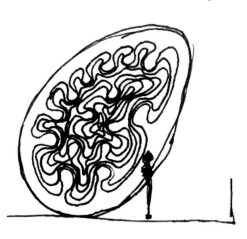

We asked ourselves if, instead of showing tiny pieces of each material, we could have a sheet of each material as tall as the gallery. If we fused sheets of this size together, we could make the world's biggest sandwich of materials and carve away at it to reveal the surfaces of the materials, like creating our own geological strata.

The form of the sandwich is a simple rectangle, the height of the gallery, 6 metres high and 3 metres wide. It contains 213 materials, each carved to reveal its surface. Every layer is different: the first one is simple and quiet, but the following layers mutate and mutate until the final one is completely contorted.

To make sense of the project and to be able to build it, we needed a single massive drawing representing all the layers at the

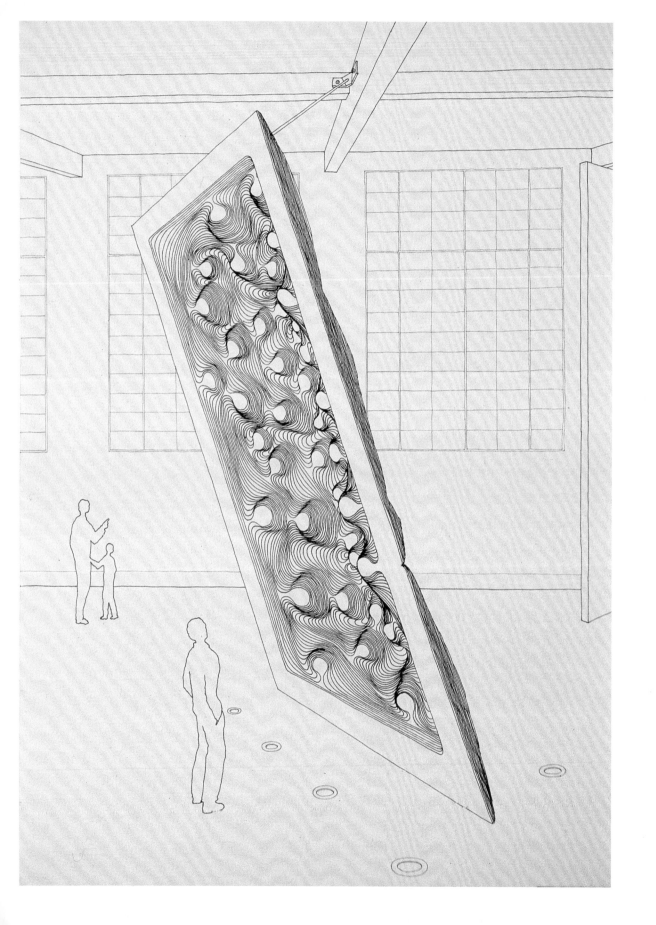

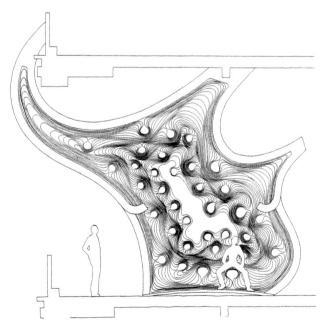

545

same time. We assumed that a computer might be able to help us with the design but we found that the lines generated by a computer had no spirit. In the end, to get the quality of curves that we wanted, a very patient designer in the studio spent three months hand-drawing each one of the thousands of metres of lines into a computer.

The project was logistically challenging. As each layer was made from at least ten pieces, the project consisted of more than 2,500 unique elements. We had layers of different types of plastic, textiles, wood, stone, papers, rubber, glass, copper, gold leaf, materials made by recycling other materials and materials used in the aerospace industry. They were sourced from different suppliers and many were donated, requiring lengthy correspondence. Every layer was a different shape and thickness and cut by different companies. On top of that, many of the materials did not come in sheet form, so we had to convert them into flat layers before they could be cut to shape. There was a huge amount of project information to manage and many opportunities for things to go wrong.

The Welding Institute advised us on the project, pointing out that we needed to be careful about the order of the layers. Because certain materials generate an electrical charge when they sit next to each other, we were at risk of creating a giant battery.

The piece was assembled layer by layer on the floor of the Science Museum, lying on its front, a process that took many weeks. Then the 4-tonne piece was hoisted up, allowing us to see it for the first time, while a member of the team played a sailors' shanty on the accordion: 'Heave ho and up she rises!' The Materials House is about as visually rich as it is possible to be. You look at it and your eye is full.

Christmas Card

*How much work can you get the
Post Office to do for 21 pence?*

IN MY FIRST SATURDAY JOB, which was in the packing depart-
ment of a mail order cycling equipment supplier, I was once
sent to the nearby post office to buy £2,000 worth of postage
stamps. The sheets of tiny rectangles with perforated edges
and Queen's heads on them looked charming and precious and
it seemed funny that a sheet of two hundred £5 stamps, worth
£1,000, was the same size, had the same high print quality and
carried an equal number of Queen's heads as the sheet of two
hundred halfpenny stamps, worth just £1.

Years later, I wondered how the Post Office would react
if we used as many stamps as possible on our Christmas cards
to make up the value of a second-class stamp, which at that time
was 21 pence.

Our idea was to create Christmas imagery by arranging
twenty-one one-penny stamps in the shape of a Christmas tree, stuck down on
to a piece of card, with the address written at the bottom, as if it was the pot
of the tree. As the Post Office has to postmark every stamp with the date and
place of posting so that nobody can use it again, the postal workers were forced to
decorate our Christmas trees with circular postmarks that looked like Christmas
tree baubles. If halfpenny stamps had not already disappeared from circulation,
we could have made our trees from twice as many stamps.

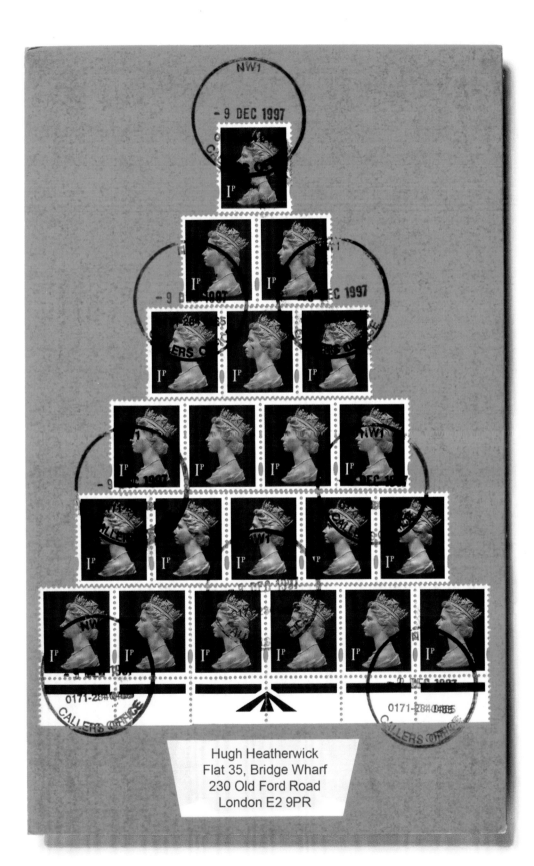

Hugh Heatherwick
Flat 35, Bridge Wharf
230 Old Ford Road
London E2 9PR

Autumn Intrusion

1997

*How can a shop window display
relate to the architecture of its shop?*

HARVEY NICHOLS IS A DEPARTMENT STORE in London famous for its special window displays. The studio was asked to design the windows that would celebrate Autumn 1997 Fashion Week. As we started to think about the project, it seemed to us that in the world of fashion retail, you could choose almost any theme for the windows – Mickey Mouse or giant Airfix kits – as long as it attracted attention. But we had never seen a window display that made a connection with the architecture of the building.

We felt that there was seldom a logical link between the design of a shop and the architecture of the building that sits on top of it. London is full of ornate Victorian buildings that appear to have had their ground floors pulled out from underneath them and replaced with a modernist slice of retail. Harvey Nichols, though, is unusual because it has stone columns that come all the way down between its windows and attach it to the pavement. It is a detached, free-standing building, rather than part of a street of shops, and occupies an important corner.

We wanted to create a design that was specific to the architecture of the Harvey Nichols building, something that could not be done with any other shop. Instead of treating its twelve windows as twelve separate display cabinets, we began looking for a single idea that could bring them together.

Although glass is associated with the idea of transparency, the contents of shop windows are often veiled or even obscured by the light that reflects off these large panes. Rather than putting objects in the boxes behind the glass and allowing the glass in these windows to be their jailer, we began to think about finding a way to escape the confines of the shop window. We started to imagine that there was no glass and that our installation was allowed to burst out into

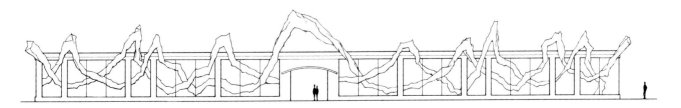

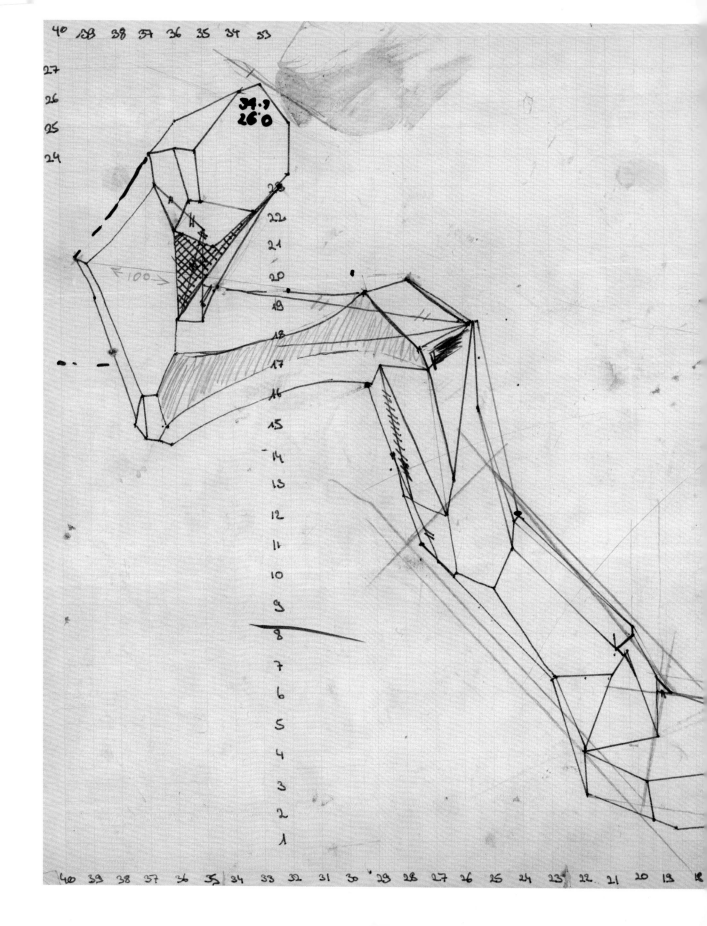

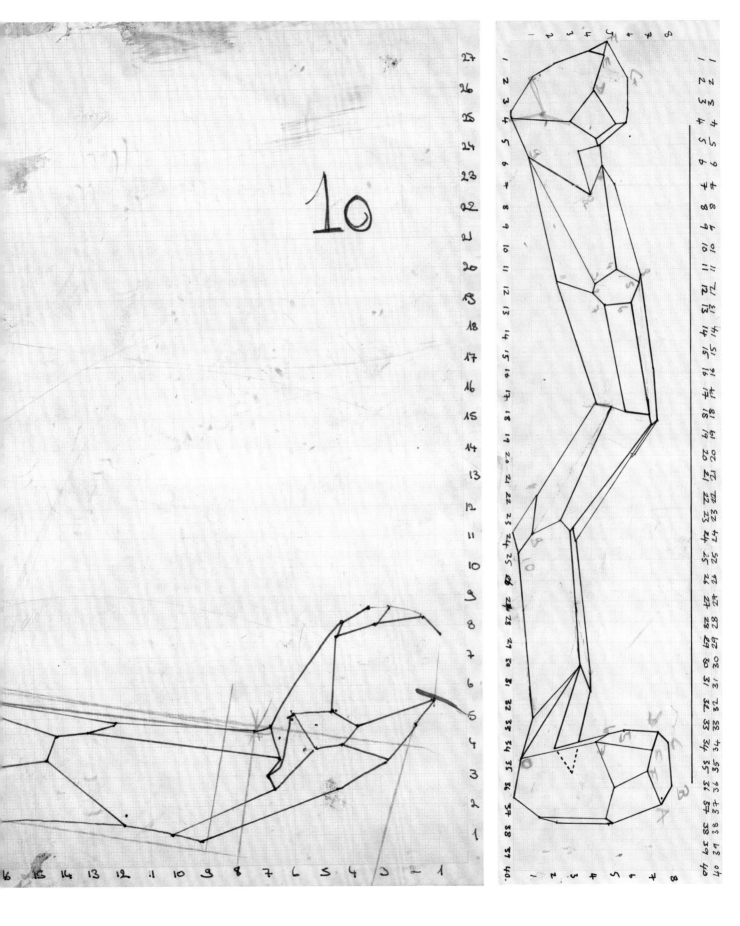

10

the street and steal space from the pavement, as well as making a connection with the façade of the building and drawing attention from around the corners.

The idea that we developed was to stitch all twelve window spaces and the façade into a single composition using an element that wove in and out of the stone pillars, extending beyond the boundaries of the shop, rising up the front of the building and protruding beyond its corners. Rather than the flowing, passive language of a snake or ribbon form, we wanted this element to feel muscular and unpredictable, a dynamic, wriggling and struggling form that is deliberately awkward and stubborn, consciously changing and contorting as it goes where it wants to go.

The only way to design such a dynamic form was for me to carve it in polystyrene, using a sharp kitchen knife. The process was too intuitive for me to be able to instruct somebody else and the piece evolved as I carved and experimented. Unless the knife was razor sharp, the polystyrene pieces would rip into bobbles.

We had six months and six people to build this huge object. It had to be strong enough to withstand the particularly strong winds in this part of the city but light enough for us to build and suspend it. We could have made it from fibreglass and painted it, but we didn't want it to give the impression of a painted simulation of something else; it needed materiality and craftsmanship. Instead, we created a special composite material consisting of an expanded polystyrene core and a veneer of aeroply, the extremely thin birch plywood that was originally developed for constructing aeroplane wings. Like the cross-section of a bone, this combination had great structural efficiency: tensile and compressive strength on its outer surfaces and a lightweight, aerated structure in the middle. The aeroply also had warmth and silkiness.

I carved two identical models of the project at 1:20 scale: one stayed in the studio and the other went to a warehouse in east London, where our team was building the project. Today, we might use three-dimensional digital technology to scale up this form, but this was not available to us then, so we had to divide the sculptural form into sections and scale up each complicated shape by hand.

We placed the miniature pieces on graph paper and made plan and elevation drawings for each one, which we scaled up on to a giant grid marked on the floor and walls of the workshop. Once we understood the geometry of each piece, we bonded and carved vast blocks of polystyrene with hot wires until we had the right form. Each piece was then veneered with acroply, which was a highly skilled job to do cleanly on such a scale and required a craftsmanship that was closer to cabinetmaking than set building. One by one, as they were completed, the pieces were stored in the neighbouring building, which happened to be London's last surviving lighthouse. Finally, working with a rigging company over a series of ten nights, the pieces were put in place, where they remained for two months.

Millennium Bridge

*Can the character of a bridge change
as you cross it?*

TO CELEBRATE THE MILLENNIUM, a decision was taken to build a new foot-bridge over the River Thames in London and the studio entered the anonymous competition that was held to find a design.

Seeking not only to create a route but also to make public spaces over the river, we came up with a proposal based on the difference in the character of the two banks at either end of the bridge. The northern end of our bridge would emerge from a narrow slot between the buildings below St Paul's Cathedral and land on the south side of the river in a wide open space, next to the former Bankside Power Station, which was in the process of becoming the Tate Modern art gallery. The bridge could, we thought, reflect the vastly differing qualities of these environments, one corporate and one artistic, by transforming itself as it crossed the river.

Researching the dynamic forms made within moving liquids, we developed a bridge that, like water thrown from a bucket, left the north bank in a shape that was tight and directional and then became wider and more generous as it travelled towards the south bank, breaking down into eddies and undulations that created significant public spaces and contained stopping points and performance areas, as well as a direct route for people in a hurry.

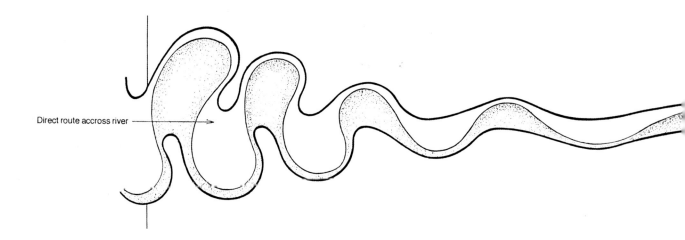

Direct route accross river

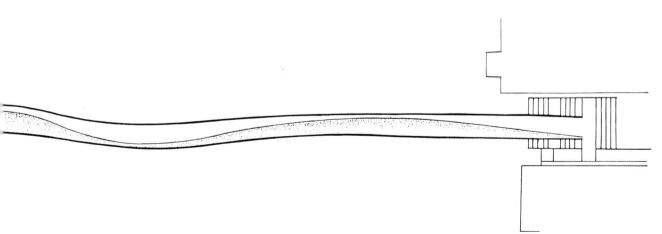

Hate Seat

*How can a strip of folded
paper lead to the design of
a functional object?*

THE ORGANIZERS OF AN EXHIBITION at Belsay Hall in Northumberland invited
the studio to design a piece of furniture. We experimented with paper folding,
wondering whether a single folded strip could become a functional object.

The idea was for a piece of furniture formed from a single strip of wood
that made the seat, legs and back of a bench, by folding its ends down, along,
around and up. If we angled the fold lines slightly off the perpendicular, the strip
formed a subtle spiral that intersected itself as it folded.

Like the classic love seat, the bench is rotationally symmetrical, but instead
of gazing into each other's eyes, the couple sit with their backs to each other,
although, in the event of a reconciliation, they can sit in the middle side by side.

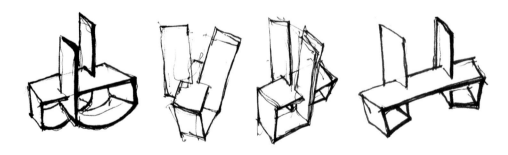

Complete Christmas Tree

What does a whole Christmas tree look like?

FINLAND WAS DONATING A FORTY-YEAR-OLD, 20-metre tree to stand outside the Design Museum in London at Christmas, and we were invited to design decorations for it. Because the project involved cutting down and killing a tree, we wanted to treat it with respect. Instead of covering it with Christmas kitsch, we looked for a way of celebrating the tree itself.

Rather than chopping it off at the ground, we decided to excavate it and bring the whole tree to London, with its entire root system intact. Like decorating the tree with candles, we would then decorate this forty-year-old tree with forty one-year-old trees in gilded pots. These could later be replanted, replacing an older tree, which would die, with forty young ones.

As conventional digging machinery would have damaged the roots, we worked with the Finnish fire brigade to wash the tree out of the ground. A deep trench, 20 metres in diameter, was dug around the tree. Then the firemen connected their hoses to a nearby river and, with 100,000 gallons of water, carefully washed the soil away from the bottom of the tree, having first anchored it in place with a crane to prevent it from toppling over. The roots were more extensive and delicate than people had thought: a vast, lace-like network of filigree elements, fine hairs designed to suck up moisture and nutrients from the ground.

The tree was transported by lorry, its roots delicately packaged into bundles that looked like dreadlocks. Forty plant pots were gilded with gold leaf and attached with steel arms to the main tree trunk, each fitted with a light source to illuminate it and the whole tree. The roots spilled out over the plinth and on to the riverside walkway. Their bark was beautifully patterned and had the quality of snakeskin.

...d Thomas Heatherwick has been invited to decorate this year's tree. The 40 year old tree comes from a sustainably managed... ...January allowing them to continue growing

Shelving for a Jade Collection

Can a windowsill be more useful?

THE STUDIO WAS COMMISSIONED BY A FAMILY in north London to design display shelves for their collection of carved jade objects. Because the wall on which they wanted to display the collection was dominated by three narrow, horizontal windows that looked like letterboxes, we felt that any new piece of furniture needed to relate to these windows.

Our solution was to treat the windows as if they were eyes and grow the display units out of each one like eyelids. The bottom eyelids pulled out to make surfaces on which to display the objects and the top eyelids stretched up to the ceiling to cast light downwards on to the collection, the intention being to symbolically draw in the light from outside.

The finished pieces were fabricated in the studio's workshop, combining a steel structure with a twisting birch veneer surface.

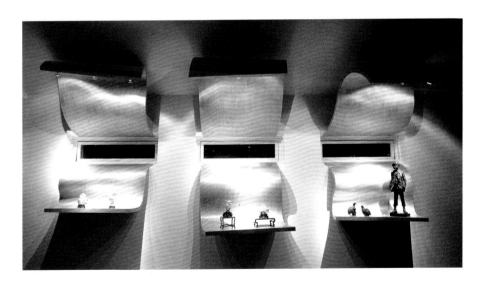

Conran Shop Window Display

Can the design of a shop window display evolve like a doodle?

FOR THE WINDOWS OF THE CONRAN SHOP in London, the studio was asked to produce a display of four hundred pieces of kitchen equipment, a collection of disparate objects – spoons, cloths, bins, kettles, brooms – all different sizes and made of all kinds of materials. We wanted to get away from the conventional format of using a separately designed set of shelves to exhibit the objects.

Experimenting with drawing, I drew one of the objects and wrapped a line around it. I kept going and added in another object and put another line around that. Disturbed by the accumulation of objects, each new line reacted to the previous lines. By obeying a small artistic rule, a design evolved. The rule gave you some control but as you carried on adding more and more disturbances, you did not know exactly what the whole thing was eventually going to look like.

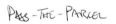

PASS-THE-PARCEL

It reminded me of visiting furniture factories in Sweden, which were set in the forests that supplied them with timber, and hearing that they often found bullets embedded in the grain of this wood. At some point in the trees' lives, bullets had got lodged deep in their trunks but the wood had carried on growing around them, accommodating the bullets like an infection that disturbs a tree's growth rings. I liked the idea of inserting imperfections into something that would otherwise be perfect.

Working on the floor of the studio, we grew each piece by incorporating the objects layer by layer, wrapping them in the cheap, corrugated cardboard that comes in rolls and is used for packaging. There was no final design. We designed the pieces as we made them, deciding where to put a saucepan or a toaster and then reacting to what happened next. All we could do was to try to steer the design as we allowed the series of forms to make themselves, gradually incorporating 12 kilometres of cardboard.

The finished pieces were in place for ten weeks and resembled slices through a vast pass-the-parcel game package.

Kielder Boathouse

Can a floor become a roof?

INVITED BY AN ART CONSULTANT to propose a project for the area around Kielder Water, the vast manmade lake in Northumberland, the studio suggested a boathouse with a jetty for a boat to pull up against and a roof to protect people from rain while waiting for the local ferry service.

Instead of creating a conventional jetty with a separate covered structure, we made the end of the jetty become the canopy, curling itself round and over to form a shelter, developing a connection between functional elements that are normally separate. The boathouse was to be constructed entirely from glass: thousands of identical glass sheets bonded together using high-performance, transparent, ultraviolet adhesive.

We imagined this as a crystalline form suspended above the water, reflected in it and illuminated at night. Although the technology that would make this project possible was still in development, it came out of the studio's interest in the structural use of glass and was the beginning of the idea for a glass bridge (pages 420–25).

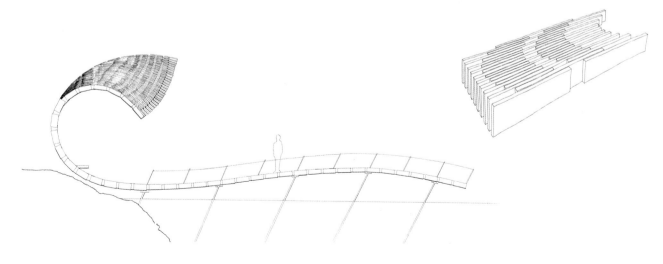

Film Festival Ticket Office

Can straight pieces of wood make a curved building?

THIS IDEA FOR A SMALL BUILDING from which to sell tickets for a film festival developed out of research and experimentation with small temporary buildings, such as kiosks, pavilions and gazebos.

Following tests with interleaving piles of wooden pieces, we developed a 10-metre structure that consists of four V-shaped stacks of wood which curve upwards, crossing through each other and converging at the top into two V-shaped peaks. The planks form buttresses and walls, which in turn become the structure and the roof.

A supplier of sustainable timber offered to source some of the fragrant wood from a cedar of Lebanon tree that had blown over in a gale. Using identical straight lengths of wood meant there would be little waste and the timber would be easy to reuse after the project was dismantled.

Christmas Cards

1994

*How can you send appreciation
by post?*

TO SHOW OUR GRATITUDE to people who had supported us or worked with us, the studio began sending out special cards at Christmas. Each year, we looked for ways of turning inexpensive materials into postable objects.

Our earliest cards were little more than decorative test pieces. The first one came from experimenting with the studio's new rotary trimmer, a piece of office equipment for cutting paper, which, when used to slice card very finely, produced tiny, twisted slivers. Another card was an object made by taking a stack of birch plywood strips and weaving them through each other. As we carried on looking for ways to send love, we became interested in the process by which they were sent, the rituals of posting and receiving a card, and found that the subject of our Christmas cards became Christmas cards themselves.

For seventeen years, we produced the cards in our workshop, setting up mini-production lines that allowed us to repeat the making processes several hundred times, using tools, jigs, devices and systems that we invented and constructed. When we had 350 cards to make and each one needed 52 holes in it,

we had to construct a jig with which we could drill 15,600 holes (or bond 6,300 stamps to each other or stick 7,500 small envelopes together). We would suddenly find ourselves becoming experts in stamp adhesive, manila stationery paper and casting from a postbox. Each year, the staff of the Special Handstamp Centre, a department in the vast Royal Mail sorting office at Mount Pleasant in north London, helped us get the cards through the postal system.

574

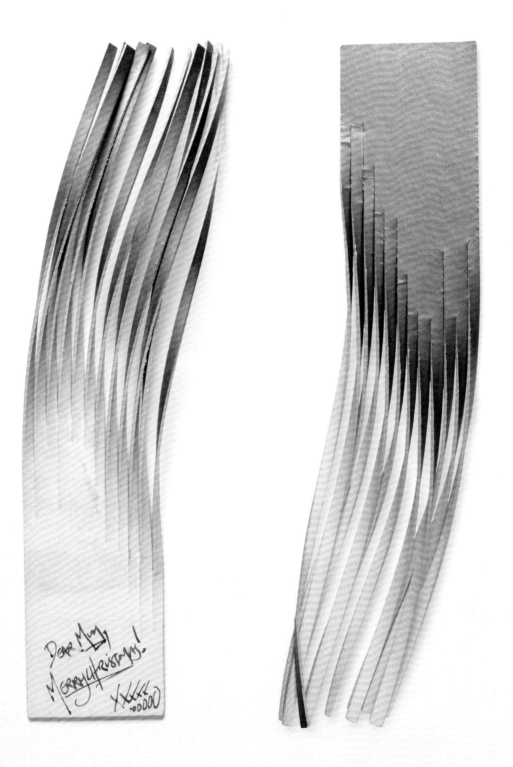

Montblanc Diary

Can each day's page in a diary be a different shape?

A LUXURY GOODS COMPANY asked the studio to design a limited-edition diary. Influenced by the technique of cutting finger-holds into the edges of dictionaries and encyclopaedias to identify their alphabetical sections, we decided to treat the book as if it was a block of wood and to sculpt undulating curves into its long edge. In the manner of traditional bookbinding, this carved surface was gilded with gold leaf. Breaching the conventional rectangular extents of the book by carving it in this way made it sensuous to handle and gave a unique shape to the page for each day of the year.

Sleeping Policeman

*How can you make a sleeping
policeman work harder?*

OBSERVING THAT BRITAIN'S STREETS were filling with miscellaneous items of street furniture and infrastructure, such as barriers, traffic monitoring cameras, bollards and electricity boxes, we wondered if there was a way to reduce the number of these objects by combining their functions.

Our idea was to take a sleeping policeman, the sausage-like lump across a road designed to slow cars down, and twist it up and over the pavement. As well as controlling the speed of the traffic, it would make a pair of cantilevering benches. It could be made from terrazzo, a polished concrete containing pieces of marble.

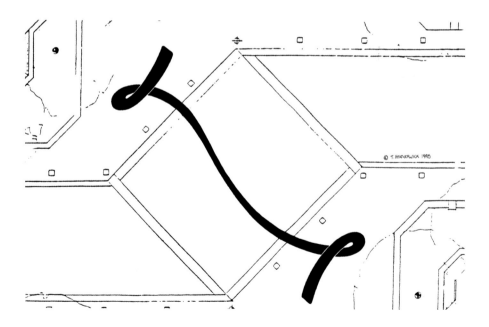

© T. HEATHERWICK 1995

Log

1994

Can you expand a tree trunk?

THIS TEST-PIECE CAME FROM SEEING tree trunks in Sweden that had been felled and split into planks. To allow moisture to escape from the green wood, the logs had been put back together with small pieces of wood inserted between each plank to let air circulate between each one. These reassembled logs were no longer round in section but stretched into ovals. It occurred to me that you might be able to stretch a log like this in more than one direction while still holding it all together.

Using a bandsaw, I repeatedly sliced a log lengthwise, stopping before each piece was completely severed, and then, having turned the log through 90 degrees, sliced it from the other end so that these cuts went through the log in a perpendicular plane.

As the slices were fanned out using spacers, first one way and then the other, it made a geometrically interesting object that remained a single piece of wood, with the expanded texture of its bark continuing across the splayed edges of the slices.

Business Card

Can you make someone eat your business card?

WITH MY MASTER'S COURSE coming to an end and the degree show approaching, I wanted to find a memorable way to give people my contact details, while also making a connection with the pieces I was showing. As it was a hot summer and my work would be exhibited outdoors, it occurred to me to create a business card that was also a refreshment.

Because I missed those bad jokes that you used to find on British ice lolly sticks I decided to design and manufacture an ice cream and put my name and telephone number on the stick. My first idea, a form that appeared to have been crushed, like a piece of clay, in the recipient's hand, looked unappetizing, so I rationalized it into a twisted shape that fitted the licking area of the end of a tongue.

To make six hundred lollies, I made a set of twelve wooden formers, from which I made trays of plastic moulds using the college's vacuum-forming machine. A south London ice cream-making company gave me access to their factory by night for a month, and allowed me to use their ingredients and machinery. From a factory-full of flavours, I chose vanilla cream for the lollies, with their tips dipped in chocolate.

For the sticks, I bought wooden tongue depressors from a medical supplier and used my cooker to heat a branding tool that had been acid-etched for me to burn my details on to them. Every morning, throughout the two weeks of the show, I took outside a second-hand freezer that I had bought. If

people wanted my business card, they had to eat the ice cream to find out my name, telephone and fax number.

Windsor Great Hall

How do you design a new piece of heritage?

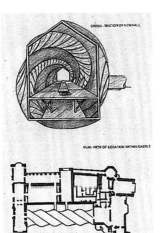

WHEN THE GREAT HALL at Windsor Castle, the British Queen's weekend home, was destroyed by fire in 1992, there was a debate about whether to rebuild the hall or replace it with something that reflected the present time. A competition was held for ideas and, working with a fellow student from the Royal College of Art, I produced quick drawings for an idea that used both the existing materiality of the monumental castle – a palette of historic materials such as carved wood, stone and stained glass – and the same high level of craftsmanship that had been used to build the previous hall.

An elongated space like this hall gives your eye the pleasure of appreciating the pattern and perspective that comes from the repetition of details growing smaller as they recede into the distance. Our proposal involved taking that splendid space and twisting it through 360 degrees from one end of the hall to the other, while leaving the floor a flat surface suspended within its length. We imagined that the new space, constructed with exceptional craftsmanship using traditional materials, would offer the most remarkable view as it spiralled away from you.

In creating this hall, our Royal Family would be expressing confidence in contemporary ideas while retaining the richness of historic materiality and craftsmanship in its realization.

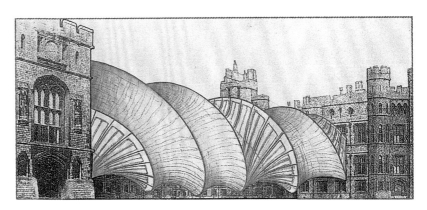

Gazebo

1994

Can you make a building using only two components?

WHEN I BEGAN MY POSTGRADUATE COURSE at the Royal College of Art in London, I wanted to continue researching and experimenting with ways of making buildings. During the summer break, I was commissioned to make a piece of furniture, a 4.5-metre timber bench, which was the test piece for Extrusions (pages 274–83). At one point, there had been hundreds of pieces of plywood piled up, ready to be glued together. Playing with these stacks, I found that if I distorted them, tilting them towards each other until they were almost toppling over, but then interleaved them as if shuffling playing cards, the stacks could support each other structurally. It seemed possible that this idea might work on an architectural scale.

The gazebo consists of two stacks of birch plywood L-shapes, 6 metres high, which curve outwards and then in towards each other. As they meet, they mesh together for support, passing through each other and continuing upwards. The exact form of the curve, which follows the shape of a person's back, was an experiment in finding the most comfortable shape possible to lean against as you sit inside the structure.

The building was an experiment in setting a rule and letting that make the design. It is made from one main component, an elongated element with a gentle curve. Six hundred of these identical elements are stacked up, each layer separated by a circular disc spacer, to form the interlocking stacks. These two components form sophisticated details by themselves as the two stacks slide into and past each other. The ceiling has a visual richness and intricacy, formed by nothing more than the merging of the piles.

By alternating the elements with spacers and leaving gaps within the layers, I could halve the quantity of plywood I needed and therefore halve the cost. The gaps formed by the spacers gave extra interest to the structure by allowing the piles to slip through each other while remaining intact. The final pieces were hand-cut from fifty 8 x 4-foot (244 x 122-cm) sheets of marine ply, using an efficient cutting pattern for the sheets of plywood that produced virtually no waste.

It was possible to build this project only because I met Sir Terence Conran. He visited the Royal College and I showed him a model of the idea. Understanding that there was not enough space at the Royal College to build anything of this size, he generously invited me to live at his house in Berkshire and construct it at his furniture workshops, with the help of Dominic Raffler, a student from the year below.

The finished piece has an unusual optical quality. From close up, where you can only see through the slats at your eye level, the building appears to be a solid object, but it becomes progressively more transparent as you move further away and the slats become parallel relative to your line of vision. From a distance, the interplay of lines produces an unexpected moiré effect. Altering your point of view by bending your knees causes the appearance of animated phantom curves within the structure.

For the graduation show, the project was brought to London and assembled outside the college in Kensington. At night, its partial transparency allowed the brightly illuminated Royal Albert Hall to be seen through it. After this, Terence Conran gave the gazebo a permanent home in Berkshire.

587

589

Bench

*How can a seat encourage
better posture?*

WHILE TAKING LESSONS in the Alexander Technique, a discipline based on understanding habits of body movement and posture, I became increasingly aware of the way that when people sit in chairs, they tend to slump against the backrest. I started to think about whether it would be possible to design a comfortable outdoor seat without a backrest.

The idea is a tapered slab that comes out of the ground with its top edge folded to form a seat. It allows you to sit with your back straight and relaxed, because the seat is set higher than a normal chair. Also, its surface slopes forwards rather than backwards and its curved shape supports the base of your spine. The forward tilt not only makes the seat easier to get up from but also sheds rainwater, so puddles do not form on it.

To make the bench, I worked with craftsmen who were skilled in the traditional craft of making terrazzo, the concrete material that consists of marble chips set in cement and polished. I carved the pattern for the seat out of wood and car body filler, and this was used to make moulds to cast the final concrete pieces.

Twisted Cabinet

How can a test piece lead to the design of a piece of furniture?

THE PROJECT BEGAN AS AN EXPLORATION of geometrical form. As a student, I was experimenting with a machine tool called a bobbin sander, which consists of a spinning abrasive cylinder, mounted vertically on a work table. I liked this machine because it did not allow you to shape things into flat planes, but forced you to carve different kinds of surfaces.

While the objects I was carving originated from a rigorous geometry of straight lines, they produced forms with twisting surfaces. I made versions that twisted in opposite directions and put them next to each other and found that, if the pieces were hinged along their straight edges, they could combine to make a screen – but that if I combined four of these elements, I could make a cabinet with schizophrenic doors. When they are opened halfway, the bottoms of the doors look as if they are nearly open, while the tops still look almost closed.

After setting up the studio, my first project was to handmake a large version of the cabinet from heavy pieces of oak, for an exhibition. To have it ready in time, I was obliged to carve for sixteen hours a day, seven days a week, for four months. The finished cabinet was the height of a person and needed four people to lift it. It was strapped to the roof rack of my car (ready to travel to the exhibition), when I found a man in a suit, standing in the street, examining it. He turned out to be the local undertaker and he insisted that I had a successful career ahead of me as a coffin-maker.

Plank

*Can a plank of wood also be
a piece of furniture?*

WHEN I WAS A STUDENT at the Royal College of Art, we were asked to design and make a coffee table, using the leftover pieces of wood in the materials store. Even though I don't drink coffee I began thinking about taking a single plank from the storeroom and seeing if it was possible to make it into a whole piece of furniture.

Experimenting with folding long pieces of paper that had the proportion of a plank, I found that if I folded the paper several times, at a slight angle to the direction of the plank rather than straight across it, the strip would make a spiral. Instead of colliding, the two ends would go past each other, making a form with a curious rotational symmetry.

The outcome of this process was an ordinary plank with a secret. It can lean against a wall or lie flat in a pile of other planks, like a piece of wood at a timber merchant. At any moment it can be folded up to make a side table or a seat and then fold out again, returning to its raw state as a plank.

The complexity was in how to make the plank hinge. It had to fold, be strong as a piece of furniture and have joints that were almost invisible when the plank was folded out flat. It took many experiments and a surprising degree of precision craftsmanship to solve this. Having made two of these myself, I was later approached by a specialist manufacturer with a proposal to produce it in limited quantities.

Arts & Business Award

How can you increase the impact of thirteen small objects?

WHEN I WAS A STUDENT, I won a competition to design thirteen awards, which would be presented at the National Theatre in London to businesses that had sponsored the arts in an innovative way. Small awards would make little visual impact in an auditorium of this size, whereas a single large object would stand out better. And if this single object were able to break down into thirteen individual awards, the winners would feel they were part of something beyond their individual achievement.

The idea was to make a grand chalice of polished metal, 1 metre across, formed from thirteen identical abstract objects, which interlocked like an Islamic pattern based on repeated tessellating geometry. During the ceremony, the cup would gradually be dismantled as the thirteen award-winners each received a segment. I liked the idea that the chalice would exist again only if the winners got together for a reunion.

One of the awards was given to Diana, Princess of Wales. It had been announced that morning that this would be her last official public appearance because, the week before, a photographer had got into her gym and taken an intrusive and embarrassing picture of her lifting weights, which had been published around the world. I said, 'Princess Diana, I am supposed to present you with this award, but it's a bit heavy.' Despite the strain she was under, she laughed and said, 'Don't worry – I do weights!'

Interlocking Book

Can you do joinery with books?

WHILE CUTTING AND SHAPING pieces of wood for other projects, I was interested in the idea that single sheets of paper are thin and delicate whereas hundreds of sheets put together and bound into books turn into dense blocks. Was it possible to treat these solid lumps of paper in the same way as planks of wood?

Using woodworking tools, I found that I could make a simple joint and connect two books by cutting channels in both books and slotting them together. Joined together, they lock into each other to form a self-supporting structural composition. When they are pulled apart, the small missing section on each page gives the text an unusual composition. This idea is a good way of expressing the connection between two books with related subject matter, such as two-way language dictionaries or a novel in two parts, and it was taken forward for a two-volume edition of *Mrs Bridge* and *Mr Bridge* authored by Evan S. Connell and published by Penguin as a limited edition of one thousand copies.

City Gateway

*Can a monument be made
from the ground?*

CONCERNED THAT THE ASSOCIATION with ugly 1960s social housing blocks had given concrete a bad image, the British Cement Association held a competition, asking students to propose new ways of using concrete. Picking a notional site, I imagined a major road that needed both a pedestrian route underneath it and a landmark to signify that this highway was the gateway into an area.

The proposal was to manipulate the land on either side of the road by first cutting into the ground, in order to excavate the ramp that leads down to the foot tunnel, and then lifting the pieces of ground and peeling them back to create a pair of arching forms, rising 80 metres into the air on either side of the road. As the elements curl back, they reveal their undersides to be raw and highly textured, a surface we had never seen before in cast concrete.

The project was a first attempt to explore both how large structures might be integrated into a landscape, rather than stuck on top of it, and the architectural use of giant texture.

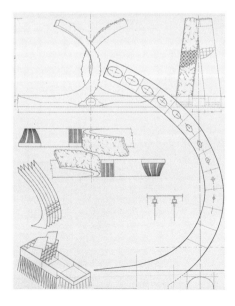 

Pocket Knife

*Can something dangerous
also be a piece of jewellery?*

WHEN I WAS AT THE ROYAL COLLEGE OF ART, a whisky manufacturer asked us to design a gift that could be given out with their bottles.

Remembering a small collection of pocket knives owned by my grandfather, I decided to try to design a new one that did not damage the fingernails as it was being opened and that revealed more of the dangerous bit of a folding knife, without it being dangerous.

The final idea was to mutate a conventional pocket knife, making it easier to open but still protecting you from the sharp part when closed by making the body of the penknife dance around its blade.

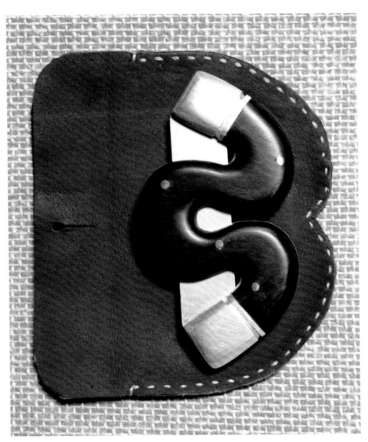

Upholstered Furniture

Can furniture upholstery have the qualities of an animal's skin?

WHEN I WAS A STUDENT IN THE EARLY 1990S, I became interested in the use of upholstery in furniture. In existing upholstered furniture pieces, the familiar formula seemed to be that designers thought of shapes and then other people made soft versions of them. Since a craftsman could make almost any form you drew by carving it in foam and then cutting and sewing fabric as necessary to fit over it, there was little meaningful relationship between a design and its fabrication.

It appeared to me that it might be possible to allow an upholstered shape to emerge through the process of experimenting with upholstery materials instead of drawing it in advance. Rather than imposing my will on the materials, could the materials impose their will on the design?

The Chinese Shar-pei is a breed of dog that has so much more skin than it needs, relative to the quantity of muscle and bone that it has, that its coat forms velvety creases, furrows and wrinkles like living upholstery. Thinking of this, we developed the idea of constructing furniture by manipulating a flat, foldable skin of laminated fabric and upholstery materials.

With a fellow student, I created small maquettes of the concept, going on later to make full-sized test pieces in the studio, using large, laminated sheets of fabrics and foams. Through this experimentation, we found that, as it rippled and rucked up, the manipulated material produced incidental forms similar to those found in nature, which at that time seemed to be a fresh visual language for upholstery.

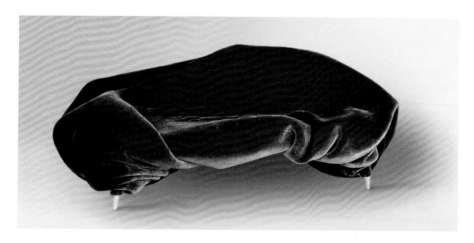

Pavilion

1992

How can a student make a real building?

AT THE TIME WHEN I WAS STUDYING at Manchester Polytechnic, the world of designed products and furniture had recently come alive with new ideas. Many young students aspired to design chairs and lights like the famous practitioners whose work they saw in magazines and exhibitions. Although interesting things were happening in the context of small objects, I felt that this kind of energy and originality was not being applied in the design of new buildings.

Because I was intrigued by design at every scale, from the smallest objects to the largest, I had chosen to study design instead of architecture, but continued to have a particular focus on buildings. I wanted to know if the kinds of ideas, techniques, materials and craftsmanship that were usually applied on smaller scales could be made

to work on a much larger scale. Since it was part of my degree course to research and write a dissertation, I took the opportunity to look at the apparent disconnection between the practice of architecture at that time and the practical craft of making. This led directly to my decision to use the final year of my course to try to design and make a full-sized piece of architecture.

I was interested by a category of building that seemed to have been overlooked. In Victorian times, there had been a craze for constructing fascinating, tiny buildings – pavilions, follies and gazebos – within the grounds of country estates.

This scale of building appealed to me because it did not fit neatly into the conventional categorizations of architecture, sculpture or design. In the absence of a client, I took on the challenge of building at this scale by myself.

At that time, in the 1980s, there was a strong reaction in Britain against the postwar architecture of concrete city blocks, which resulted in demands for new architecture to be 'in keeping' with the country's heritage of buildings from the past. The pressure to make new buildings look similar to the older buildings that sat next to them seemed to be having a paralysing effect on design in the present. But I wondered if I could side-step this need to conform to an existing context by making my building both transportable and temporary.

As there were only nine months left of my course, I needed an idea for a building that could be designed, engineered and built in this time. The problem with being my own client and having no site was that, as long as it was achievable, the concept could be anything. I explored many ideas but it was hard to find a reason to choose any one of them. The idea that stood out was a version of something ordinary, a derelict farm shed that I had once seen in Northumberland, in the north of England. My eyes had been trying to make sense of its pitched roof, which had subtly distorted because the ground it stood on had subsided.

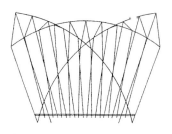

My final idea was an extrapolation of this: a normal building with a pitched roof that has been twisted down so much at its opposite corners that the roof starts to become the walls. At each end, there is a set of three 4-metre-high doors, which rotate to open, while leaning both sideways and outwards. I chose to make the walls, windows and roof using a restricted palette of materials, consisting of timber, aluminium and clear polycarbonate. I was excited about exploring the idea of producing twisted glazing, something I had never seen done.

A young structural engineer, Aran Chadwick, who taught on the architecture course, took an interest in what I was trying to do. Computer-aided design was in the early stages of development and he had specialized software at his home, where we worked together in the evenings and every weekend, to model the building and make the detailed calculations that were needed.

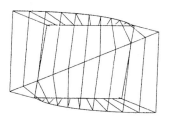

As there was no ready-made architectural product available for constructing twisted glazing, I had to invent a new system for twisting, holding and waterproofing the structure's polycarbonate window panels. It took a combination of screw fixings, rubber sealing strips and 2 kilometres of Velcro to hold in place the twisted panels, with the enormous tension in them.

Having no money to buy materials, I was helped by a tutor who had recently set up a sponsorship department, and who worked with me to get thirteen sponsors to donate materials worth many thousands of pounds.

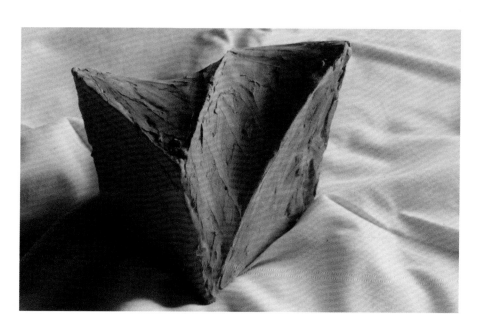

Building the pavilion was a collective effort. For three months, the course technician, a skilled machine engineer, worked alongside me machining the metalwork for the project. A student from the year below, Jonathan Thomas, also worked with me on the project for half the year, excited by the prospect of making a full-sized building. He was also good at motivating other students to help us. The only place we could construct the pavilion was outdoors in a courtyard in the college, where we had to work in full sight of everyone in the cafeteria, with the rain of Manchester pouring down on us. In the end, even the caretakers helped.

The pavilion was never meant to be a permanent structure. The aim of the project was simply to make any building at all; if it lasted a year, I was happy. After the degree show in Manchester, we took the pavilion to London and rebuilt it outside the Business Design Centre in Islington. It was on show for two weeks and was later bought by the Cass Sculpture Foundation in Sussex, where it was put on permanent display.

I later explored the possibility of translating the Pavilion's twisted roof form into a modular building system that used a series of left- and right-handed versions of the Pavilion, with vertical sides, pushed together in different configurations to create covered spaces with three-dimensional tessellating roofs.

Pair of Seats

1991

Symmetry or asymmetry?

WONDERING IF IT WAS POSSIBLE to form a seat and a back from a single ribbon-like strip, I had used Sellotape and copper wire to make a tiny model of a chair that had an enjoyable dynamic asymmetry. I then became interested to find that the addition of a second chair, a mirror image of the first, seemed to act as a stabilizing force to convert the unbalanced form of the single chair into a pleasingly symmetrical composition with an obvious aesthetic harmony.

Rather than using measurements or drawings to fabricate the two chairs, I worked by eye, cold-bending the steel bar using jigs and bending dogs. Each time I welded a piece to one chair, I would do the same to the other. Working with the lengths of metal, I found that trying to make them twist or spiral too quickly produced a confused and mangled mess, and that the only way to make a satisfying sinuous form was to allow the metal bars to curve in only one plane at a time.

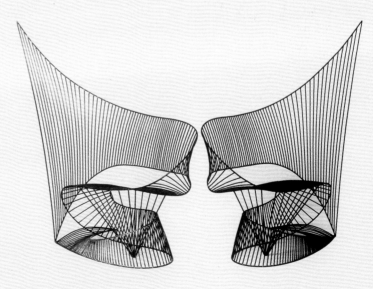

Clay Test Pieces

*With no predefined idea and
a material that lets you make
any shape you want, how much
three-dimensional complexity can
you give a form in a few seconds?*

Clay Study for a Water Sculpture

With an idea in your head and a material that lets you make any shape you want, how much three-dimensional complexity can you give a form if you work at it for several weeks?

Vessels

*Can friction alone hold the
pieces of an object together?*

THE DESIGN FOR THIS OBJECT came from experimenting with a bandsaw to make lots of cuts in a piece of wood, in close proximity to each other, without cutting through the wood completely. I found myself transforming the wood into something with two textures, the comb-like quality of the cut area contrasting with the smooth section in between.

Once I had made three identical wooden pieces, I gradually slid them into each other and found that, as the cuts interleaved, they formed a subtle and beautiful corner detail. With so much surface area between the touching pieces, the elements gripped each other with enough friction to make it possible to gently bend their surfaces and hold them in a form that resembled a vessel. Later, I made a metal version using laser cutting, which at that time was a relatively new industrial technique.

616

Cabinet

*When a tutor sets a project to design
a piece of furniture using a single
sheet of MDF, what can you make?*

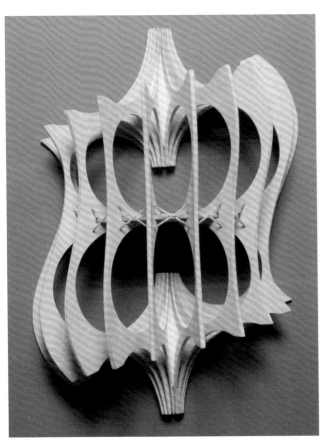
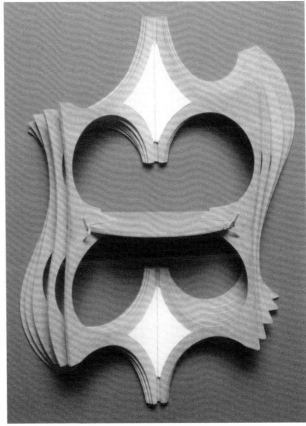

Chain Experiments

*What different forms can link
together and articulate to create
a chain?*

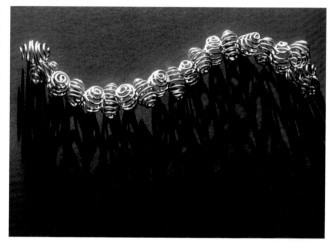

SPOTTING ROLLS OF COPPER, aluminium and brass wire in the materials store at college, I began taking long pieces home at weekends and sitting for hours with pliers bending and cutting them, to experiment with repetition, geometry and interlinking elements. While some of the things I made came from looking for different ways to articulate the movement between two interconnected elements, with others I was just exploring the forms that wire would allow itself to be turned into.

Two of the tests were based on interlinked spirals. One was made with a two-dimensional element which, unlike a conventional chain, created more than one point of contact between each link. Another worked in a similar way but consisted of three-dimensional spirals with rounded forms that swivelled through each other.

618

Slipcast Tile

How much three-dimensionality can you give to a repeating ceramic tile?

Test Pieces

Where can ideas come from?

WHILE I WAS STUDYING, I developed a particular way of thinking through making. Instead of always starting with a drawing or a discussion, I used the making of test pieces in the workshop to find ideas. Adopting a spirit of purposeful aimlessness, I was trying to avoid needing an outcome. Although giving myself permission to experiment, I remained open and receptive to the possibilities that the materials in my hands were offering, ready to convert them into something useful.

For me, most of these experiments were mini-mission statements for architectural projects. Making them, I was wondering how each one might translate to the scale of a building or piece of furniture, or thinking about how a twist or joint or texture could become an element such as a roofing membrane or cladding system. I also found that working on this restricted scale to develop ideas for buildings forced me to maintain the clarity and simplicity of an idea.

What is shown in the following pages is a selection of these test pieces. One was an experiment with wood-turning on as large a scale as possible. Having got a green tree trunk from staff of the local council woodyard, I managed to fit this into the college lathe and, at great danger to myself and onlookers, found that I was able to carve into the huge piece of spinning wood and produce an enormous turned wooden object, which was also interesting when it was cut in half.

On a placement with the college's embroidery course, I experimented with the possibilities of creating three-dimensional form using fabrics, holding a piece of calico and wondering what kind of forms I would get if I repeatedly twisted it in different places. Another fabric experiment was to iron heavily starched calico into multiple pleats using an industrial iron. This made the fabric behave like structural origami and transformed it into a twisted geometrical form.

Sometimes I made test pieces to explore specific design ideas. Imagining forms for the roofs of buildings, I investigated tensile surfaces by dipping wire into a liquid plastic that hardened into three-dimensionally curving surfaces. In another test, I was wondering if there was a way to make a seat that could be a bed and explored the idea of surrounding a rolled-up single mattress with a frame that makes a back and arms, as well as acting as a clip to keep the mattress rolled up. Another time, I was looking at how the part of a chair you sit on could also be what the chair stands on.

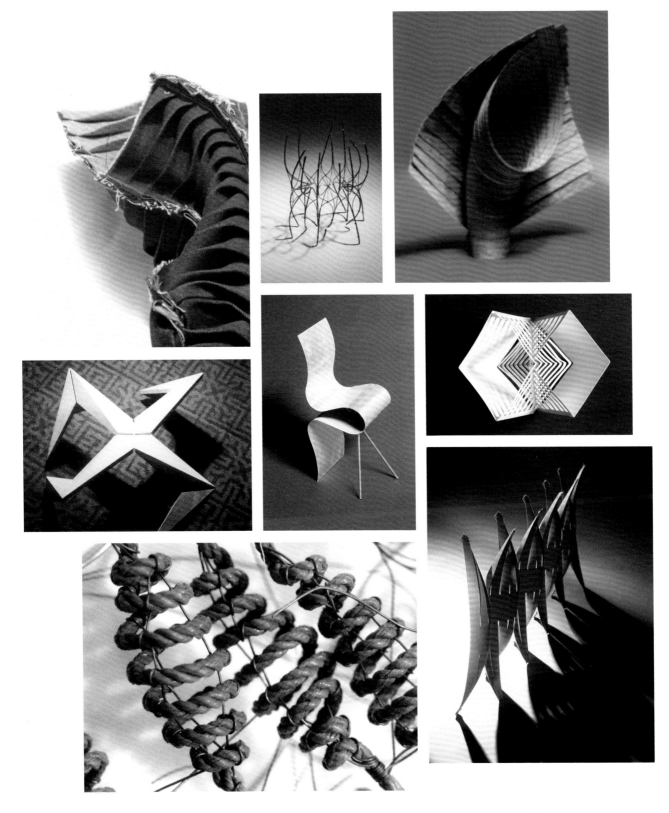

Working with cardboard, I developed a folding mechanism that allowed the card to hinge so that the cuts in it moved past each other in an interesting way. The spiralling rope form came from combining rope, a flexible material, with a more rigid element, wire. I also used copper wire to explore the potential for making structural forms.

Experimenting with making loops in identical-length strips of oak wood veneer using an office stapler to secure the loops, I found that fitting the pieces together produced a form that opened out and leaned forward as the relative proportions of the loops changed. Again working with thin wood, I manipulated a single sheet of quite bendy plywood into a free-standing screen. And finally, as part of the geometrical carving experiments that developed into the Twisted Cabinet (pages 592–93), I produced two pieces using the offcuts that had been removed from the main element, before it developed its twisted curving surfaces.

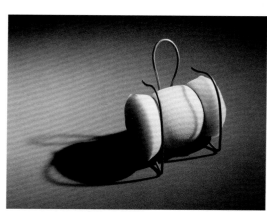
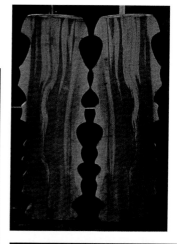

Throne

*Can the suspension system of
an old-fashioned pram lead to
the design of a chair?*

Project-Makers

1000 Trees
COMMISSIONER: Shanghai Kai Xuan Men Real Estate Co Ltd.
COLLABORATORS: Basilica De La Sagrada Familia, UEL, Alan Chandler, Ingrid Hu, Wilf Meynell. CONSULTANTS: MLA Architects (HK) Ltd (Local Architects), Arup (Structural Engineer), P & T Architects & Engineers Ltd (Mechanical & Services Engineer), Wah Heng Glass Group (Façade Consultant), Shanghai Institute of Architectural Design & Research (Local Design Institute), GDC (Retail Consultant), Urbis Limited (Landscape Architect), Speirs and Major Associates (Lighting Consultant), Rider Levett Bucknall (Cost Consultant), Inhabit Group (Façade Consultant), Mode (Branding Consultant), Van Den Berk (Horticultural Advisor). HEATHERWICK STUDIO: Lisa Finlay, Jimmy Hing Leung Hung, Christian Álvarez Gómez, Jeremy Backlar, Sarah Borowiecka, José Cadilhe, Yuxiang Cao, Rodrigo Chain, Linus Cheng, Leo Cheung, Ruggero Chialastri, Leonardo Colucci, Fergus Comer, Vincenzo D'Auria, Thomas Glover, Tamsin Green, Antonin Hautefort, Le Ha Hoang, Hao-Chun Hung, Thomas Impiglia, Jessica In, Linnea Isen, Panagiota Kotsovinou, Wendy Lee, Nicolas Leguina, Shan Li, Virginia Lopez Frechilla, Débora Mateo, Vichayuth Meenaphant, Dimitrije Miletić, Craig Miller, Sayaka Namba, Philipp Nedomlel, Regina Ng, Claudia Orsetti, Daniel Portilla, Thomas Randall-Page, Ryszard Rychlicki, Emmanuelle Siedes, Osbert So, Skye Yuxi Sun, Nicholas Szczepaniak, Cliff Tan, Kenneth Tagoe, May Tang, Ezgi Terzioglu, Chris Tsui, Ivan Ucrós Polley, Paula Velasco Ureta, Kaijun Wang, Paul Westwood, Simon Winters, Eda Yetis, Kelin Yue, Xirong Zheng. **Page 224**

Aberystwyth Artists' Studios
COMMISSIONERS: Aberystwyth Arts Centre, Aberystwyth University. SPONSORS: Aberystwyth University, The Arts Council of Wales, Welsh Assembly Government, Aberystwyth Arts Centre. CONSULTANTS: Packman Lucas (Structural Engineer), Max Fordham

Consulting Engineers (Mechanical and Electrical Engineer), Adrian Tester (Building Services Engineer), Davis Langdon (Quantity Surveyor), B3 Safety (CDM Coordinator). MAKERS: Heatherwick Studio Construction (Main Contractor), A. L. L. Hughes & Sons (Subcontractor), Lowfields Timber Frames (Prefabricated Timber Frames), Renotherm (Spray Foam Insulation), EOM Electrical Contractors (Electrics), Edwards & Owen (Plumbing), AWS Turner Fain (Glazing), NaturaLight Systems (Glazing), Gareth Pugh Steel Framed Buildings (Guttering). HEATHERWICK STUDIO: Tom Chapman-Andrews, Peter Ayres, Lucia Fraser, Julian Saul, Ole Smith, Craig Stephenson. **Page 366**

Airo
COMMISSIONER: IM Motors
STUDIO TEAM: Thomas Heatherwick, Stuart Wood, Thomas Glover, Charlotte Bovis, Adam Brown, Alfredo Chavez, Leo Cheung, Mi Ding, Raquel Diniz, Kelli Fontana, Hannah Francis, Uwe Frohmader, Ross Gribben, Nathalie Harris, Marcus Hawk, Fabian Hubner, Sam Johnson, Matthijs la Roi, Kelvin Lam, Freddie Lomas, Ariadna Lopez, Stuart Macalister, Matthew Magee, Charlotte McCarthy, Francis McCloskey, Dirce Medina, Ian Ng, Wojciech Omiljanowski, Hannah Parker, Theophile Peju, Riccardo Petruzzi, Luke Plumbley, Ji Qi, Manuel Ramos, Matthew Robson, Elisa Simonetti, Rahel Stephanie, Cassandra Tsolakis, Blue Tuohy. **Page 58**

Al Fayah Park
COMMISSIONER: Salama Bint Hamdan Al Nahyan Foundation. CONSULTANTS: RAPM (Project Managers), AKT II (Structural Engineers), GHD (Landscape Architects), Royal Botanical Gardens Kew, Transsolar (Climate Engineers), BEEMME (MEP Consultants). HEATHERWICK STUDIO: Mathew Cash, Etain Ho, Alexander Laing, Michael Lewis, Frederick Pittman, Tom Selby, Ondřej Tichý, Sophia Tang. **Page 240**

Arts & Business Award
COMMISSIONERS: Arts & Business, Arthur Andersen. MAKERS: Essex Replica Castings, Opal Signs. **Page 596**

Autumn Intrusion
COMMISSIONER: Harvey Nichols. SPONSORS: London Docklands Development Corporation, M-real Corporation (formerly Metsa-Serla), 3M. COLLABORATORS: Ron Packman, Jonathan Thomas. CONSULTANTS: Packman Lucas (Structural Engineer), Elektra (Lighting Designer). MAKERS: Heatherwick Studio, Vertigo Rigging (Installation), Tim Fishlock, Louise Raven, Julian Saul, Joanna Scott, Miri Heatherwick, Stewart McCafferty. **Page 550**

Azabudai Hills
COMMISSIONER: Mori Building Company
HEATHERWICK STUDIO: Thomas Heatherwick, Neil Hubbard, Michael Lewis, Steven Ascensao, Ian Atkins, Jordan Bailiff, Laura Barr, Juno Baumgarten, Gabriel Belli Butler, Elena Blanco, Einar Blixhavn, Nic Bornman, Erich Breuer, Paul Brooke, Adam Brown, Megan Burke, Mark Burrows, Adriana Cabello, Calum Campbell, Darragh Casey, Mat Cash, Wang-Fung Chan, Andrew Chard, Michael Cheung, Kacper Chmielewski, Wai Chun, Chi Chung, Jesse Connuck, Silvia Daurelio, Aurelie de Boissieu, Etienne de Vadder, German De La Torre, Dimitrije Dica Miletić, Alex Dickie, Ana Diez Lopez, Danny Dimbleby, Raquel Diniz, Alberto Dominguez, Alice Dousova, Ben Dudek, Lisa Finlay, Alex Flood, Kelli Fontana, Tryfon Foteinopoulos, Harriet Gargrave, Moira Geddes, Antonin Hautefort, Marcus Hawk, Hayley Henry, Etain Ho, Charlotte Hodges, Aziz Hoque, Ho-Ping Hsia, Naida Iljazovic, Katerina Joannides, Peter King, Nilufer Kocabas, Andre Kong, Ayumi Konishi, Gergely Kovacs, Paalan Lakhani, Francis Lam, Kelvin Lam, Ruby Law, Nicolas Leguina, Ivan Linares Quero, Nick Ling, Kanru Liu, Elli Liverakou, José Marquez, Charlotte McCarthy, Andy McConachie, Sayaka Namba, Jacob

HEATHERWICK STUDIO: Stuart Wood, Neil Hubbard, Tim Miller, Tan Sohanpall. **Page 258**

London Olympia
COMMISSIONERS: Deutsche Finance International, Future Olympia (Operator), YOO Capital.
CONSULTANTS: Adamson Associates (Architect of Record), Buro Happold (Accessibility), Campbell Reith (Civil Engineer), Desco (MEP), Eckersley O'Callaghan (Façade Engineer), Gardiner & Theobald (Cost, Principal Designer and Project Manager), Gerald Eve (Planning), LDA (Landscape Architect), Laing O'Rourke (Main Contractor), McBains (BREEAM), MLM (Building Control), Momentum Transport (Transport), Olsson Fire (Fire), REEF Associates (Façade Access and Maintenance), Robert Bird Group (Structure), SPPARC (Architecture), SWECO (Vertical Transportation), Vanguardia (Acoustics), Want Marketing (Marketing). COLLABORATORS: Cake Industry (Design & Engineering), Habito (Timber Design & Furniture), Morris Singer (Fine Art Foundry), Seele (Facade Specialist). HEATHERWICK STUDIO: Thomas Heatherwick, Eliot Postma, Carlos Parraga-Botero, Ian Atkins, Alyaa Azhar, Ángela Bailén López, Juno Baumgarten, Charlotte Bovis, Joe Brennan, Erich Breuer, José Cadilhe, Calum Campbell, Darragh Casey, Mat Cash, Kacper Chmielewski, Grace Chung, Teodor Cozma, Alex Dickie, Danny Dimbleby, Raquel Diniz, Alberto Dominguez, Ben Dudek, Andre Ford, Tryfon Foteinopoulos, Hannah Francis, Olivia Fricker, Harriet Gargrave, Ragavendran Gowrisankar, Ross Gribben, Nathalie Harris, Kong Hoang, Laurens Jacobs, Fanos Katsaris, Madhav Kidao, Michael Kloihofer, Alexander Laing, Kelvin Lam, Barbara Lavickova, Freddie Lomas, Ariadna Lopez, Stuart Macalister, Matthew Magee, Consuelo Manna, Marco Mazzotta, Andrew McConachie, Charlotte McCarthy, Francis Mccloskey Lopez, Andy McConachie, Irene Mennini, Craig Miller, Alfonso Monedero, Alex Murarescu, Pippa Murphy, Nabiha Naciri, Philipp Nedomlel, Ian Ng, Naoko Omasa, Claudia Orsetti, Hannah Parker, Silena Patsalidou, Gabriel Piovanetti, Luke Plumbley, Olivia Reid, Emmanouil Rentopoulos, Almu Rodriguez, Silvia Rueda Cuellar, Luis Sacristán Murga,

Deyan Saev, Mario Andre Sampaio Kong, Luke Squires, Mary Suen, Ángel Tenorio, Ondřej Tichý, Anca Trestian, Blue Tuohy, Si Wah Dong, Cong Wang, Paul Westwood, Skye Yuxi Sun. **Page 78**

Longchamp Store
COMMISSIONER: Longchamp.
COLLABORATORS: Jean Cassegrain, Philippe Cassegrain. CONSULTANTS: Packman Lucas (Structural Engineer), Atmosphere Design Group (Executive Architect), Building Structural Engineering Services (Executive Engineer), Gilsanz Murray Steficek (Executive Engineer), HDLC Architectural Lighting Design (Lighting Designer), O'Dea Lynch Abbattista & Associates (Mechanical and Electrical Engineer), Outsource Consultants (Expeditor). MAKERS: Shawmut Design & Construction (Main Contractor), Hillside Ironworks (Staircase Steelwork), Imperial Woodworking Enterprises (Woodwork), Talbot Designs (Glass Panels), Decca (Furniture).
HEATHERWICK STUDIO: Tom Chapman-Andrews, Rachel Hain, Jem Hanbury. **Page 396**

Maggie's Yorkshire
CLIENT: Maggie's
CONSULTANTS: Abrahams and Carlisle (Joiner), AKT II (Structural, Civil and Transportation Engineer), Balston Agius (Landscaping), Blumer-Lehmann AG (Timber Construction), Butler & Young (Mechanical and Electrical Engineer), CDM Scotland (Clean Development Mechanism Consulting), Kendrews, Light Bureau (Lighting Design), Max Fordham (Environment Engineer), Olsson Fire & Risk (Fire and Risk Consultant), P.P. O'Connor (Construction), Robert Lombardelli Partnership (Cost Consultant), Sir Robert McAlpine (Construction and Civil Engineer), John Wright Electrical (Electrics). HEATHERWICK STUDIO: Thomas Heatherwick, Mat Cash, Neil Hubbard, Rebeca Ramos, Ángel Tenorio, Nick Ling, Ian Atkins, Peter Ayres, Alyaa Azhar, Mark Bagguley, Jordan Bailiff, Lucie Beauvert, David Bellis, Einar Blixhavn, Charlotte Bovis, Erich Breuer, Adam Brown, Mark Burrows, Keti Carapuli, Darragh Casey, Francesco Cavaliere, Michael Chomette, Jesse Connuck, Tom Coupe, Etienne de Vadder, Alex Dickie, Raquel Diniz, Alberto Dominguez, Ben Dudek, Lisa Finlay, Alex Flood, Matthew Gilbert,

Phillip Hall-Patch, Etain Ho, Kong Hoang, Juan Ignacio Oyarbide, Sara Jaafar, Catherine Jones, Peter King, Nilufer Kocabas, Gergely Kovacs, Francis Lam, Barbara Lavickova, Hyein Lee, Nicolas Leguina, Nick Ling, Elli Liverakou, Freddie Lomas, Abel Maciel, Luis Miguel Samanez, John Minford, Alfonso Monedero, Sayaka Namba, Philipp Nedomlel, Charmaine Ng, Ian Ng, Naoko Omasa, Juan Oyarbide, Hannah Parker, Monika Patel, Gilberto Pedrosa, Tayra Pinto, Luke Plumblcy, Gabriel Piovanetti, Jeff Powers, Enrique Pujana, Manuel Ramos, Silvia Rueda Cuellar, Deyan Saev, Luis Samanez, Gabriel Sanchiz, Ahira Sanjeet, Ahad Sheikh, Wendy Smith, Rahel Stephanie, Cliff Tan, Takashi Tsurumaki, Ivan Ucros Polley, Dominic Vadra-Edwards, Antoine van Erp, Ruth Vatcher, Paul Westwood, Brandon Whitwell-Mak, Charles Wu, Meera Yadave, Skye Yuxi Sun, Aysha Zahid, Artur Zakrzewski, Pablo Zamorano, Chen Zhan. **Page 154**

Masdar Mosque
COMMISSIONER: Foster + Partners.
COLLABORATOR: Foster + Partners.
CONSULTANT: WSP Group (Structural Engineer). HEATHERWICK STUDIO: Mark Marshall, Neil Hubbard, Andrew Taylor, Abigail Yeates. **Page 292**

Materials House
COMMISSIONER: The Science Museum.
SPONSORS: Royal Society of Arts & Commerce, Arts Council of Great Britain, Arts Lottery, materials donated by more than 80 companies.
COLLABORATOR: Jonathan Thomas.
CONSULTANTS: Packman Lucas (Structural Engineer), Clare Cumberlidge (Art Consultant), Ben Eastop (Art Consultant). MAKERS: MAKE, Vertigo Rigging (Installation), GFM (Profile Cutting). HEATHERWICK STUDIO: Kieran Gaffney. **Page 542**

Millennium Bridge
COMMISSIONERS: London Borough of Southwark, *The Financial Times*.
COLLABORATOR: Ron Packman.
Page 560

Montblanc Diary
COMMISSIONER: Montblanc. **Page 576**

Nanyang Technological University Learning Hub
COMMISSIONER: Nanyang Technological University (NTU).

COLLABORATOR: Sara Fanelli.
CONSULTANTS: CPG consultants
(Lead Architect), TY Lin (Structural
Engineer). MAKERS: New Con Builders
(Main contractor), LWC Alliance Pte
Ltd (Concrete façade). HEATHERWICK
STUDIO: Ole Smith, Peter Ayres, Ashley
Clayton, Jeronimo Garcia, Helen Lee,
Shan Li, Simon Ng, Juan Oyarbide,
Paul Robinson, Danai Sage. **Page 182**

Notting Hill Residential Tower
COMMISSIONERS: Land Securities,
Delancey. COLLABORATOR: Conran &
Partners. CONSULTANTS: Ramboll UK
(Structural Engineer), Hill International
(Project Manager), King Sturge
(Planning Consultant), Knight Frank
(Property Advisor), Arup (Façade
Consultant), Hoare Lea (Mechanical
and Electrical Engineer), Colin
Buchanan (Transport Consultant).
HEATHERWICK STUDIO: Tom
Chapman-Andrews, William Aitken,
Jeg Dudley, Abigail Yeates. **Page 334**

Olympic Cauldron
COMMISSIONER: LOCOG
(London Organising Committee of
the Olympic and Paralympic Games).
COLLABORATORS: Martin Green,
Catherine Ugwu, Bill Morris, Stephen
Daldry, Mark Fisher, Hamish Hamilton;
Piers Shepperd, Scott Buchanan and
team; Patrick Woodroffe and team;
Danny Boyle, Suttirat Larlarb, Mark
Tildesley, Tracey Seaward and team;
Kim Gavin, Es Devlin and team;
Bradley Hemmings, Jenny Sealey and
team; Rick Smith, Karl Hyde and team.
CONSULTANTS: Stage One (Structural
Engineer, Mechanical Engineer), FCT
(Flame Engineer), London 2012
Ceremonies Technical Team, Robbie
Williams Productions (Project Manager),
Scott Buchanan (post-tender Project
Manager). MAKERS: Stage One,
FCT (Flame Engineer and Fabricator),
Contour Autocraft (Copper Elements).
HEATHERWICK STUDIO: Katerina
Dionysopoulou, Andrew Taylor.
Page 174

Pacific Place
COMMISSIONER: Swire Properties.
COLLABORATORS: Ron Packman, Fred
Manson. CONSULTANTS: Wong & Ouyang
(Executive Architect and Structural
Engineer), Hugh Dutton Associés
(Concept Engineer), Isometrix (Lighting
Designer), Mode (Graphic Designer),
Andreas Hiersemenzel (Glass Consultant).

MAKERS: Gammon (Main Contractor),
Yearfull Contracting (Interior
Contractor), BSC (Timber Benches),
Whitton Casting (Lift Buttons).
HEATHERWICK STUDIO: Mathew Cash,
Fergus Comer, Claudia Hertrich, Alex
Jones, William Aitken, Chloé Ballu, Tom
Chapman-Andrews, Jennifer Chen,
Christos Choraitis, Christian Dahl, Bim
Daser, Jeg Dudley, Melissa Fukumoto,
Rachel Glass, Jem Hanbury, Ingrid Hu,
Neil Hubbard, Adelina Iliev, Alexander
Jackson, Anna Jacobson, Ben Johnson,
Abigail Kendler, Johan Kure, Helen Lee,
Elizabeth Leidy, Virginia Lopez Frechilla,
Liz Middleton, Craig Miller, Tim Miller,
Lukasz Szczepanowicz, Ana Taborda,
Andrew Taylor, George Thomson, Leisa
Tough, Peter Webb, James Whitaker,
James Wignall, Abigail Yeates, Tom Yu,
Dandi Zhang. **Page 348**

Pair of Seats
STUDENT WORK. COLLABORATORS:
Miri Heatherwick, Plymouth University.
Page 612

Paper House
COMMISSIONER: Royal Borough of
Kensington & Chelsea. COLLABORATOR:
Toby Maclean. CONSULTANTS: Packman
Lucas (Structural Engineer), TALL
Engineers (Structural Engineer),
Manage (Project Manager). MAKERS:
Guttridge (Frame), 2D3D (Fit-out).
HEATHERWICK STUDIO: Stuart Wood,
Mark Burrows, Rachel Hain. **Page 454**

Paternoster Vents
COMMISSIONERS: Mitsubishi Estates,
Stanhope. CONSULTANTS: Packman
Lucas (Structural Engineer), Waterman
Partnership (Engineer), Eric Maddox
(Lighting Designer), Mace (Project
Manager). MAKER: Graham Welding.
HEATHERWICK STUDIO: Kieran Gaffney.
Page 490

Pavilion
STUDENT WORK. SPONSORS: British
Alcan Extrusions, G. E. Plastics,
Selectus, Permabond, Dunlop, GSC
Group of Companies, Angle Ring,
Crucial Trading, Mage Fasteners,
Europanel, Sellotape. COLLABORATORS:
Jonathan Thomas, Aran Chadwick.
MAKERS: Jonathan Thomas, students,
tutors and technicians of the Manchester
Polytechnic three-dimensional design
course. **Page 606**

Plank
COMMISSIONERS: Keen, Benchmark
Furniture. COLLABORATOR: Steuart
Padwick. MAKERS: Opus Magnum,
Benchmark Furniture. **Page 594**

Pocket Knife
STUDENT WORK. COLLABORATOR
& MAKER: Julian Saul. **Page 603**

Rolling Bridge
COMMISSIONERS: Paddington Basin
Development Corporation, Chelsfield.
COLLABORATOR: Ron Packman.
CONSULTANTS: Packman Lucas
(Concept Engineer), SKM Anthony
Hunts (Structural Engineer), Solent
Fluid Power (Hydraulics), Primary
Fluid Power (Hydraulics), DJW
Consulting (Hydraulics), Mace
(Project Manager and Planning
Supervisor), Gardiner & Theobald
(Quantity Surveyor), Montagu Evans
(Planning Consultant). MAKER:
Littlehampton Welding. HEATHERWICK
STUDIO: Kieran Gaffney, Stuart Wood.
Page 436

Salviati Glass Furniture
COMMISSIONERS: Salviati, Vessel
Gallery. CONSULTANT: Simon Moore
(Artist Liaison). MAKER: Salviati.
HEATHERWICK STUDIO: Stuart Wood.
Page 404

Shelving for a Jade Collection
COMMISSIONER: Undisclosed.
COLLABORATOR: Jonathan Thomas.
MAKER: Heatherwick Studio. **Page 566**

Sheung Wan Hotel
COMMISSIONERS: Lucid Rich, Kush.
CONSULTANTS: Spence Robinson
(Executive Architect), WT Partnership
(Cost Consultant), Siu Yin Wai &
Associates (Structural Engineer),
Far East Consulting (Electrical and
Mechanical Engineer). HEATHERWICK
STUDIO: Peter Ayres, Alexander Jackson,
Alex Jones, Ole Smith, Robert Wilson,
Tom Yu. **Page 300**

Sleeping Policeman
COMMISSIONER: Holly Street
Public Art Trust. COLLABORATOR:
Ron Packman. **Page 578**

Slipcast Tile
STUDENT WORK. **Page 619**

630

Space Garden
COLLABORATOR: Aurelia Institute
HEATHERWICK HTUDIO: Stuart Wood,
Charlotte Bovis, Raquel Diniz, Alice
Dousova, Marcus Hawk, Irene Hsu,
Matthew Magee, Edward Meyers,
Miranda Musson, Olga Rienda. **Page 16**

Spun
COMMISSIONER: Magis
(Rotation-moulded Plastic Edition).
COLLABORATOR: Haunch of Venison
(Metal Edition). MAKERS: Magis
(Rotation-moulded Plastic Edition),
Anthony Moore (Metal Edition),
Marzorati Ronchetti (Metal Edition),
Coventry Prototype Panels
(Metal Edition). HEATHERWICK STUDIO:
Stuart Wood, Mark Burrows,
Jonathan Sturgess (Metal Edition).
Page 326

Stem
CLIENT: American Hardwood
European Council (AHEC) and Design
Museum. MAKER: Benchmark.
HEATHERWICK STUDIO: Thomas
Heatherwick, Stuart Wood, Tom Glover,
Philipp Nedomlel, Ian Ng. **Page 66**

Street Chandelier
COMMISSIONER: London Borough
of Southwark. **Page 514**

Temple
COMMISSIONER: Shingon-hu Buddhist
Organisation. COLLABORATORS: Kaoru
Okamura (Translator), Trevor Laidler
(Visualizer). CONSULTANTS: Packman
Lucas (Structural Engineer), Mawatari
Kogyo K. K. (Executive Architect),
Master Bros (Project Manager),
Neuplatz (Project Manager),
Theo Theodorou (Design Agent).
MAKER: Royal National Throat Nose
and Ear Hospital (3D Scanning).
HEATHERWICK STUDIO: Kieran Gaffney,
Rachel Hain. **Page 480**

Test Pieces
STUDENT WORK. **Page 620**

Throne
STUDENT WORK. **Page 623**

Towers of Silence
COMMISSIONER: Bombay Parsi
Punchayet. CONSULTANTS: Adams Kara
Taylor (Structural Engineer), Rider
Levett Bucknall (Cost Consultant).
HEATHERWICK STUDIO: Peter Ayres,
Craig Miller. **Page 254**

Tree of Trees
COMMISSIONER: Queen's Green
Canopy. CONSULTANTS: RISE
Management Consulting.
COLLABORATORS: Smith and Wallwork
Ltd (Structural and Infrastructure
Engineering), Format Engineers Ltd.
(Engineering), Barcham Trees PLC
(Tree Specialists), Cleveland Steel &
Tubes Ltd. (Steel). MAKER: Millimetre
Ltd (Manufacturing). HEATHERWICK
STUDIO: Thomas Heatherwick,
Stuart Wood, Tom Glover, Ian Ng, Nick
Ling, Freddie Lomas. **Page 26**

Turning Trees
COMMISSIONER: Mitsubishi Estates
Limited. CONSULTANTS: Modus
Operandi (Art Consultant), Van den
Berk (Trees). HEATHERWICK STUDIO:
Stuart Wood. **Page 486**

Twin Roundabouts
COMMISSIONER: London Borough
of Barking & Dagenham. SPONSORS:
European Regional Development Fund,
Arts Council of Great Britain, Arts
Lottery. COLLABORATOR: Maisie Rowe.
CONSULTANTS: Packman Lucas
(Structural Engineer), London
Borough of Barking & Dagenham
(Highway Engineer), Geoff Wood (Art
Consultant). MAKER: Alfred McAlpine.
HEATHERWICK STUDIO: Kieran Gaffney,
Rachel Hain, Sarah Kaye. **Page 528**

Twisted Cabinet
COMMISSIONER: Benchmark Furniture.
COLLABORATOR: Steuart Padwick.
MAKER: Benchmark Furniture.
HEATHERWICK STUDIO: Stuart Wood.
Page 592

UK Pavilion
COMMISSIONER: Foreign &
Commonwealth Office of the
Government of the United Kingdom.
SPONSORS: Foreign & Commonwealth
Office, UK Trade and Invest, British
Council, Department for Communities
and Local Government, Department
for Environment, Food and Rural
Affairs, Department for Business,
Innovation and Skills, England's
Regional Development Agencies,
Department for Culture, Olympics,
Media and Sport, AstraZeneca, Barclays,
BP, Diageo, GKN. COLLABORATORS:
Casson Mann, Philip Dodd, Andrew
Cahn, Mark Jones, Ian McCartney,
John Sorrell, Paul Smith, Wolfgang
Stuppy, Albert Taylor. CONSULTANTS:

Adams Kara Taylor (Structural
Engineer), Atelier Ten (Environmental
Engineer), Safe Consulting (Fire and
Risk Engineer), Architectural Design
& Research Institute of Tongji
University (Executive Architect),
RHWL (Executive Architect), Troika
(Walkway Exhibition Designer),
Adriana Paice (Project Coordinator),
Davis Langdon & Seah (Quantity
Surveyor), Mace (Project Manager).
MAKERS: Mace, Suzhong Construction
Group, Mike Smith Studio.
HEATHERWICK STUDIO: Katerina
Dionysopoulou, Robert Wilson, Ingrid
Hu, Jaroslav Hulin, Stuart Wood, Peter
Ayres, Jem Hanbury. **Page 308**

Universidad EAN
COMMISSIONER: Universidad EAN.
HEATHERWICK STUDIO: Eliot
Postma, Manuel Ramos, Adam Brown,
Harriet Gargrave, Kelvin Lam, Kate
Le Masurier, Stuart Macalister, Francis
McCloskey, Flavio Medeiros, Luke
Plumbley, Elisa Simonetti, Vito Sugianto,
Simone Tchonova. **Page 22**

Upholstered Furniture
COLLABORATOR: Anna Maria Feniello.
HEATHERWICK STUDIO: Stuart Wood,
Mark Burrows, Zeinab El Mikatti,
Mike MacVean. **Page 604**

Vessels
STUDENT WORK. **Page 616**

West Bund Orbit
COMMISSIONER: Hongkong Land &
Ping An Group. COLLABORATORS:
Arup (Structural Engineer), Inhabit
Group (Facade Engineer), James Corner
Field Operations (Landscape Designer),
LPA (Lighting Consultant), Ronald Lu
& Partners (Executive Architect),
Robotic Plus (BIM Consultant), Sync
Cloud (BIM Consultant), Tianhua
(LDI), WSP (MEP Engineer), Wutopia
Lab (Interior Designer).
HEATHERWICK STUDIO: Thomas
Heatherwick, Neil Hubbard, Marco
Mazzotta, Francis Ng, Kacper
Chmielewski, Leo Cheung, Teodor
Cozma, Raquel Diniz, Alice Dousova,
Kong Hoang, Aziz Hoque, Marcus
Hawk, Stuart Macalister, Consuelo
Manna, Craig Miller, Philipp Nedomlel,
Nicolas Ombres, Luke Plumbley, Jeff
Powers, Brando Posocco, Ji Qi, Skye
Yuxi Sun, Mary Suen, Matthew Taylor,
Ashley Tso. **Page 52**

Image Credits

All images © Heatherwick Studio unless otherwise indicated.

Alamy: 22, 28, 43 (top left), 80 (centre and bottom left),
Alinari/TopFoto: 32 (top)
Joe Almond: 189 (bottom), 190 (bottom), 191, 194-195
Anthony Hunt Associates: 421
Archives of Pearson Scott Foresman/Wikimedia Foundation: 112 (bottom)
Courtesy of ArtLyst.com: 178 (bottom)
Arts & Business: 596–599
Arup: 162-3, 168, 171, 172-173
Assembly Studios: 344 (bottom left, bottom right), 345
Iwan Baan: 118-119, 125, 126-127, 196-197, 202-203, 204, 205, 206-207, 222-223, 214-215, 259, 261 (centre right), 262 (top right), 263 (right), 264-267, 308, 314 (top left, bottom), 316-317, 318 (bottom right), 320, 321 (bottom), 324-325, 348, 350, 351 (bottom left, bottom right), 353, 354, 355 (bottom left, top right, bottom right), 356-357, 358 (bottom), 359 (bottom), 360-361
David Baluizen: 496-497
Roger Bamber: 382 (top)
Rob Barty: 11 (top left)
BBC Photo Library: 423 (top left), 444
Benchmark Furniture: 592 (top left), 593
Bombay Sapphire: 218
Chris Brown: 284
China Central Television courtesy of the British General Consulate, Shanghai: 315
David Cleveland: 69 (bottom)
Cristiano Corte, Marzorati Ronchetti: 7, 331 (top)
Devisual: 34-35, 44, 46-47, 49, 51 (top)
Raquel Diniz: 13 (third left), 14-15, 17, 19, 25 (top), 26-27, 29, 30, 31, 32-33, 40 (top right), 60 (bottom), 64 (centre), 65, 70-71, 76, 77, 82 (bottom right), 83, 86, 87, 88-89, 93, 94, 95, 96, 97,

98-99, 104, 108-109, 137, 138, 139
ECADI: 50 (bottom) 51 (bottom)
Edwardian Inventions by Dale & Gray, 1979: 9 (top left)
ESO: 11 (third left)
Estudio Nod: 23, 24
Catherine Evans: 378, 384
Sarah Fanelli: 189 (top)
Foreign & Commonwealth Office: 321 (top)
Fosun Foundation: 50 (top left, top right)
Fraunhofer ITWM: 169 (bottom)
FreeFoto.com: 443 (centre left)
Friends of the High Line: 112 (top)
Getty Images: 8 (top right), 11 (second left), 11 (bottom left), 175 (left), 178 (centre right), 180-181, 438 (bottom right)
Stephen Gibson: 8 (bottom right)
Isobel Goodacre: 329
Graham Carlow Photography: 318 (top right)
Len Grant: 457, 461, 462, 463, 466-467
Jonathan Gregson: 380-381
Rick Guest: 512, 513
Hasbro Ltd: 508
Marcus Hawk: 128-129, 140-141
Luke Hayes: 134
Homes and Communities Agency: 9 (bottom left)
Neil Hubbard: 92 (bottom left)
Hufton + Crow: 102-103, 107, 135, 148 (bottom), 150, 151, 152-153, 154-155, 158, 159, 160, 161, 182-183, 190 (top), 192, 193, 221
John Hughes: 330 (bottom), 331 (bottom)
I M Motors: 58-59
istock/Vincent Song: 52 (top)
Henryk Tomasz Kaiser: 604 (top right)
KnifefishSC: 156 (bottom right)
Nikolas Koenig: 396, 400 (centre right)
LakeRidge Photography: 488 (right)
Jon Lasiuk: 144 (bottom)
Nic Lehoux: 400 (bottom left)
Yijia Li: 40 (bottom right)
Library of Congress Prints

and Photographs Division, Washington, D.C., Frank and Frances Carpenter Collection (LC-USZ62-116669): 226 (top)
Liz Ligon: 149
Whitney Loewen: 10 (third right)
Longchamp Paris: 503, 507
Lucas Digital: 319 (top left)
Magic Car Pics: 9 (third left)
Peter Mallet: 274, 280, 281, 326
Manchester Evening News: 465
Mary Evans Picture Library/ ILN: 80 (top)
Kenji Masunaga: 100-101
Daniele Mattioli: 313 (top left, top right, bottom right), 314 (top right), 322-323
Christoper McAnneny: 122, 123, 124 (top right and centre)
Phil Captain 3D McNally: 277 (top)
Mir: 41, 43 (bottom), 45
Mori Building Co. Ltd: 90 (top)
MURANUK for Goodwood Festival: 61, 64 (bottom)
Luis Sacristán Murga: 4, 38 (top right), 39, 42
William Murray: 382 (bottom left), 383 (bottom right)
Museum of English Rural Life, University of Reading: 10 (second right)
Scott Nash: 13 (bottom left)
Navigator Films: 198 (bottom)
News Licensing: 179 (top right)
PA Images: 174, 176 (left)
Cristobal Palma: 454
Ema Peter: 110-111, 114, 116 (bottom), 117
Mark Pinder: 460 (bottom), 511 (bottom right), 563
Pollinger Ltd, Estate of Mrs J. C. Robinson: 9 (second left)
Pxfuel.com: 43 (top right)
Qingyan Zhu: 229, 230-231, 232-233, 234, 235, 236, 238-239
Reuters/Pawel Kopczynski: 177
Deyan Sayev: 36 (top)
Salviati: 406, 407
Samuel Dorsky Museum of Art, State University of New York: 250
Edwina Sassoon: 446, 447 (second left)
Timothy Schenk: 142-143, 147,

148 (top)
Norbert Schoerner: 449
Kevin Scott: 113, 116 (top)
Shutterstock, gary718: 48 (top)
Sinclair Knight Merz: 439 (top)
Slashcube: 37
Susan Smart: 332-333
Andy Smith: 36 (bottom)
Steve Speller: 362, 363, 364-365, 436, 440, 441, 442, 448, 450-451, 470-471, 479 (bottom), 479, 491, 494-495, 501, 508, 530 (second left, bottom), 532-533, 539, 540-541, 532, 547, 550, 555 (top left), 558-559, 566, 567, 568, 571, 590 (bottom), 591, 594, 595
Sophie Spencer-Wood: 584
Andy Stagg: 385, 386-387
George Steinmetz: 438 (top left)
© John Sturrock, used courtesy of King's Cross Central Limited Partnership: 130 (top), 133
Edmund Sumner: 368 (bottom), 369, 370-373, 390, 392, 393, 394-395
Swire Properties Ltd: 349 (top left)
TALL Engineers: 419
Hilton Teper: 198 (top)
Tian An: 224-225, 237
Tokaen, Ushijima: 90 (bottom)
TopFoto, Alinari: 144 (top)
University College London Science Lab: 414-415
Kikuko Usuyama: 400 (top left)
Tom Vack, Magis: 328 (top right, second right, bottom right)
V&A Waterfront Museum, Cape Town: 201 (top)
© Victoria and Albert Museum, London: 80 (bottom centre), 179 (bottom right)
wearenarrativ: 78-79, 84 (bottom), 85
Jasper White: 72, 73 (centre right and bottom), 74, 75, 178 (left), 179 (centre left), 240, 241 (top right), 248, 249, 272 (bottom), 288, 298, 306-307, 319 (bottom left), 328 (top left), 340 (bottom left), 341, 343, 346-347, 389, 412, 413, 419, 426-427, 428, 429, 431, 432 (bottom left), 433, 486 (bottom right), 489, 492 (top), 504-505, 506, 534, 535,

536, 537, 538, 549, 554 , 574, 575, 576, 577, 580, 582 (top right), 600, 601, 623
Wikimedia Commons: 80 (bottom right)
Adrian Wilson: 400 (top right, bottom right), 401, 402-403
Worthing Herald: 285
Wright Bus: 261 (top left)
Jintai Zhang: 38 (bottom left, bottom right),
Qingyan Zhu: 53, 54-55, 56, 57

Considerable efforts have been made to trace the rights owners of the material reproduced in this book, but in some cases we have regrettably been unable to do so. We would be pleased to insert an appropriate acknowledgment in any subsequent reprint of this book.

Heatherwick Studio
1994–2024

Diego Aboal
Zaakir Adia
Shantha Adivhalli
Daniel Agahi
David Agostini
Luis Aguirre Manso
Sanjeet Ahira
Ike Aigbogun
William Aitken
Sam Aitkenhead
Abi Ajiboluwa
Dima Alawneh
Alice Aleksandrovits
Nabil Allaoui
Sinead Allchurch
Simone Altmann
Christian Álvarez Gómez
Maura Ambrosiano
Sofia Amodio
Tammy Amornkasemwong
George Amponsah
Andreas Anagnostopoulos
Paul Andrew
Julin Ang
Amittai Antoine
Camille Archilla
Nick Armitage
Nick Arthurell
Steven Ascensao
Zara Ashby
Oma Ashley Benjamin
Doris Asiamah
Jokin Astorkia
Sogol Atighehchi
Ian Atkins
John Attenborough
Simona Auteri
David Aviram
Radu Axinte
Joan Ayguade
Peter Ayres
Alyaa Azhar
Jeremy Backlar
Mark Bagguley
Sabeena Bagol
Ángela Bailén López
Jordan Bailiff

Chloé Ballu
Stuart Bannocks
Elaine Baptiste
Sofia Bark
Stefano Baroffio
Paul Baron
Laura Barr
Melanie Bartle
Stefania Batoeva
Janice Baumann
Juno Baumgarten
Jan Baybars
Antonia Beard
Mikel Beaumont
Lucie Beauvert
Ramona Becker
Matt Bell
Gabriel Belli Butler
Marie Benages
Vito Benjamin Sugianto
Simone Berardelli
Andreja Beric
Liz Betterton
Leena Bhanderi
Carolina Biegun Elgue
Andrew Bigwood
Daisy Billows
Eleanor Bird
Ben Bisek
Elliott Bishop
Clara Bismuth
Elena Blanco
Einar Blixhavn
Carrick Blore
Camille Booth
Nic Bornman
Sarah Borowiecka
Charlotte Bovis
Isobel Bracegirdle
Nikki Brane
Joseph Brennan
Erich Breuer
Keeshia Briscoe
Paul Brooke
Polly Brotherwood
Tyler Brown
Adam Brown

James Budgen
Veljko Buncic
Megan Burke
Mark Burrows
Aleksandar Bursac
Victor Bustos
Jennifer Butler
Adriana Cabello Plasencia
José Cadilhe
Calum Campbell
Julia Cano
Yuxiang Cao
Keti Carapuli
Darragh Casey
Pat Casey
Mat Cash
Tom Castle
Aaron Cattani
Francesco Cavaliere
Rodrigo Chain
KaYu Chan
Brisa Chander
Tom Chapman-Andrews
Taz Chappel
Michael Charbonnel
Andrew Chard
Lucy Charlton
Kyriakos Chatziparaskevas
Alfredo Chavez
Jennifer Chen
Yü Chen
Linus Cheng
Doris Cheong
Daryl Cheung
Leo Cheung
Michael Cheung
Chia Chi Yeh
Ruggero Chialastri
Chun Chiu
Kacper Chmielewski
Michael Chomette
Christos Choraitis
Krina Christopoulou
Paul Chu
Yao Jen Chuang
Chi Chung
Grace Chung

Carly Circuitt
Khanyo Cishe
Ashley Clayton
Kate Close
Sally Cohen
David Cole
Natalie Cole
Kathleen Coleman
Daniel Coley
Griffin Collier
Josh Collier
Leonardo Colucci
Louise-Anne Comeau
Fergus Comer
Rosie Connors
Jesse Connuck
Lizzie Cooper
Amy Corrigan
David Costa
Alex Cotton
Tom Coupe
Holly Cowan
Teodor Cozma
Nerma Cridge
Jacob Crittenden
Annie Croll
Jessame Cronin
John Cruwys
Teodor Cuciureanu
Megan Cumberland
Jonathan Curtis
Pola Czynczyk-Gottesman
Vincenzo D'Auria
Christian Dahl
Ruth Daniels
Jonny Darkes
James Darling
Bim Daser
Silvia Daurelio
Enzo D'Auria
Leila Davis
Pennie Daws
Ken Day
Jason Day
Jacob de Berker
Aurelie de Boissieu
Aliénor de Chambrier

Paulo de Costa
German de la Torre
Etienne de Vadder
John Deeny
Demitris Demetriou
Amaia Diaz
Jordina Diaz Ferrando
Laurie Dickason
Sophie Dickerson
Alex Dickie
Ana Diez Lopez
Danny Dimbleby
Mi Ding
Raquel Diniz
Kristine Diola
Katerina Dionysopoulou
Pinar Djemil
Irem Dokmeci
Alberto Dominguez
Victoria Dong
Alice Dousova
James Dowling
Matteo Dragone
Jenny Draxlbauer
Vivienne Du
Ben Dudek
Laurence Dudeney
Jeg Dudley
Nina Due
Robert Dunbar
Christina Dyrberg
Olga Dziewulska
Eyal Edelman
Julia Edwards
Andrew Edwards
Dave Edwards
Zeinab El Mikatti
Bee Emmott
Max English-Merrick
Sarah Entwhistle
Felipe Escudero
Samuel Evans
Danielle Eveleigh
Norman Faizal
Thomas Farmer
Pam Fauchon
Sheu Fei Hoe

Montana Feiger
Amber Fenley
Lucca Ferrarese
Chiara Ferrari
Francis Field
Federica Filippone
Lisa Finlay
Mark Finzel
Alexandra Fioux
Tim Fishlock
Ian Fitzpatrick
Xavier Flores Moncunill
Catherine Flowers
Kelli Fontana
Andre Ford
Alexandra Forward
Tryfon Foteinopoulos
Hannah Francis
Konrad Frankowski
Lucia Fraser
Lauren Fresle
Olivia Fricker
Andrew Friedenberg
Eran Friedland
Uwe Frohmader
Claudia Fruianu
Melissa Fukumoto
Wang Fung Chang
Giulio Gabrielli
Kieran Gaffney
Hattie Gallagher
Liam Gallagher
Brandon Gassner
Lily Galt Mcloughlin
Emma Game
Jeronimo Garcia
Harriet Gargrave
Aimee Garner
Moira Geddes
Zoe Gibbs
Matthew Gilbert
Rachel Giles
Frank Gilks
Sarah Gill
Victoria Gill
Marion Gillet
Rachel Glass
Thomas Glover
Maya Golan
Maxim Goldau
Amanda Goldsmith
Wayne Gordon
Paloma Gormley
Raga Gowrisankar
Fernando Graca
David Grant
Emer Grant
Sarah Grant
Tamsin Green
Ross Gribben
Adam Grice
Erick Grijalva
Stefano Grisoglio
Michael Gryko
Anjie Gu

Jan Guell
George Guest
Shah Gul
Kara Gurney
Nao Guy
Le Ha Hoang
Bahia Haddam
Ellen Hägerdal
Daniel Haigh
Rachel Hain
Karim Hallak
Phillip Hall-Patch
Trond Halvorsen
Paulene Hamilton
Shaun Hamilton
Jem Hanbury
Ben Hanson
Tim Harris
James Harris
Amira Hashish
Blaire Haslop
Antonin Hautefort
Benoit Hauviller
Marcus Hawk
Matilda Hawthorne
Jonathan Haycox
Chen He
Lucy Heale
Elena Heatherwick
Hugh Heatherwick
Marisa Heatherwick
Miri Heatherwick
Moss Heatherwick
Thomas Heatherwick
Vera Heatherwick
Max Heine-Geldern
Anna Heinrickson
Matthew Heitel
Francis Henderson
Hayley Henry
James Hepper
Lucy Hermon
Antonio Herrero
David Herriotts
Claudia Hertrich
Shannon Hewlko
Will Hicks
Alicia Hidalgo
Sabine Hielscher
Mathew Hill
Andy Hillman
George Hintzen
Milan Hirani
Lisa Hirst
Etain Ho
Kaowen Ho
Winki Ho
Charlotte Hodges
Laura Hoggan
Dan Hollands
Matthew Holloway
Ben Holmes
Christopher Hon Ming Lam
Aziz Hoque
Paz Horn Robinson

Steven Howson
Catalina Hoyos Pareja
Ho-Ping Hsia
Irene Hsu
Ingrid Hu
Carmen Hu
Xuanzhi Huang
Neil Hubbard
Fabian Hubner
Anna Hughes
Jaroslav Hulin
Hao-Chun Hung
Jimmy Hung
William Hunter
Ben Hutchinson
Juan Ignacio Oyarbide
Naida Iljazovic
Sajid Ikram
Adelina Iliev
Marina Illum
Thomas Impiglia
Jessica In
Linnea Isén
Amer Ismail
Alice Ives
Ibuki Iwata
Sara Jaafar
Alexander Jackson
Ben Jacobs
Laurens Jacobs
Anna Jacobson
Catherine James
Ollie James
Michael James Matsell
Scott Jarvie
Pawel Jaskulski
Elliot Jefferies
Yao Jen Chuang
Dominique Jenkins
Roberta Jenkins
Samantha Jenkins
Holly Jerrom
Miguel Jimenez
Zhiting Jin
Ye Jin Lee
Katerina Joannides
Christophersen Johan Kure
Alecia John
Anya Johnson
Ben Johnson
Kara Johnson
Rebecca Johnston
Gareth Jollands
Alex Jones
Catherine Jones
Chris Jones
Jonathan Jones
Syafiq Jubri
Sonila Kadillari
Maria Kafel-Bentkowska
Eva Kamali
Toms Kampars
Ayesha Kapila
Martynas Kasiulevicius
Noor Kassam

Fanos Katsaris
Sarah Kaye
Helene Kazan
Kevin Kelly
Isabelle Kelly
Abigail Kendler
Charlie Kentish
Catherine Kenyon
Agnes Kerecsanin
Flora Kessler
Madhav Kidao
Kate Kilalea
Peter King
James Kirkpatrick
Valerly Kisyuk
Stephen Klesel
Michael Kloihofer
Alex Knanh
Saige Knowles
Nilufer Kocabas
Josh Koenekoop
Willem Kok
Andre Kong
Makiko Konishi
Ayumi Konishi
Marko Koops
Dimitra Kotsi
Panagiota Kotsovinou
Ioanna Kougia
Gergely Kovacs
Bori Kovacs
Catherine Kullberg
Christophersen
Pallavi Kumar
Johan Kure
Kyp Kyprou
Matthijs la Roi
Alexander Laing
Maya Laitken
Paalan Lakhani
Francis Lam
Ming Lam
Kelvin Lam
Chloe Lamb
Darren Lamb
Nyheke Lambert
Keely Lanigan
Jonas Larsen
Adrienne Lau
Carol Lau
Margot Laudon
Barbara Lavickova
Ruby Law
Yue Law
Beau Lawrence
Cath Layton
Edith Le Grand
Kate Le Masurier
Changyeob Lee
Helen Lee
Viviane Lee
Wendy Lee
Zoe Lee
Hyein Lee
Latifa Lee

Nicolas Leguina
Elizabeth Leidy
John Lenehan
Sacha Leong
Noeline Leong
Michael Lewis
Shan Li
Vivien Li
Amy Li
Justin Li
Yijia Li
Mavis Lian
Julian Liang
Colin Lievens
Eric Lim
Hendrick Lin
Raina Lin
Iván Linares Quero
Nick Ling
Chia Ling Chung
Jeroen Linnebank
Pascoe Lintell
Kanru Liu
Ko-Cheng Liu
Pin Liu
Elli Liverakou
Ning Loh
Freddie Lomas
Jakeline Londono
Virginia Lopez Frechilla
Ariadna Lopez Rodriguez
Clare Lowther
Pikyan Luk
Connie Luk
Jakob Lund
Malin Lundin
Stuart Macalister
Hamze Machmouchi
Evonne MacKenzie
Stevie MacKinnon-Smith
Toby Maclean
Simon Macro
Mike MacVean
Kevin Madigan-Reeve
Matthew Magee
Michael Magennis
Helen Maier
Clare Manassei
Sogi Mangalsuren
Consuelo Manna
Fred Manson
Michele Manzella
Ana Margarita Wang Zúñiga
Rosanna Marks
José Marquez
Mark Marshall
Kirsten Martin
James Martin
Stepan Martinovsky
Brooke Mason
Josh Mason
Débora Mateo
Tomomi Matsuba
Gemma Matthias
Gayle Mault

Marco Mazzotta	Sarunas Nekrosius	Emma Pettit	Dani Rossello Diez	Toby Startup
Christopher McAnneny	James Ness	Remi Phillips-Hood	Leon Rowan	Edward Steed
Stuart McCafferty	Francis Ng	Andrea Piazza	Maisie Rowe	Hannah Steenson
Charlotte McCarthy	Regina Ng	Clara Pierantozzi	Genny Rowson	Amy Stein
Francis McCloskey Lopez	Simon Ng	Gabriel Piovanetti	Silvia Rueda Cuellar	Rahel Stephanie
Andy McConachie	Charmaine Ng	Frederick Pittman	Urzsula Russek	Craig Stephenson
Sean McCormick	Ian Ng	Ross Plaster	Fergus Ryan	Rosslyn Stewart
Andrew McDowell	Wiley Ng	Emily Platzer	Stephanie Ryan	James Stirrat
Garvan McGrane	Jonathan Nguyen	Luke Plumbley	Ryszard Rychlicki	Sebastian Stoddart
Miranda McInerney	Leah Nichols	Ondrej Pokoj	Ville Saarikoski	Chris Stone
Tom McKeogh	Karen Nicolao	Julio Poleo	Joanna Sabak	Holly Stringer
Andrew McMullan	Marie Nihonyanagi	Fabio Porcu	Luis Sacristán Murga	Anna Strzelczyk
Abigail McNeill	Alexandra Nikolova	Daniel Portilla	Deyan Saev	Jonathan Sturgess
Tom Meacock	Jenine Noble	Abigail Portus	Tereza Safarikova	Mary Suen
Edwina Meade	Erika Nokes	Brando Posocco	Danai Sage	Skye Yuxi Sun
Flavio Medeiros	Ella Norris	Naya Posotidou	Siba Sahabi	Juliette Sung
Dirce Medina	Wojtek Nowak	Eliot Postma	Kong Sai Hoang	Daniel Swann
Vichayuth Meenaphant	Alice O'Hanlon	Luis Potter	Gabriel Sanchiz	Tilly Symonds
Kim Megson	Jack O'Kelly	Raphaela Potter	Sarah Sandercock	Nicholas Szczepaniak
Ruth Mellor	Cara O'Sullivan	Fernando Poucell	Ahira Sanjeet	Lukasz Szczepanowicz
Joseph Melvin	Riona O'Sullivan	Dimitra Poulokefalou	Pablo Santos	Ana Taborda
Lisa Melvin	Alexandra Oberrotman	Jeff Powers	Julian Saul	Akari Takebayashi
Jorge Xavier Méndez-Cáceres	Valentina Occhini	Matthew Pratt	Ian Saunders	Chloe Tam
Irene Mennini	Ilias Oikonomakis	Max Prav	Emric Sawyer	Elias Tamer
Posy Metz	Michele Oke	Gemma Pretorius	Heidi Schaefer	Lucy Tams
Dirk Meuleneers	Mira Oktay	Lucy Priest	Louisa Schmolke	Cliff Tan
Edward Meyers	Sabrina Oliveros	Enrique Pujana	Hannah Schneebeli	Yue-Ying Tan
Dimitrios Michas	David Olomata	Kabir Purewal	Billy Schreiber	May Tang
Liz Middleton	Karol Olszewski	Umesh Qarmar	Abigail Scott Paul	Sophia Tang
Luis Miguel Samanez Carrillo	Naoko Omasa	Ji Qi	Polley Sebastian Ute	Willow Tang
Paul Milan	Nicolas Ombres	Sarah Quinn	Zuleika Sedgley	Neal Tanna
Dimitrije Miletić	Wojciech Omiljanowski	Phoebe Radford-Hodgkins	Thomas Selby	Andrew Taylor
Craig Miller	Barakat Omomayowa	Vuk Radovic	Asako Sengoku	Matt Taylor
Tim Miller	Kao Onishi	Manuel Ramos	Ana Serrano	Simone Tchonova
Benjamin Mills	Satoko Onisi	Rebeca Ramos	Feruzi Shabani	Ussumane Tchuda
Siobhan Milne	Leonora Oppenheim	Thomas Randall-Page	Alexandra Shah	Nicole Teh
Jody Milton	Claudia Orsetti	Ryan Ras	Dina Shahar	Ángel Tenorio
John Minford	Marwah Osama	Miyong Rathe	Sunil Sharma	Ezgi Terzioglu
Holly Mitchell	Melissa Osborne	Louise Raven	Richard Sharp	Chris Thomas
Rosie Mitchell	Calvin Osei	Alex Rayner	Eyal Shaviv	James Thomas
Hilary Moir	Cameron Overy	Chris Rea	Ahad Sheikh	Joseph Thompson
Nader Mokhtari	Ron Packman	Jethro Rebollar	Ken Sheppard	George Thomson
Alfonso Monedero	Julia Pagni	Alex Reddicliffe	Don Shillingburg	Emma Thorn
Matthew Montague	Giuliano Pairone	Zora Redl	Tracy Shum	Tom Thornton
Bruce Morgan	Christopher Palmer	Emma Reid	Tin Shun Tsoi	Athena Thrasyvoulou
Sinead Morgan	Pinelopi Papadimitraki	Olivia Reid	Emmanuelle Siedes	Jie Tian
Glenn Morley	Sofia Papageorgiou	Hana Reith	Elisa Simonetti	Ondřej Tichý
Matthew Morris	Hannah Parker	Yanni Ren	Phoebe Simpson	Shannel Tilbury
Francesca Morroni	Warren Parker	Emmanouil Rentopoulos	Ailsa Sinclair	Jordan Tobin
Darya Mortazavi	Giovanni Parodi	Arturo Revilla	Helen Siu	James Tomkins
Chloe Mostyn	Carlos Parraga-Botero	Kate Revyakina	Jill Skulina	Sharon Toong
Tony Mullins	Monika Patel	Harriet Ridout	James Smith	Ray Torbellin
Alex Murarescu	Silena Patsalidou	Olga Rienda	Ole Smith	Ana Torrecilla
Pippa Murphy	Beajle Pattni	Kimberly Riley	Thomas Smith	Leisa Tough
Owen Murray	Conor Paul	Stefan Ritter	Wendy Smith	Jacqueline Townsend
Miranda Musson	Ebru Payne	Paul Robinson	Luke Snow	Fabrizio Tozzoli
James Mustill	Adam Peacock	Sandra Robinson	Osbert So	Colleen Tracey
Diana Mykhaylychenko	Ben Pearce	Marta Robinson	Tan Sohanpall	Lucas Trapa
Nabiha Naciri	Gilberto Pedrosa	Matthew Robson	Sharn Somasiri	Anca Tristan
Sayaka Namba	Theophile Peju	Almu Rodriguez	Rachel Song	Natasha Trumic
Mira Narun	Lorenzo Pellegrini	Miguel Rodriguez	Ricardo Sosa-Mejia	Miltos Tsakiris
Irina Nazarova	Katherine Penney	Paco Rojas	Flavio Sousa Monteiro	Ling-Li Tseng
Chioma Ndeze	Joanna Penneycard	Bethany Rolston	Gemma Spencer	Ashley Tso
Jacob Neal	Dylan Perera	Péter Romvári	Will Spink	Cassandra Tsolakis
Philipp Nedomlel	Riccardo Pertruzzi	Mirren Rosie	Luke Squires	Chris Tsui

636

Takashi Tsurumaki
Blue Tuohy
Ivan Ucrós Polley
Rebecca Ullah
Paloma Uriel
Sebastian Ute
Dominic Vadra-Edwards
Enol Vallina
Antoine van Erp
Jasper van Oosterhout
Athanasios Varnavas
Akrivi Vasilopoulou
Ruth Vatcher
Ivan Vegas Martin
Marcos Velasco
Paula Velasco Ureta
Guido Vericat
Silvia Vian
Bettina von Kameke
Harry Vos
Ruby Wai
George Wainwright
Tabitha Walker
Michael Wallace
Marcus Wallbaum
Alma Wang
Daniel Wang
Cong Wang
Junyi Wang
Kaijun Wang
Peng Wang
Zhan Wang
Marta Wasenczuk
Dominik Watracz Yarocki
Peter Webb
Daniel Weidler
Adrian Weidmann
Ying Wen Teh
Georgina Wesley
Adam West
Paul Westwood
James Whitaker
Lisa White
Simon Whittle
Brandon Whitwell Mak
James Wignall
Nadia Wikborg
Thomas Williams
Kyle Williams
Wendy Williams
Genevre Wilshire
Craig Wilson
Robert Wilson
Holly Wilson
Jerzy Wiltowski
Scott Winchester
Simon Winters
Pricilla Wong
Stuart Wood
Helen Wren
Andrew Wright
Douglas Wright
Jonathan Wright
Emma Wright
Charles Wu

Lu Xia
Sherry Xiao
Yexin Xiong
Mei Xue
Meera Yadave
Christine Yan
Abigail Yeates
Stephanie Yee
Choon Yen Yap
Eda Yetis
Wen Ying Teh
Chris Yoo
Sophie Young
Hannah Young
Tom Yu
Kelin Yue
Chen Yue
Chiara Zaccagnini
Aysha Zahid
Artur Zakrzewski
Pablo Zamorano
Edgar Zandberg
Chen Zhan
Dandi Zhang
Fei Zheng
Jiazi Zheng
Xirong Zheng
Lijing Zhou
Ollie Zhu
Qiheng Zhu

Special thanks for their work on this edition to:
Lucas Dietrich
Helen Fanthorpe
Frank Gallaugher
Robert Heath
Adam Hooper
Catherine Hooper

Acknowledgments

HEATHERWICK STUDIO has been making for three decades. Whether it's a new city district or a one-off Christmas card, we've always pushed ourselves to make places or things that are joyful and encourage connection.

Along the way there have been many special people who have helped us enormously as the studio has grown in confidence and capacity, and through inevitable teething problems and growing pains. This list of thank yous will always be imperfect, but I want to acknowledge some of the incredibly talented individuals who have been critical parts of the journey.

Terence Conran gave me encouragement to keep going when I was struggling to find my way at the Royal College of Art, and then even gave me somewhere to live while I built Gazebo (pages 584–9) for my degree show. He was unique, not only for his championing of excellence in design, but also for understanding how to make new ideas accessible to the greatest number of people.

Over thirty years the studio has moved from being me by myself in 1994 to a team of 240 people today. This wouldn't have been possible without the studio's partners and domain leaders: Matt Bell, Mat Cash, Laurence Dudeney, Lisa Finlay, Neil Hubbard, Kyp Kyprou, Nick Ling, Ruth Mellor, Craig Miller, Eliot Postma, Gemma Pretorius, Elisa Simonetti and Stuart Wood. Each of them has provided wisdom, energy and extraordinary commitment as the studio has grown.

The studio has also been supported by the involvement of its associates who, as friends and mentors, have contributed amazing expertise and enthusiasm. The engineer Ron Packman has a unique place in the studio's narrative as a true collaborator in the endeavour of having ideas and the adventure of putting them into practice. So too has my father Hugh Heatherwick, who helped us understand the meaning of excellence within our own organization. We've also enjoyed a warm and valuable relationship with architect Fred Manson, who spends a huge amount of time with us, provoking, questioning and encouraging.

For their collaboration, friendship and support, the studio and I would also particularly like to thank:

Ron Arad, Francis Archer, Alexa Arena, Iwan Baan, Ross Bailey, Rachael Barraclough, Patrick Bellew, Len Blavatnik, Mike Bloomberg, Erica Bolton, Danny Boyle, Pat Brown, Yonca Dervisoglu, John Burke, Andrew Cahn, Tristram Carfrae,

Jean Cassegrain, Daniel Charny, Edmund Cheng, Craig Cohon, DJ Collins, Jay Cross, Zhikang Dai, Stephen Daldry, Mary Davidge, Linda Davies, Mervyn Davies, Lucas Dietrich, Barry Diller, Gerard Evenden, Tony Fadell, Sara Fanelli, Mala Gaonkar, David Giampaolo, Kate Goodwin, David Green, Martin Green, Stewart Grimshaw, Guangchang Guo, Morwenna Hall, Dee Halligan, John and Cynthia Hardy, Patti Harris, Peter Hendy, John Hitchcox, Brent Hoberman, Brooke Hodge, Dorothea Hodge, Bernard Holmes, Bingyi Huang, Father Christopher Jamison, Ed Jarvis, Simon Johnson, Mark Jones, Hanif Kara, Mami Kataoka, Michelle Kaufmann, George Keliris, Keith Kerr, Pearl Lam, Chloe Lamb, Jiyoon Lee, Laura Lee, Patrick Lee, Seow Hiang Lee, Xin Li, Changfeng Ling, Weng Ling, Stuart Lipton, Christian Louboutin, Kai-Yin Lo, Victor Lo, Joanna Lumley, Roger Madelin, Pritpal Mann, Eileen Mannion, Nader Mokhtari, Paul Morrell, Tyler Morse, Daniel Moylan, Ravi Naidoo, David Nelson, Catherine Nikolaou, Mark Noble, Greg Nugent, Midori Omori, Coen Van Oostrom, Larry Page, Eugenio Perazza, Herbert Perico, Sundar Pichai, Gavin Pond, Ruth Porat, Mary Portas, Jane Quinn, David Radcliffe, Jemma Read, Vicky Richardson, Stephen Ross, Maisie Rowe, Sarah Sands, June Sarpong, Edwina Sassoon, Joanna Scott, Kevin Sheekey, John and Frances Sorrell, Steve Speller, Will Storr, Jiwei Sun, Albert Taylor, Diana Taylor, Abraham Thomas, Jonathan Thomas, Adrian To, Shingo Tsuji, Alejandro Vadia, Alan Yentob, Madelyn Wils, Michael Wolff, Robert Wong, Jane Wood, Jochen Zeitz and Dawei Zhang.

The studio is a group of phenomenally talented and hard-working people, a group of enthusiasts who inspire collaborators, specialists, advisors and commissioners to go further than they might otherwise do. Every person who has ever worked at the studio is named on the previous pages, and to each one of you, an immense thank you.

Finally, this book is dedicated to the imaginative vision of clients, commissioners and authorities who demand that projects are special.

On the front cover: Little Island, New York.
Image © 2024 Hufton + Crow

On the back flap: Little Island, New York.
Image © 2024 Timothy Schenk

First published in the United Kingdom in 2012 by Thames
& Hudson Ltd, 181A High Holborn, London WC1V 7QX

This revised and updated edition published in 2024

This edition first published in the United States of America
in 2024 by Thames & Hudson Inc., 500 Fifth Avenue,
New York, New York 10110

Thomas Heatherwick: Making © 2012, 2013, 2015
and 2024 Heatherwick Studio

Text contributions
2024 Edition: Rachel Giles and Kim Megson
Previous editions: Maisie Rowe

Heatherwick Studio
Project management: Rachel Giles
Photography: Raquel Diniz
Picture research: Cecilia Mackay

And also: Charlotte Bovis, Kyriakos Chatziparaskevas,
Teodor Cozma, Jessame Cronin, Tom Glover, Aziz Hoque,
Jimmy Hung, Ibuki Iwata, Alecia John, Michael Lewis,
Stepan Martinowsky, Francis Ng, Ian Ng, Leah Nichols,
Jenine Noble, Eleanor Norris, Edward Meyers, Craig
Miller, Owen Murray, Carlos Parraga-Botero, Manuel
Ramos, Olga Rienda, Matthew Robson, Bethany Rolston,
Luis Sacristán Murga, Mary Suen, Matthew Taylor,
Jordan Tobin, Ray Torbellin, Xirong Zheng, Carmen Zhu.

All project dates refer to the year commissioned.

British Library Cataloguing-in-Publication Data
A catalogue record for this book is available from
the British Library

Library of Congress Control Number 2024936857

ISBN 978-0-500-29716-2

Printed and bound in China by C & C Offset Printing Co. Ltd

FSC
www.fsc.org
MIX
Paper | Supporting
responsible forestry
FSC® C008047

Be the first to know about our new releases,
exclusive content and author events by visiting
thamesandhudson.com
thamesandhudsonusa.com
thamesandhudson.com.au